J. P. Wheeldon

Freshwater fishing in Great Britain other than Trout or Salmon

J. P. Wheeldon

Freshwater fishing in Great Britain other than Trout or Salmon

ISBN/EAN: 9783337146955

Printed in Europe, USA, Canada, Australia, Japan

Cover: Foto ©Lupo / pixelio.de

More available books at **www.hansebooks.com**

International Fisheries Exhibition
LONDON, 1883

FRESHWATER FISHING

IN

GREAT BRITAIN

OTHER THAN TROUT OR SALMON

BY

J. P. WHEELDON

LATE ANGLING EDITOR OF "BELL'S LIFE"

LONDON
WILLIAM CLOWES AND SONS, Limited
INTERNATIONAL FISHERIES EXHIBITION
AND 13 CHARING CROSS, S.W.

1883

LONDON:
PRINTED BY WILLIAM CLOWES AND SONS, LIMITED,
STAMFORD STREET AND CHARING CROSS.

INDEX.

	PAGE
INTRODUCTION	3–7

ROACH FISHING.

	PAGE
Rods	8
Lines, hair *v.* gut	8
Floats—shotting, &c.	9
Bait of various kinds	9
Ground baiting	10
Various methods of fishing	10–12
Localities where fish are found	12, 13
Swims in summer and winter	
Blow-line fishing and daping	13

BARBEL FISHING.

	PAGE
Difference between Thames and Trent fishing	15
Selection of swims	16
Biting and baiting	17
Dodges in barbelling	18
Baiting the swim	19
Various methods of fishing	20
Rods	21
Winches	22
Lines and casting	23
Dressing	24, 25
Colour of gut bottoms	25
Fitting up leger tackle	25
Hooks	26

TROUT FISHING.

	PAGE
Localities where fish are found	27
Weir fishing	27, 28
Rods	28
Traces, flights, &c.—colour of gut	29
Binding and joining	30
Spinning leads, etc.	31
Flights, and baiting them	32
Artificial baits	33
Casting	34
Live Baiting	35

PIKE FISHING.

	PAGE
Rods	37
Lines and Reels	38
Baiting, spinning flight	39
Likely places for casting	40
Live baiting	41
Old-fashioned theories	42
General tackle	43
Baiting	44
Floats and baits	45
Snap tackle	46
Paternostering	47
Striking	48, 49

PERCH FISHING.

	PAGE
Derwent perch	50
Description and handling	51
Localities where fish are found	52
Rods, winches, and hooks	53
Baits	54
Worm fishing	55

CARP FISHING.

	PAGE
Description	56
Localities where fish are found	57
Baits	58

	PAGE
Potato fishing	59
Methods of fishing	60

CHUB FISHING.

Description and localities where found	62
Likely places	63
Rods and reels	64
Gut bottoms and legering	65
Baiting	66
Cheese, paste, greaves and shrimps	67

TENCH FISHING.

Likely localities	69
Tench tackle, and using it	70
Bait	71

BREAM FISHING.

	PAGE
Description	72
Localities where found	73
Thames fishing	74
Tight corking and hooks	75
Ground baiting	76
Legering and baits	77
Cooking bream	78

DACE FISHING.

Description, and localities where found	79
Bottom fishing and baits	80
Likely places	81
Fly fishing for dace	82
Blow-line fishing	83
Ant flies	84
DISCUSSION	85–88

International Fisheries Exhibition
LONDON, 1883.

CONFERENCE ON TUESDAY, JULY 31, 1883.

LORD ABINGER in the Chair.

FRESHWATER FISHING IN GREAT BRITAIN OTHER THAN TROUT OR SALMON.

I HAVE the honour to submit for your approbation a few remarks based principally upon practical knowledge, and having reference to the pursuit of angling for what are commonly called "the coarse fish" of this country.

This class of sport is, very deservedly, popular in the extreme, and day by day, I think, grows in the public estimation. The reason for such popularity is not difficult to find, inasmuch as in great towns, such as London, or indeed in any manufacturing centre, the man who either inherits or cultivates a taste for angling, becomes a student in a charming and health-giving pastime, not necessarily expensive to one of limited monetary resources, yet one which, followed out faithfully and observantly, is, I believe, the invariable means of developing any latent disposition to good. Coarse fish angling has also another distinction of its own. It is particularly the sport of the poor man. Salmon fishing, with all its gloriously moving incidents by "flood and field," is a branch of English sport nearly entirely confined to the wealthier classes. Trout fishing is almost, if not quite as exclusive. There is hardly a yard of trout water within hail of any large town but what is at once monopolised, either by its owner, or by some one who can afford to pay a high price for the privilege of fishing it. In the case of the coarse fisher this state of affairs takes an altogether different aspect; because the very poorest amongst the community can, if he so pleases, and thanks to that binding law which is the result of long-continued user, hie him to the banks of such noble rivers as the Thames and the Lea, and there fish to his heart's content. I am not about to tell you that he is certain to obtain sport sufficient to repay him for his trouble and possible outlay. That is a question in these modern days, and amidst the riot and hurly-burly caused by those angler's pests—steam launches—and the greatly increased traffic of the river, which must always remain merged in obscurity, until, at any rate the close of the day. An acute mind will naturally reflect that the same ratio of reasoning applies to all classes of fishing, and I am by no means prepared to gainsay it. In the Thames, however, such a reflection comes home with tenfold force, and it only shows how keenly the love of angling is developed in the bosoms of many men, how patient and long-suffering fishermen are, as a race, and how content with the hope even of small mercies, when throughout the season the great railway stations are crowded every week with whole battalions of the rank and file of the angling army.

It is, however, at the London, Brighton, and South Coast Railway Station, and that at Liverpool Street, on the Great Eastern Line, that the most extraordinary sight in connection with the coarse fishermen of London is to be seen on every Sunday morning.

It may be that mention of the selected day may offend the "unco guid" section of polite society; but it must be remembered, as a set-off, that nine out of every ten of the great crowd gathered round the Booking-Office window are recruits from the still greater host of workers with bone, muscle, thew and sinew, to whom loss of time during the working hours of the week means not only loss of bread, but perhaps the loss of some small delicacy to a sick and ailing child. Thus it would seem particularly hard to attempt restraint upon such men in the gratification of their simple pleasures, nor is it by any means certain that they do not imbibe far more real good through their vigil by the river's side, than if they had donned the carefully saved suit of go-to-meeting broadcloth, and dozed drowsily and drouthily over a drawling, doctrinal dissertation, delivered by a divine of the "Stiggins" type. Rest assured if there be a sick baby, the little one is rarely forgotten, and smoke-grimed Daddy, all the better and healthier in soul and body for his twelve hours' rest from the roaring forge, gathers her or him, as the case may be, a bonny bundle of wild blossoms which he takes home with him as the topmost layer of the cargo in his roach basket.

The approaches to either of the lungs of the great Wen which I have spoken of, are indeed a wonderful sight. Gathered there are pale-faced weavers from Spitalfields, with flexible delicate fingers, cane-chair workers, with hard and horny hands; brawny, swart hammermen, and stout-limbed big-muscled strikers, both of them probably from some neighbouring foundry. Then there are dyers and curriers with the stain of their calling set indelibly on their skins, together with workers, perhaps from a white lead factory with that tallowy, unhealthy complexion inseparable from such a life of toil. Amongst these there are a few, but a very few, smartly dressed clerks with their sweethearts, and these probably eye the hundreds of fishermen wonderingly as upon an introduction to a strange development of human nature. Later on, this latter section of the holiday throng will be found tea-drinking in shady Broxbourne arbours, or watching the fisherman with a curiously developed interest as he plys his delicate tackle. Look round carefully through the ranks of thronging piscators, and any one may see for himself that they are all anglers of one stamp. It is curiously strange, but none the less strange than true, that nine out of every ten of the anglers of London are all wedded to the pursuit of roach fishing. Every man there has a long 18-ft. rod in its jean case, and with this is tied up the handle of his landing net. His rod is invariably slung across his shoulder, and dependent from the butt, and resting on his broad back is the well-known basket or box seat without which the true roach fisher never sets out.

It may perhaps be well at this point to consider why it is that the modern rodster is apparently attached so much to this particular branch of the sport. The answer is, that it is at once the prettiest and most skilful branch of angling in the world, as well as that which is most easily attainable ; and to see such men at work on the Lea as Hackett, Bates, Da Costa, or my old friend Tom Hughes, whose show of fish at this exhibition is second to none, in their particular style, or Theaker or Bailey upon the Trent, is to see one branch at least of the true poetry and craft of angling.

It will be impossible within the limits of time at my command to enter fully into all the mysterious ramifications attaching to many branches of the silent craft. One or two of them however I must touch upon, and knowing that roach-fishing is the most popular of all branches, I venture to deal with that first.

Now at the outset I may tell you, gentlemen, who may

not, possibly, have seen roach fishermen at work on the Lea, something about the manner in which they set to work. In the first place, I think it might be well to consider the rod, which is usually one of 18 feet in length, built of the very best white Carolina or West Indian cane. The best rods are invariably made as free as possible from burrs and knots, the cane being specially picked for their manufacture. Stiffness and pliability throughout their entire length is one great thing which is always looked to, and yet they have an immense amount of give and take in the very fine, yet short, top joint, and the immediate connecting joint. That is a very essential qualification in a rod devoted to the special branch of angling with which I am dealing. Previously, I think, to the famous match between Woodard, the champion of London, and Bailey, an equally great fisherman on the Trent, there was no such thing as real thorough roach rods made at any time, or at any rate rods made especially for roach-fishing, and specially with regard to the habits of the fish. They were simply bamboo bottom rods, and not half so much attention was given to their manufacture. But upon the occasion of this famous match, which excited an immense amount of interest at the time, a great impetus was given to that particular branch of the craft, and for months and months nothing else was talked about in London angling circles but roach-fishing and fishermen. Directly following this leading affair, match followed match amongst lesser luminaries of the angling world, and presently a maker named Sowerbutts, of Commercial Street, brought out a first class rod for roach-fishing, and he it was perhaps who gained an enormous reputation as being the first man who made roach rods in their present excellent form and finish.

There is no doubt he studied the particular play and style of rod necessary for this kind of fishing. Then he was followed, and imitated also, by a host of other makers, until in the present day, and amongst such traders as Carter and Sons of St. John Street Road, Alfred of Moorgate Street, and last, but not least, a little maker I have known something about lately, named Gold, of Waterloo Road, and who I think makes as good a class of rod as it is possible to obtain for this particular branch of fishing, there is small appreciable difference to be found in the quality of their manufactured goods. Generally, then, a rod for roach-fishing should be lengthy yet full of equable spring—tapered beautifully from the broad butt, built of the very lightest white pine, to the slender cane and lance-wood top, as light as possible in the hand, with no superfluous weight attached in the shape of rings, or heavy metal fittings, and altogether a perfect weapon suited for a very perfect branch of the art of angling. I have no belief in general all-round rods. A salmon rod should be a salmon rod and nothing else, and a roach rod ought to be equally distinct.

I may now, perhaps, properly discuss the question of roach lines, and I may also at this point premise that a really good and skilful roach fisherman almost invariably uses tight tackle. He seldom or never condescends to the use of running tackle, save, it may be, by operators upon the Trent. There has been a considerable controversy during the last few years in the columns of the 'Fishing Gazette,' and other sporting journals, with regard to the advantages of gut over hair. For my own part I never could see that there was any strikingly great advantage derived from the use of hair in roach-fishing, and particularly when the chances were that one was likely to get hold of a heavy chub or barbel in the same swim—save it might be from the sportsmanlike desire to kill one's fish with the lightest possible tackle. Therefore, I think a nice round fine gut line is as good a tackle as one could possibly use. Roach-floats are invariably made from either quill or reed, and they are selected as a matter of course with regard to the depth and character of the water which it is intended to fish. Nicely shaped wooden floats are favourites also, but, carrying little shot, they are only suitable for swims of medium depth. There is a considerable amount of difference in the manner in which the roach-float is shotted, as against other floats used for other purposes. For instance, it matters very little if the perch or chub-float wants the completing shot to effect its perfect balance, but the roach-float cannot possibly be shotted too deeply down, so long as the immediate tip of the float, which I may explain is the top of the white quill and the cap, swims steadily and nicely over the surface of the stream. That is the very best character that a roach-float can possibly assume. It should be shotted down to the point, when three or four shot corns more, over and above the weight of the bait itself, would assuredly swamp it.

I will now go to the question of baits. For roach-fishing they are few in number and very simple, and without touching upon the question of pearl barley, wheat, shrimps, wasp grubs, silk weed, or any other of the many various baits which kill at certain times, I think I may say that one of the best kinds of bait one can possibly use, is a paste made of stale crumb of bread just moistened, and worked up in the palm of a cleanly hand. A very excellent paste is likewise made of an arrowroot biscuit, from which the outside brown crust has been scraped off, until the inner and white interior only is left. Slightly moistened with fair water, this biscuit works up into a capital white paste, which is at times especially killing. Gentles, again, during the winter time, are a capital all-round bait, and the same may be said of the tail of a lob worm, or small red worm, either in summer or winter, when floods have caused a rise in the streams, and probably a course of coloured waters. Ground bait, which is usually a very expensive matter in various other methods of fishing, is in roach-fishing very simple and inexpensive. The roach-fisher seldom uses anything but a stiff paste made of bread and bran. He soaks his bread over night, and in the morning squeezes the surplus water away, and then adds to it a quantity of bran, working it up in his hands, until he gets a stiff paste as tough and hard as putty. He baits his swim with pieces of this ground bait about as large as a pigeon's egg, or a good sized walnut. That is quite sufficient for the purpose of baiting a roach swim. On the Lea they have a practice which I have found wonderfully good at times, when roach are exceedingly shy, and when they will not take a bait under any conditions, and that is this. When these experienced operators have baited their hook with an ordinary piece of paste or with gentles, they take a little of this tough ground bait, and nip it immediately over the two shots which are usually put on the bottom length of hair or gut, about two inches above the hook. When the float is thrown gently up-stream, the extra weight causes it to sink, but the rodster lifts it carefully along until it gradually reaches the point where the roach are supposed to be lying. The whole way it comes down the stream, this little bit of bread and bran keeps flaking small particles off along its downward track. This is especially attractive to roach, and practice has frequently proved that they will then feed a great deal better than they had been doing previously, when the simple bait itself had been floated time after time down the swim. Now, the roach is a particularly quick and active fish in its habits. It follows the bait down, and I believe sucks it in as it goes down the stream, taking hold of it with the peculiarly shaped prehensile upper lip. That upper lip of the roach is precisely like the hood of a perambulator. I believe those big, aldermanic fellows, sly and wary as courtiers, cautiously protrude their upper lip, and, hunger getting the better of them, suck the bait in. But the instant they get the bait into their mouths, and they detect that there is anything foreign about it, that instant they reject it. That shows the importance of the float being shotted down until the very lowest depth of its floatability has been secured. You see it will hardly bear one corn more shot, and when these artful old roach follow the bait down-stream, when they look at it even, to stretch one's imagination a little, much less touch it, instantly the float gives way, and there is a little sharp dip. Now, the good roach-fisherman is marvellously quick in hooking his fish, and from start to finish it is a bit of finished wrist-action entirely. He fishes with this long 18-foot rod—which I have attempted to describe to you—and it is curious and beautiful to see the accuracy with which a crack roach-fisherman will hook fish after fish with merely a little upward jerk of the wrist. The line is very short; indeed, from the point of the float to the top of the rod, it is usually not more than a couple of feet in length, and consequently, this short length being kept taut throughout the float's downward journey, the slightest upward stroke is sufficient to hook the wariest old roach, so long as it is done at the proper moment of time. Miss that moment, and one might just as well not strike at all.

There is a considerable difference between the various styles adopted upon the three rivers, viz., the Lea, the Thames, and the Trent. That upon the Trent is called "stret pegging" in some cases, "tight corking" in others, and is always founded upon the midland fisherman's excellent theory of fine and far off. It is questionable, however, whether this is quite so good as the Lea style. Roach-fishing on the Thames at any rate is practised from a punt by fishing with a long light line and a short rod. The punt angler on the Thames almost invariably uses running tackle, but in the Lea and most other rivers I think the best anglers use that class of tackle which experience tells them is the most useful, viz., a long rod with a tight line, and that I am well assured is the finest and most artistic principle of roach-fishing.

Now, with regard to the rivers in which roach are found. I think the finest roach I ever saw or heard of came respectively from the Avon and Stour, one being a Dorsetshire and the other a Hampshire river. The Lea, in days gone by, was also a famous roach stream, although in later years I think its angling capacities have not been quite so good. There are also excellent roach in the Mole, a beautifully quaint little stream, its banks teeming with thoughtful associations with the works of dead and gone poets, while the Colne also is a charmingly productive stream whose fish are strikingly handsome specimens.

One word now upon swims, and then I will close this branch of freshwater fishing.

It is likely enough to strike even the most unreflective mind, that there should naturally be a great difference between the swims selected for almost any class of fishing during the heats of summer, and those picked out during the rigours of the winter season. Some men there are, however, who never learn. Others, who do, soon gather together the fact that there is a considerable difference in the style of water which should be selected by rodsters at various times of the year. As a matter of fact, roach are ground-feeding fish, seldom or never taking bait except on the bottom of the river. It does not follow, however, that roach in the great heats of the summer do not take flies and insects on the surface of the river, because they will do so beyond all question. So will they also take baits presented at mid-water, or off the bottom, at times. They affect two different classes of water during the summer and winter. Some of the best roach swims in the more pleasant portion of the year are almost invariably found near large beds of weeds, at sharp swims at the tails of mill streams—not too sharp for the travel of an ordinary roach-float—or where the water runs smartly without too much stream by old camp-shedding. There the roach will easily be found during the summer months. It is very frequently the practice during those months, and particularly during great heat seasons, when it is almost impossible to catch fish on the bottom of the river, to fish for them by means of dipping or daping with the live natural insect. Then there is another very killing method called blow-line fishing. That is effected in this way. The operator is armed with a long, light, pliable rod, to which is attached a line somewhat longer than the rod itself, made of floss silk. The angler has his back to the wind, and having found out where the fish are lying he waits for a breeze. His tackle consists of a little length of the finest possible gut at the end of a long length of floss silk. To the gut link is attached a small hook which he baits with a natural grasshopper or blue-bottle fly. With the rod held aloft, the baited hook in the left hand, he waits for a breeze. Presently it comes and bellies the floss silk line out in a long graceful curve which blows right over the water. He watches his opportunity until it gets directly over where the roach are possibly lying, and then, drops the baited hook gently as a bit of thistle down on the surface. That is a very killing method of taking roach when they will not by any means take a bait at the bottom of the river. Regard being had to the best time of the year for roach-fishing, the autumn, and better still, the winter months occupy the post of honour. I personally have had some of the very finest takes of roach in the winter months that man ever had in this world, and I remember upon one occasion when fishing in the Hampshire Avon I took 75 lbs. of heavy roach in 5 hours. I took them all with a tight line—not running tackle—and using an 18-foot rod over a very heavy stream of swirling water. I had some of the finest sport you can possibly imagine. There is no time better in the world than the winter time for roach-fishing. On a sharp, crisp morning, when the trees and grass are frosted all over with hoar; when you hear the robin's notes whistling out bright and clear, and the sooty rook's harsh caw sounds less strident, then is the time to go roach-fishing.

I do not say the fish will feed very early in the morning, but when the sun gets up, the hoar begins to melt, and there is a little softness in the ground, then the fish begin to feed, and the deeper the selected swim consistent with a fairly good convenience in fishing it, the better at that period of the year. The fish are in the best condition; they are lusty, plump, and glowing with radiant colour. I know of no class of fish that makes a more thoroughly good and handsome basket as the result of the angler's toil, than a rattling good basket of roach.

Barbel Fishing.

There is another highly popular branch of sport to which the London angler is deeply attached, and that is barbel-fishing. It is mostly practised on the Thames. I do not say there are no barbel in the Lea, because I know there are, and plenty of them, but as barbel-fishing is most effectively carried out on the Thames, and is possibly better understood on that river than on any other in the kingdom, I shall confine my remarks chiefly to the practice there.

Now as to the qualities of my friend the barbel. We have heard a great deal lately about the marvellous gameness of the black bass of America, and I have heard my friends Mr. Wilmot and Dr. Honeyman expatiate upon him at vast length, saying that there is no such fish in this world for game qualities. I am perfectly prepared to admit it, but I must insist that the barbel of the Thames is an equally game fish, indeed I doubt very much whether there is any fish which can possibly eclipse my old antagonist the Thames barbel. He is a wonderfully game fish; you can never call him dead until he is absolutely in your landing net. I can tell you, gentlemen, that when I have had a big barbel "hang on," to use a fisherman's slang, in a heavy weir stream, the sport has been comparable to the best fighting salmon I ever hooked in my life or ever saw hooked, considering the relative difference in the tackle used. There is a considerable difference between the style of barbel-fishing on the Trent and on the Thames, and these are the two principal rivers where barbel are fished for in the present day. The Trent fisherman almost invariably fishes with float tackles, the Thames fisherman with a leger. The difference is still greater when you listen to the conditions on which success is said to depend. The Trent fisherman tells you that unless the river is low and exceedingly bright there is no possible chance of catching barbel at all. The Thames fisherman, and I take it upon myself to say he is right, will tell you that you rarely get fish in the Thames unless the water is high and thick. The higher the water, and the

thicker the water is, short of anything like the thickest
"pea soup" condition, the better, I think, is your chance
of getting barbel. The difference between the two styles
can be easily understood, because they are so totally and
distinctly opposite. The Trent fisherman fishes with a
float, and consequently he wants low and bright water, so
that the fish for which he is angling may see the bait
and follow it down the stream. The Thames fisherman,
knowing perfectly well that the barbel, not only being a
gregarious fish swimming in shoals, but also being an
essentially ground-feeding fish, feeds his fish up to a
certain point, and then fishes for them with tackle which
lies at the bottom of the river. I am not prepared to say
that the Trent fisherman is not as good a man as it is possible to conceive, but I certainly think that taking the best
samples of the two men, and pitting them one against the
other upon the two rivers, and each fishing in his own style,
that the Thames fisherman will invariably beat the Trent
man, because after all that is said and done barbel are barbel
all the world over, and their habits are precisely similar.

Now in the selection of swims for barbel in the early
part of the summer I should prefer sharps and good scours,
because there the fish are lying beyond all question.
They are freeing themselves from parasites, cleansing
themselves from spawning operations, and there they will
occasionally feed, and you will always find them in three
or four feet of water. There is no reason why, in such
a depth as that, excellent fish should not lie. I have
over and over again seen them of eight and ten pounds in
such situations equally as well as in deeper water. As the
summer progresses and the autumn season comes on,
they shift down bit by bit into the lower waters, and get
into heavy runs under projecting clay banks or close in to

deep swims protected by camp shedding. I do not know that I can pick out a better sample of such a bank than the one well known to all Thames fishermen, called the "High bank" at Sonning. There the water runs in a very heavy stream indeed. The banks are hollowed and scoured out, presenting harbours of refuge to the fish; and during the autumn period and that of approaching winter, heavy barbel lie under those banks for shelter, and consequently it is a capital place to angle for them.

Now there is an immense difference between the bite of a barbel when he really means business and the reverse. Occasionally it so happens that when a barbel swim has been well baited, and the proper length of time has been allowed for the fish to recover after a heavy dose of baiting, before the work of the angler commences, your barbel, when he does feed, makes so little mistake about it that there is very little trouble to the angler. Then one gets the poetry of angling so far as barbel are concerned; but on the contrary, now and again, they feed in the most curious and perverse manner. In speaking of hook baiting on the Thames, the general practice is as follows: the fisherman takes a worm, dips it into a basin of sand, rolls it up, takes a big white Carlisle hook, puts it in at the head, and threadles that unhappy worm right up the whole shank of the hook. Thus the unfortunate worm is pierced clean through by the hook from end to end, leaving just a little bit of the tail wriggling at the extreme point of the hook. Now that bait being thrown into the stream upon ledger tackle, and when barbel are feeding, they will take it like a shot. Sometimes I think my friend would take a boot-jack. He seizes hold of the bait, and there can be no mistake about the fact of his bite, because he frequently pulls the rod clean down to the water. On the other hand, he does nothing of the kind. I have frequently heard Thames fishermen say to one another, "Have you had any sport to-day," and shaking their heads mournfully they say, "No, but those confounded dace have been nibbling at the bait all day long." But the nibbling probably arose from a totally different source, and it has been barbel biting when they were in that capricious mood I just spoke of, and when they only bite very gently and tenderly. Now I have a little bit of a dodge by means of which I have tried to find out the weak points of a barbel when he has been in that particularly low-spirited condition with regard to feeding. Instead of completely spoiling my worm by the process of threadling previously spoken of, I take a perch-hook, No. 8 or 9, and then a lob worm, and pop the hook right through the middle. I just nick it through the middle of the worm, and leave the two ends of the worm to work about. Now if you compare the action of those worms in a basin of water, the one being threadled right up the gut with only a little atom of lively flesh at the end of his tail, and my worm with two small punctures only made in his flesh while the rest is wriggling and curling most deliciously, I think you will agree with me that if the fish be delicate and refined in his taste with regard to worms, there can be little doubt which of the two he would be likely to prefer. I venture to think he would take mine. The Thames fisherman also, when legering, throws out the bullet and turns the rod sideways at a distinct angle, so that when the fish bites he pulls the rod right down. Well, a child even could hook him then, but sometimes, when they are not feeding, the little resistance that is offered by the rod frightens them and they are off. Now I hold my rod and bait somewhat differently. Having put the worm on I throw out the bullet, and feeling it strike the bottom I lift it up, and draw it towards me so as to get the gut bottom taut, and then drop it very gently and wind up with a swift-actioned Nottingham reel. This being done, I next turn the point of the rod so that its extreme top indicates the precise spot where the bullet lies, and place the smallest possible amount of tension on the reel, just so much only as to prevent the stream taking the line off. Consequently, when a barbel takes the worm I feel the slightest little touch and release my finger so that the line may run freely. Thus I let him take the worm, and he on his part feels no resistance whatever. Away he goes with it, and then he usually gets pepper, and it is cayenne of the first order.

A great consideration in connection with barbel-fishing is baiting your swim, and upon that depends the whole of the after success. I frequently hear of men who go down to fish the Thames, and in really good localities, where there are plenty of fish, putting in a quantity of bait over night, fishing the swim early the next morning, and the next day going home disgusted. A brother fisherman says, "Well, Jones, did you have any sport?" he says, "Not an atom; I put in 5,000 worms on the swim, and I never caught a fish." Why is that? Well, the answer is, because in nine cases out of ten a thoughtless angler puts his worms in at night, and he fishes over them the next morning. The consequence is, there is a herd of barbel inhabiting that particular section of the stream, they have all fed on those worms, and are in precisely the same position as a London alderman would be, if, after having just swallowed a huge dose of turtle-soup and venison somebody offered him a fat pork chop. You may put 5,000 or even 10,000 worms on to a barbel swim—I do not care how many there are—and allow the fish sufficient time to recover their appetites, say 25 to 30 hours afterwards, and then most certainly will you get fish, unless there is some peculiar circumstance in connection with the temperature of the air, or water, or electrical disturbances, or anything of that kind which prevents the fish feeding. I could give a curious illustration of that. I once went to fish at Mr. Worthington's weir at Sonning. I put into a barbel swim there 28 quarts of lob worms. I think there were nearly three slop pails full. I fished there 24 hours afterwards; and I may add that at that time I was the angling editor of 'Bell's Life,' and my racing chief, Mr. Henry Smurthwaite, known to every racing man under his nom de plume of "Bleys," was with me. The result of the day's fishing, after giving the barbel a really good rest after baiting, was for the two rods something like three cwt. of fish, besides some large trout and perch. I should add, however, that out of the three cwt. we only brought ten fish home, the rest being turned back into the river. Now for a few words of practical instruction.

The best known methods of capturing this essentially sporting fish are three in number, to wit—with the leger, float and clay-ball. Practice with the float may be divided into what is known as "tight" or "long corking," and fishing with the "slider"—the latter, certainly, a capital style to adopt, when deep and varying runs of water have to be attempted. I propose, therefore, to deal with the subject matter of this part of my paper in the order named at its head, making my chief point the leger. The rod used —an important item,—should, in my opinion, for convenient fishing never exceed 12, or at most 14 feet in length; for as this sport is usually pursued by its votaries from the medium of a punt or boat, as affording the readiest opportunity of reaching known haunts of the fish under notice, a rod of this length will be found far more handy and useful in a cramped space than one of greater length.

Its material is the next consideration, and, after trying rods manufactured from a variety of woods, I can find none so reliable and lasting as one of good sound cane, such as can be obtained to perfection from my friend Alfred, of Moorgate Street, himself a good and practical fisher, and hence a good man to apply to. The joints should be perfectly straight, free from flaw, and the less knots in them the better, the ferrules strong and well fitted, the rings upright, as a matter of course, thus allowing the line to run freely, when thrown out from the winch; and with regard to the action or "play" of the rod, it should neither be too stiff nor too supple. If it is very stiff it does not show by the "niggle" at the point of the top-joint, a process most popular in use, when the fish is attacking the bait, or at any rate, if they are feeding badly, the best moment at which to strike. If it is too supple, the quick stroke of the wrist necessary in driving the steel home into our tough-nosed friend's snout is frequently lost through the action being diffused too slowly through the elasticities of the weapon in use. The rod, therefore, should be fairly stiff, with a fine top, a trifle stouter than a roach top, yet with an amount of bend and give-and-take work about it as will aid the hand, wrist, and reel, in killing a good fish, should the angler be so fortunate as to get hold of one. The best advice that I can offer to a tyro in the selection of a rod is this—in buying your rod go to such men as Alfred of Moorgate Street, Gowland of Crooked Lane, Bowness and Farlow of the Strand, or Carter of St. John Street Road. Tell them exactly what you want, pay a good price at the outset, and the probabilities are that you will get a tool that with careful usage will last a lifetime. While upon the subject of rods I may mention, perhaps with advantage to my readers, the excellent rods that are to be obtained from many of the well-known Nottingham tackle manufacturers, and no one does them better than Wells, of Sussex Street, Nottingham. They are made of deal, beautifully balanced, well whipped and ringed, with substantial fittings, and for float work a man can have no better rod in his hands. For legering, however, they are a bit too "kittle," and from the frail nature of the material employed in their manufacture it is obvious that at the best of times they require a delicate hand, and an absence of anything like pully-hauly business. Otherwise a smash is about as likely to ensue as an explosion if one dropped a hot coal into a barrel of powder. In the hands of a workman these rods are simply perfection for floating, and so beautifully light that the longest day never tires. And now as to the winch, another important auxiliary. Wooden pirns, or Nottingham winches as they are more generally called, as well as those made of vulcanite, are so thoroughly well made, and so cheaply put together nowadays, that no one would dream of using any of the old-fashioned brass furniture that formerly pertained to the rod. Reels can now be had combining two actions, the one being the free, easy run, so necessary to the practice of float-fishing with a long run down-stream, the other, a check action, obtained by simply pressing a spring on the reverse side of the handles, which impels a little catch downwards, the point of the bolt-shaped catch nicking into the cogs of a wheel fitted upon the centre pin, thus obtaining the most perfect check. Pressure backwards upon the spring relieves the cog wheel, and the winch then runs upon its centre pin with the velocity of "greased lightning." Such a winch as this is the best that can be used, the only drawback being —and of course there must be something—is that if it be manufactured from wood and one gets out on a soaking day, the inner rim will swell with the wet, causing the winch to clog. I have once or twice experienced the misfortune of a "strike" on my colleague, the reel's part, brought about under watery conditions of weather, and that too at a time when the fish were, to use an angler's slang, "mad on"—a concurrence of circumstances not to be devoutly wished. It has struck me that an edge of very thin metal fitted upon the rim of the inner wheel would entirely obviate this only defect in an otherwise perfect winch. A twisted silk line is good, but a plaited line is far better; I would advise anglers, therefore, always to choose the latter. Twisted lines, unless the angler is an adept at throwing from the reel, of which more anon, kink abominably after they once become wet, and I leave it to my reader's own mind to picture the misery of a man who gets some 25 or 30 yards of line in a fearful "boggle" about twice out of three times in his attempts to throw out to a spot where the fish are taking the bait. With a plaited line it is different; and even if the angler cannot throw from the reel—a little performance that requires some practice before perfection is attained—he has only to be fairly careful and see that his coils of line are free and clear of any obstruction in the shape of twigs or stiff blades of grass if upon the bank, or the toes of his boots, or the chair legs in a punt. At the time of throwing out also, dispense with anything like a jerk when impelling the bullet to its desired destination, thus securing the ultimatum of your happiness—to wit, the free running of the line through the rings, without any tangle, or the annoyance of finding the fine line linked well round one of them, and the bullet and leger bottom flying away through space by itself, broken away from the line by the impetus of the throw, and the sudden check caused by the link aforesaid. Supposing, then, that a plaited line has been selected, I would have 100 yards of it at least on the reel for legering, and for this reason. Careful as one may be, a fine line always rots and frets more or less with hard work, and it is always advisable before commencing a day's campaign against such an undoubted hard puller as your barbel, to see that the line is in good condition. If it is not, break it away in lengths of a yard at a time, until it will stand the test of a strong, steady pull. Thus 100 yards will not be too much. Consistently with the requisite strength that is required, the line cannot be too fine, for it should be remembered, that the finer the line the less effect the stream has upon it, and the less weight will be required to keep it at the bottom. Thus it will be sufficiently patent to every rodster that the smaller the bullet used, if one can only make certain of its being upon the bottom, the more readily will the bite of the fish be distinguished, and the more likely is one to kill a large one with a light bullet that can be held taut above him, than with a heavy one, which must cause a certain amount of bend or "sag" in the line when the fish is struck and pounding away for liberty. While upon the subject of lines, and before dismissing it, I may, perhaps, add a few words upon their preservation. Nothing ruins a line, no matter how good it may be, so much as allowing it to remain on the reel for any length of time after use, and a capital adjunct to the angler's equipment will be a light wooden winder, say a foot square, that fits closely and neatly to the side of the basket. On this the line should be wound off the reel, but not in lengths overlapping each other, directly the sport of the day is over, and care should be taken that a few yards more than the quantity that has actually been in use be unwound from the reel and well dried, to provide for the great probability of the wet having soaked down amongst the silk that has been unwound during the day. When the line is thoroughly dry it may be advantageously dressed with the following preparation—as good and simple as can be used, keeping it thoroughly supple, and aiding it in water-resisting power —Take a bit of the best bees-wax that can be got, say of the size of a walnut, and a piece of the hard fat from the exterior of the sheep's kidneys, of about the same size, and melt them up together, giving the mixture frequent stirs with a stick, so as to assimilate the two substances thoroughly. When it is cold and hard, give the line a rub or two with this preparation every time it is used, and it will be found an excellent preserver of the most delicate lines. Leger bottoms should be selected from round, stout gut. Finer, of course, should be in the tackle book for use if the water is very bright, and each should be a yard in length. I have found nothing so good in the shape of colour as gut dyed of a light sorrel hue. I cannot help thinking that gut of this colour is less likely to be distinguished by the watchful, wary eye of a shy feeding fish, when lying on a sandy, gravelly bottom, than the blue gut, although I am aware that some of our best barbel-fishers pin their faith to the latter colour, and allow nothing to shake their allegiance. For my part, and having killed some barbel in my time, and at all seasons, I have found the sorrel gut giving better results than anything else. The proof of the pudding, therefore, being in the eating, I have only to add that white gut is an utter abomination. In fitting up the leger bottom, I use a length of the very finest stained gimp, of a yard in length, with a small bored shot fixed firmly upon it at the lower end, where the gut joins—this gimp being for the bullet to work upon, as I have found, over and over again, that the chafing of the bullet upon the fine silk line has caused a large amount of wear and tear, and losses of good fish, from the silk breaking exactly at the spot where the bullet worked upon it. Such experience caused me long ago to alter my tactics, and, if the gimp is selected fine enough—and it can be got nearly as fine as stout gut—and it is used with a yard of gut below it, it will not operate against the angler's success if the fish are feeding at all. If they don't feed, nothing on earth will make them. Hooks for legering, at any rate for lob-worm fishing, should be long in the shank, stout in the wire, and not too broad at the bend; they are sold at all respectable tackle shops now, with a small silk loop whipped on the shank in lieu of the usual length of gut, and are far preferable, doing away with the chance of the hook link being weaker than the gut bottom—and, again, a quantity can be carried without the chance of getting the gut links tangled and warped, a state of things frequently happening no matter how careful a man may be.

Perhaps the best hook in use at present amongst barbel-fishers is one made by Messrs. Allcock of Redditch, an eminent manufacturing firm, and called "The Wheeldon Barbel Hook." It is a white Carlisle and has a small wire loop at the top of the shank, on which it is only necessary to loop the gut bottom.

Although my paper is entitled "On Modern Fishing other than Trout and Salmon," I can hardly, in dealing with the Thames, leave the question of trout-spinning entirely out, because it is a question so strongly applicable to the Thames, and to no other river; therefore, I feel I must say half-a-dozen words even at the risk of tiring you. I think we ought, as English anglers, to feel very proud of our great home river, and of the quantity and calibre of the fish which inhabit it. I doubt very much if our friends from America or New Zealand, or any other place you like to mention, can bring forward more magnificent trout than have been taken in the Thames within the last few years. The Kennet again is swarming with trout, and as for size, I have only to point to some examples in the Exhibition. I think Lord Craven has taken trout in the Kennet up to 20 lbs. in weight, and two years ago a trout was taken in the Kennet behind Messrs. Huntley and Palmer's biscuit factory close upon 17 lbs. Neither is that an isolated instance, because within the last Thames trout season an old friend of mine, Mr. Ross-Faulkner, took a trout at Hampton Court Weir 14 lbs. 15 oz., and that is almost within the sound of the omnibuses and cabs rattling through Oxford Street. Other anglers have had splendid samples from the Thames. I might mention the names of Messrs. Allard, Hughes and Pugh amongst them, all of whom are showing grand trout at this Exhibition. I think it redounds very greatly to their credit as anglers to have caught such splendid trout. Again, Mr. Forbes, of Chertsey, a gentleman I have the honour to know, has perhaps the most magnificent collection of Thames trout that any man ever saw. With regard to trout-fishing there is a considerable amount of judgment necessary in approaching the locality that a trout inhabits. In the early part of the year you find trout on the scours near where they spawn, and they do not move up to the weirs, where they are more frequently caught, until the warm weather induces them to do so. As soon as hot weather sets in, you invariably find that trout follow the stream up further and further, getting at last to the heads of the big Thames weirs. There is a considerable amount of precaution necessary in approaching a weir. If a man goes to a weir-head where the foot-walk goes across from side to side, with a great sixteen-foot rod in his hand, and looks over the head of the weir where usually the trout are in the habit of lying, what is the consequence? Away goes your fish. Thus I may perhaps, hint at the best style to adopt under the circumstances.

To my notion a man wants two rods, so as to make his kit thoroughly complete, and so far as spinning pure and simple is concerned, I propose to speak of that branch of trout angling first, thus giving it the preference over live baiting. Not because I have fallen into the hypocritical groove which obtains in angling circles, and which enables certain very virtuous gentlemen to denounce live-baiting publicly, while they follow it up on every possible occasion in private; nor from the conviction that spinning is necessarily the purest and most sportsmanlike method of angling for large trout.

But why two rods? Well, I will give you my reasons. In punt fishing, or spinning from a boat, a long rod is often sadly in the way, and in the course of a day's casting to either side while working down a likely-looking reach where it is known fish lie, will tire and strain even a very stout arm indeed, quite as much as in a day's salmon casting, take my word for it. For such work, therefore, commend me to a rod lightly yet strongly made of sound unblemished mottled cane, 12 feet in length, with plenty of spring and play in it from butt to point, and fitted with the very best ring that ever was invented for casting or throwing purposes, viz., that brought out by Gregory of Birmingham, and at present fitted to most of the rods turned out by the celebrated firm of Allcock of Redditch. It is a perfectly simple appliance, being an arched wire whipped on at either side. The ring itself is firmly soldered into the centre of the arch; but it is absolutely out of even a careless angler's power to engender such an awful possibility as a kink, and that alone should be a sufficient guarantee of its worth to any one who has either lost, or who can imagine for one moment the diabolical and horrific grief and misery of losing, a good trout by such an unlooked-for and apparently impossible contingency.

In weir spinning the condition of things is altogether different. Here, not only is it sometimes necessary to fish at a considerable distance below one's standpoint, but a very large scope of water, every inch of it looking capable and likely ground, has to be covered. For this, therefore, give me a sixteen foot rod, pliable and springy, so that by the mere motion of the top joint alone I can keep my bait revolving smartly without taking up more than an inch or two at a time of the line.

Traces, flights and baits should have each a separate place. In connection with the first and second of these, two very necessary items, the greatest possible care should be used in the matter of their selection, for it is mainly upon their delicacy, accurate work, and powers of successful resistance to the plunging of a big and powerful fish, that the issue of the battle lies. Colour, likewise, is a great point, therefore principally choose, for trout spinning at any rate, gut of a pale smoky blue-green, if such a colour exists, a matter I am by no means certain about, and next see that it is correct and clear to the eye, free from white specks, or from knotty excrescences to the touch. Then if you have sufficient ability, and will take my advice, make your traces yourself. If not, you will not be far out by leaving them in the hands of such men as Alfred, Farlow, or Gowland.

But in their manufacture, whether it may be done at home or abroad, either carry out, or leave, positive instructions, that from top to bottom of the trace there shall not be one atom of binding in it. It is this very thing that in nine cases out of ten has been responsible for the loss of a good fish. "Godfrey Daniel!" says the fisherman, after seeing a grand fish just hooked fling himself clean out of the water and go with lightning-like speed down the run. "Godfrey Daniel! what a beauty!" Then ensues a splendid run for twenty yards, when a man's heart thumps painfully—absolutely painfully—at the bare notion of such a glorious creature becoming his own in due and proper time, and one vows "by our lady" that he shall be played as carefully, and with as gentle touch as one approaches the dear partner of one's bosom at that awful period when she's sulking for a new bonnet and can't have it. Hands up! There's another fling out of the water, and old brown-faced and horny-handed Tom Davis says excitedly and hoarsely, "Drop point on ye're rod, sir—smart, now!" and you instinctively do it as matter of course. Gone? Impossible! But it is so, and there's no getting away from it, and presently you see your own once fondly hoped-for trout leap a hundred yards in the stream below you, in the vain attempt to get rid of the half-yard of gut hanging from his jaws and the stinging triangles in his soft fleshy mouth. "Ah, gone at a bit o' binding," says old Tom ruefully at your elbow, surveying the broken trace. "Thowt so; I did by gum! It's they blessed careless coves at the shops as is to blame for half the trout as is lost;" and I entirely endorse old Tom's imaginary opinion. Therefore not a scrap of binding, if you please. It is just as easy to make small loops for the swivels, and after putting the loop through (the gut being well wetted previously), to draw them tight; and in the long run it is ten times more reliable, take my word for it. Now as to swivels and the length of the trace.

I sometimes tumble across trout-fishers up the Thames who are spinning a weir with three-quarters of a yard of gut (and that very coarse), three large jack swivels, and a great ugly lead, heavy and coarse enough for the coarsest and roughest pike fishing in private waters, where sharpset fish will often run at anything. For my own part, and knowing that if there is one fish which is especially more wide-awake and cunning than another it is an old wary Thames trout—I always start on the war-path as well and carefully armed as a man can be. I don't mean to assert, mind, as a fact, that the angler with coarse tackle never gets a fish. On the contrary, there is nothing so likely, supposing he knows from observation exactly where a trout feeds—and they feed day after day in the same spot to the fraction of a foot—that if he goes at early morning, before the weir has been disturbed by any of its paddles being drawn, and cautiously drops a biggish bait which spins well exactly over his lovely mottled nose, but that he will dash at it without an instant's reflection. That's when he is dead hungry, and then any fool can catch him. But only let him have a "bit in hand;" let him have, say, two or three bleak or dace down his throttle, just to take the sharp edge of the morning off, and rely upon it, it's the artist then, and not the chance man, that gets him even to look at a bait at all.

Thus I like a fine gut trace of full a yard and a quarter long, the lead so placed that it is a yard of trace length, and the length of the flight-link itself from the bait, and with at least five small, well made, well oiled swivels, and one double one, all set below the lead. There is no necessity for any above it; the lead is not intended to spin, and all the motion, therefore, should be below it. The more there is, and the freer it is, the less likelihood of a kink or snarl in the line. For the lead itself, nothing, in my opinion, beats the "Field lead," when mounted on an inch or two of very fine gimp, and next to that is a very good one brought out by the editor of the ' Fishing Gazette.'

As to the flight, after trying them all, I come to the conclusion that there is nothing better, perhaps, than the simple old Thames flight, with four sets of small stout wire triangles and a single liphook. The liphook is the main trouble, because, do what one will, or act as carefully as one will with it, there is always more or less chafing. I tried the liphook bound upon a short slip of starling's wing quill, the gut passing through the interior of the quill, and this answered well—for a time. Afterwards, as the gut and quill both swelled with the wet, it became simply immovable, and necessitated each fresh bait being of precisely similar size to its predecessor. Then I went back to the old-fashioned hook, with a single small loop of gut tied on the tip of the shank. This loop permits the hook to fly loose up and down the gut link, but when it is in use, and the gut thoroughly wet, a very efficient "bite" is obtained by simply lapping the gut carefully and systematically round the shank, until the liphook fits accurately to its place at the nose of the bait.

It is by no means easy to describe baiting theoretically. More may be learned by watching the operations of a really good Thames fisherman for an hour, than by all the pen-and-ink teachings in the world. However, practice, based upon a fairly good theory, may accomplish great things, so that, having first selected a clean silvery bleak—perhaps the best of all bait for a big trout, and particularly for a spinning flight—wet your fingers and hands thoroughly before handling the little fish, with a view to saving as much as possible of his brilliant silvery armour. Then nick one of the hooks of the bottom triangle exactly through the fleshy root of the tail, and precisely at the angle of the fork. That establishes a firm hold, and then, taking the lateral line as a guide, carefully fit in hook after hook upwards, towards the head, taking care that you bruise not nor tear the delicate skin, finishing off at the top triangle, which should fit nearly at the root but slightly above the pectoral fin. Draw back the liphook, hanging loose on its wet gut, measure off say half an inch for lapping, twist it carefully up until the bend of the hook touches the lips of the bait, and equally carefully put the hook through the very centre of the gristle of both lips. If it hangs straight as a die, with only a gentle curve at the tail, it will spin so as to kill a Thames trout, and if it don't, it won't ; so there you are, don't you know!

I do not like artificial baits, although I don't say that they will not kill at times. But those times are, in my opinion, and in the majority of cases, just the same as when the short trace, coarse gut angler gets a run. Even here I must make an exception in favour of one bait, and only one, and that is the 'Bell's Life' spinner, made and sold by Alfred & Son, of Moorgate Street. This is simply a really good bait, beyond all shadow of doubt, and both in the Thames and other rivers has proved its unquestionable excellence and killing powers over and over again. As an instance, I may place it on record that on the 27th of April, 1880—the first season, I fancy, in which they came into general use, and on a bitter cold day to boot—H. P. Hughes, Esq., caught at Shepperton Weir a brace of splendid Thames trout, weighing respectively 9 lbs. and 7½ lbs. In each case the trout had completely gorged the bait, taking it so thoroughly into the mouth that it required the assistance of scissors before the hooks could be cut away. A very great deal, however, of the excellence of these baits consists in the exact angle at which the tail is bent. They are sold, I fancy, with the tails fashioned sheer across, and this won't spin, or anything approaching it. The tail should be bent slightly over with the thumb and fingers of the right hand until it assumes a very gentle downward sweep or angle from slightly below the point or root of the dorsal fin to about the line of the ventral fin, or where the ventral fin should be. With this bait I have killed many good fish, both in the Thames and Kennet, a few years ago, and I shall try them again with certainly renewed confidence.

In casting, I think nothing will beat the good old-fashioned Thames plan, of holding a coil of line in the left hand, and throwing from that, save it may be that the stream is sufficiently heavy and strong to permit the use of a heavy lead, and then one can throw from the reel—best plan of all. In any event, have no loose line about either the bottom of the punt, or on your knees, if sitting on the weir beam with your legs dangling over in space. The end, in the event of a run, may be summed up in one sentence, viz., total loss of temper, and the continued and frequent use of a word which distinguishes say the mother of a thorough-bred foal, for the rest of that day on every possible or impossible opportunity. Remember that the least possible movement of the bait is sufficient. Do not let it remain stationary, or spinning in one position long together, because to the discriminating eye of an old and judiciously educated trout, particularly of the order *Trutta Tamesis*, such a course of procedure would look odd, to say the least of it. Rather work it slowly and very gently in and out and round about every little eddy and curl, and quickly across those dark, oily-looking patches between foamy runs.

I approach the subject of live-baiting in fear and trembling, because I am half afraid that its very mention may bring a hurricane about my devoted head, and heaven knows, having had some experience of married life, I don't want that. Still, I know full well that there are scores of people ready to howl indignantly and defiantly against any one even breathing a word about live-baiting in connection with Thames trout-fishing, yet who are the very first to put it in practice when they are clear of the lens of public scrutiny. I live-bait myself, and shall continue to do so, for three very good and sufficient reasons. In the first place I beg to assert that there is ten times more real skill and science displayed in killing a good trout with my live-bait tackle than with all the spinning tackle in the world, because it is fifty times at least more delicate and fragile. In the second place, because, in spite of lamentations with upheld, shocked, and horrified hands, by sundry virtuous and "unco guid" howlers, I fail utterly and entirely to see anything unsportsmanlike in it; and, for the third, and perhaps most important of all, because I know perfectly well that, good as my chances are in a weir or rough stream with spinning bait, in wide, open, still reaches such as the very biggest trout lie in nowadays, it is at least twenty to one on the live-bait tackle as against that for spinning. Aye, and there is yet another reason, and that not the least of them either. Wherever it is known that a big trout feeds—and there is not a trout in the Thames whose home is not spotted to the fraction of an inch—there sits day after day either a professional fisherman with a customer, or without one—it is quite immaterial which, in the majority of cases—or some riverside loafer, whose only mission is to catch that trout by hook or by crook—crook preferred—and straightway convert his bones and body into beer and "bacca." Now, why should I, whose trout-fishing, cut it as fine as may be, costs at least a pound a day on the Thames, run less chance possibly than the very man who writes to tell me of a trout in such-and-such a place, and who very likely has run him, pricked him hard, or in some few cases absolutely caught him and sold him the day before ; or of the individual who values the splendid fish by just so many pots of beer and no more, who knocks him ruthlessly on the head, in or out of condition, and who has been at him morning, noon, and night from the first peep o' day on the opening of the season ?

Now here's the pattern of my tackle, any one is welcome to it, and if there be any who in time to come can tell me they have killed a ten-pounder on it fairly and squarely, no one will say more heartily—" Here's t' thee, my lad, and more power to your elbow," than he who pens these lines. First for the rod. It is a little 12-foot Nottingham barbel rod, made of deal, with a lancewood top, light, springy and handy. My reel is a wooden one, holding 200 yards of very fine silk, such as would be used for chubbing with pith and brains, or with cheese in the autumn and winter months. I have a bottom of three yards of finest gut—a very fine tapered fly cast is best—with, at the extremity, two small fine-wired perch hooks bound on the bottom strand, the lower two inches from the upper. One shot only—size No. 3—is put on the gut—4 ft. from the bait, so as to steady it in the stream. Just above the gut, and on the silk running line, is a bit of pear-shaped cork as big as a barbel bullet, sufficient only to buoy the line in a slight degree. On the upper of the two hooks is liphooked a live bleak ; the other hook flies loose, or, as I fancy, clings to the side of the little bait. If you can find and kill a big trout with this—fairly and squarely, mind, taking all the chances of submerged roots, boughs of trees, weed-beds or sunken piles—never mind anybody growling, but tell them to go and do likewise. There is not one in twenty who can, you bet.

PIKE FISHING (SPINNING).

I may now perhaps give you my ideas with reference to pike-fishing, and in the first place I think that a pike-fisher's equipment should, with regard to rods, consist of two—one being kept solely for spinning. This rod, being not more than 12 to 14 feet in length, is built so as to be more limber, and consequently has more "spring" in it than the other, which may be kept for paternoster work, trolling upon rare occasions, and live-baiting. A stiff rod for spinning—to my mind the most artistic method that can be adopted—is simply comparatively useless. The top, and indeed the rod generally, should give freely to the upward sweep of the arm when throwing, the rod being held tightly and easily in the right hand, while the butt is planted firmly in the hollow of the groin. Thus it materially helps in the direction to be obtained, and the length of the cast. Having a solid butt (which I prefer to a hollow one), the rod may yet be obtained as light and handy as is consistent with the work in hand; and any of the well-known London makers may be thoroughly depended on for workmanship. Upright or standing rings, as a matter of course, are a *sine quâ non;* without them it is impossible to throw to any distance without the line "kinking" and knotting up in a horrible tangle—perhaps the most annoying thing of all on a cold day, and when fish are feeding. The line used for spinning should be 60 or 70 yards in length, not *too* thick, thoroughly waterproofed, and well made and substantial in quality and strength; for it must be borne in mind, that it has to undergo more friction in the length used for casting than any other running line. The length named will be found amply sufficient for ordinary waters, such as the Thames or Trent, where the fish taken are usually of the ordinary size, though were I fishing some of the Irish lakes, or the private inland waters of England, where the fish have the reputation of being monsters, I should perhaps take care to have a bit more on the reel. The winch to be used is really very much a matter of fancy, although, for my own part, I prefer the plain wooden Nottingham reel to any other, for its ease in manipulation, and the rapidity with which one can reel up slack line. A reel I have lately seen, and one of the most recent manufacture, is a Nottingham reel combining two actions—the one being the smooth, easy run so necessary in "long corking," the other attained by pressing a spring on the reverse sides of the handles by which a cog is set to work giving check action instantaneously. The "flight" mounted upon fine gimp should have a set of three or four triangles and one moveable single hook. In baiting this flight of hooks, care should be taken to use dace, gudgeon, roach or bleak, whichever may be preferred, of a size proportionate with the length and fit of the flight of hooks used, as nothing tends so much to the ugly "wobbling" of a bait in the water as an over-sized fish badly mounted. Supposing then that a suitable bait is found, the bottom triangle is firmly fixed by the penetration of one of the hooks only in the extreme root of the tail, just where the flesh joins the rays; then, holding the dead fish firmly between the thumb and fingers of the left hand, so bend or curve the body that the tail assumes a clear and distinct sweep. Keeping it thus, force the point of one of the next set of triangles nicely, and without displacing the scales, into the body of the dace, so that the tail is kept firmly in the position desired. The other triangle is fitted into its place, whilst the small sliding hook is pulled down the gimp, and fixed through the nose of the bait, thus keeping all in the required position. Let us still further suppose, then, that the angler is at the waterside, and about to make his first cast. First, one word of advice as to approaching the side of a weir or river. Wherever you may be intending to angle use extreme caution—it is never thrown away—and tread as though you were in the backwoods and dreaded to hear the twang of an ambushed Indian's bowstring. Rely upon it that fish nowadays are *not* to be caught as they were in the days of Walton and Cotton; they get more and more subtle and cunning every day. Where there were ten anglers ten years ago there are now a hundred; the consequence is that every bit of fishable water is fished to death by anglers of every grade, from the rank duffer with a coarse gut line, enormous cork float and a big hook with a brandling impaled thereon, and sitting right over the water, yet who still, with a true fisherman's soul, hopes to catch that whacking perch that he saw an hour ago chase some gudgeon out of that deep hole and on to the shallows at his very feet, to the real artist, who fishes the hole with fine Nottingham tackle but little later, and takes glorious perch one after the other under "big float's" very nose, much to the latter's astonishment. So he puts his primitive tackle down to wonder at the other's skill, delighted if he can even manipulate the landing-net when an extra "big 'un" comes to bank.

Pike in fine open weather lie close in to the side, and under cover of projecting banks, tree-roots, and beds of water-flags and reeds. In colder weather they seek the shelter of the deeps. As a matter of course, if the angler approaches full in view, and with heavy and incautious tread, the place where a fish is lying, it becomes almost equally certain that the fish sees him long before he is close to his abiding place; and with one stroke of his great tail, he shoots out of the shallows and into the deeper portions of the river. So let us then "softly tread, 'tis hallowed ground," and having gained a likely spot, reel off some loose line, letting it fall clear of roots, grass, stumps, and rushes, to the left hand, and cast quietly, with as little splash as possible, if on a fine quiet day—on a windy day it doesn't matter—first to the right and then left, until converging to the centre. If the water has been fairly covered, and these preliminary casts need never be more than 10 or 12 yards from the side, and if further success does not attend you, draw off yard by yard from the reel, until a long cast, yet well within your power of rod and arm, has been attained. Never attempt to overdo it, because it always results in failure, and the tyro who tries to do a tremendous throw, will find that the extra momentum simply brings his line into a glorious tangle, and a very nice thing in fishing is a real, downright tangle—soothing to the feelings, very! As soon as the bait touches the water after the cast has been made, draw it across and against the current, with long regular strokes, with the left hand, avoiding a jerky motion, and taking care to keep the point of the rod well down, almost touching the water. The moment the point of the rod is raised, it causes the bait to spin nearer the surface, which is not to be desired, save in shallow, weedy waters. Spin the bait right up to your feet, and do not be in a hurry to get it out of the water for a fresh throw, for it often happens that both jack and perch will follow the bait out from the deeps, and take it quite close home; in fact, within sight. When a jack strikes the bait—of which fact there is usually little doubt on the angler's part, for it is plainly perceptible to the touch—strike him gently, yet still hard, so as to fix the hooks well within his bony jaws, and, having hooked your pike, it must then be very much a matter of discretion and judgment how you handle him. If you are fortunate enough to get hold of a really big fish, remember that, although pike as a rule do not go with the rattle and dash of a freshly-hooked salmon, or trout even, nor have they the dogged pertinacity of a barbel, they have—and particularly big fish—an immense amount of muscular strength, and no liberties must be taken with a good one "just on." Keep a tight line on your prey; keep him, if it is possible, as far away from the beds of weed as you can, and at the earliest opportunity get his head out of the water, and well up, giving him the benefit of a "back wash," as the rowing men say, down his capacious throat. Watch him keenly and warily, and give him hand and reel instantaneously if he makes a determined rush, taking care that no slack lies loosely about to get entangled in coat buttons or your feet. When your fish shows by his rolling, with his broad flat side to the surface, that he is fairly settled, lead him to a convenient place where the water shallows, and, bringing him to the side by the aid of the *reel*, and not the hand, get him close in, and gaff him with all speed.

LIVE-BAITING.

Under the head of live-baiting, the pike-fisher embraces several varieties of angling, chief among them being the well-known and most common method of fishing with a living fish bait attached to a hook and trace, and suspended in the water by the buoyancy of a big cork float. In large pools or meres, or indeed in any waters where there is little or no current, this style of pike angling is the easiest, and consequently the most idle. After baiting the hook, the angler can put his rod down and leave the bait to play its own part, which it generally does if lively and attractive; but it always seems to me a far less amusing method, apart from the science displayed, than spinning, or paternoster work, while it cannot be doubted, supposing one has a cold wintry day to fish in, which of the two is better calculated for keeping up the necessary caloric at any rate. A rod for live baiting should be stiffer in its action than the spinning rod, and one of 14 feet, light and handy, will be found long enough for anything, with well-made upright rings of good size, through which the line can run freely. A pike rod with small or moveable rings, is an abomination, and not to be tolerated at any price, and it certainly seems strange to think that nowadays, with all the vast improvements that have been made in sporting tools, one could find any man so conservative in his opinions as to be firmly wedded to the use of one of the old-fashioned rods in preference to a modern one. That there are such men in the world is beyond all question, for it was but the last season that a dear old friend of mine, whom I have preached to any number of times, yet in vain, was out "jacking" with me and lost three or four good fish through using a miserable old rod with moveable rings. The line "kinking" with the wet, ran freely for a moment or two and then got into a lovely "boggle" round one or other of the rings. A guess at what ensued, with a good fish running, is not difficult. The same dear old "buffer" persists in using a muzzle-loader on "the first," whilst every one else has their Boss or Grant, with breech action, and modified choke, and all the rest of it, and then he grumbles at being left behind! while the major, as he crams his cartridges in, mutters, politely muffling his tones, however, something about "D——d old muff!" Given, then, a suitable rod, a plain check winch, or, better still, a "Nottingham" holding plenty of line, from 70 to 100 yards at least, is the next desideratum. It will be noticed that I advocate more line on the winch for live-baiting than I do for spinning. Why? I fancy one of my readers' queries. For this simple reason—a fish striking at a spinning bait is hooked, or should be, there and then; and, unless he is a veritable mammoth, he will, by careful management, succumb under 30 or 40 yards' run; but in live-baiting, unless one is using snap-tackle—of which more anon—a fish may run fully that quantity off the reel, before he reaches his *sanctum sanctorum*, and before absolutely pouching the bait. A much finer line can be used in live-baiting than when adopting spinning measures, because there is far less friction, hence less wear and tear; and my idea is that tackle cannot be too fine. Half the fun consists in the satisfaction that ensues in knowing that you have settled a "grouser" with a thread, as opposed to "the barge rope and pully-hauly system." The next thing to consider, then, is the "trace," which should consist of fine gimp, or better still, stout gut, with three or four swivels in its length, to assist the bait in its gyrations. These swivels, and their free working, are important elements in jack-fishing, so that at the end of a day it is worth while for a piscator to see that they are dry, and indeed all metallic portions of his tackle, before putting them aside. Care in this particular is never thrown away. Touching live-baiting, and when adopting the old-fashioned, and, I am glad to say, nearly played-out method with live-bait and a double hook, it is made so as to lie flat and close to the side of the fish. This is attached to the trace either by a spiral screw or a wire running round a portion of the extremity of the bottom swivel, or by a sort of snap. I certainly prefer the spiral apparatus. With the double hook, the infamous baiting needle comes into operation, and is used by looping the loop of the hook-link into the eye of the needle—the latter being made with a flat sharp point at the other end. Then holding your dace tenderly, "as though you loved him," insert the point of the needle just beneath the skin at the edge of the gills, carry it through, taking care not to wound the flesh under the surface of the skin, and bring the point of the needle out behind the rays of the dorsal fin, drawing the gimp through, noting that the hook lies flat and close to the side of the fish—then pop him at once into the bait can. Jackmen using the single hook simply hook their bait through the upper lip or the back fin; but this is a style which finds little favour with a good pikeman. All being arranged, attach the hook-link to the gimp trace, and you are ready so far as the baiting is concerned. The trace should, of course, be sufficiently leaded or weighted, to ensure the bait being kept well down, and without giving it an opportunity of rising too often to the surface, which they frequently have an unhappy knack of trying to do. Much depends, with regard to the lead, and its weight, upon the size of the bait used, and also upon the depth and character of the water. Personally I strongly disapprove of side-hook fishing, and only speak of it because fish will occasionally take a bait upon this tackle when they will look at nothing else. The float used must also depend, so far as its size is concerned, upon the buoyant power required, but it is a good maxim never to use one larger than is absolutely necessary, nothing being more likely to scare a shy-feeding fish than to find that he is dragging a lot of unknown apparatus behind him. Besides that, a smaller float, supposing it to be a weedy water, is the less likely to be "hung up" during the preliminary canter. I prefer an oval-shaped float, bored, of course, and with a quill through it, through which the running line is passed, and a wooden peg fitting firmly into the orifice of the quill, keeps all tight—particularly as the action of the water causes the peg to swell. Many anglers use the above float and one or two smaller floats, called "pilots," which prevents the line "bagging" immediately round the float, and from twisting, and they are doubtless a useful adjunct. In windy, boisterous, and very cold weather, the nearer one's bait swims to the bottom the better, as the fish—the larger ones especially—under such circumstances always resort to the deeps, while on fine, mild days they will be found more in the shallows; and it has seemed to me that on such occasions, when the wind and atmosphere is nipping keen, live-bait fishing in the deepest portions of the river is more likely to command success—from the fact that the fisher goes at once into a likely stronghold. A big gudgeon, carefully put on the hook, is, when the water is bright, as good and attractive a bait for pike as can well be used—he is, besides, a tough and game little fish, and, if uninjured when thrown into the water, has another qualification, which makes him valuable,—he always seeks the bottom. In thick water, he is, from his sombre colour, not so good a bait as the more silvery dace. This latter fish, as well as small chub, are also excellent as pike baits, and good-sized bleak as well, but bleak are an excessively delicate fish, and require most careful handling in any case of live-baiting, and if hurt in the least degree, soon "turn it up." Small carp furnish a good, lasting bait, and in an emergency, the gold-fish bowl may be emptied — this, however, only on high days and holidays, for it will be found an expensive luxury. Nothing can be more certain than that a lively, hard-working bait is immeasurably superior in its killing powers, in opposition to a spent or weary bait, so that the angler should always endeavour to have his lure in the very best possible condition. It is equally certain however that there are times when pike are so ravenously "on," that I am almost inclined to believe in a chance of a run if one used an old boot for a bait. Given a run, there is not the least necessity to wait "ten minutes;" pay out the line freely, and when he stops he'll pouch it in three or four, or not at all. If after stopping he moves on again, strike him at once. A great disadvantage in the method of live-baiting with side-hook is the certain tearing of the skin, and consequent disfiguration of the bait, as well as the chance of killing small fish. All this is obviated by the use of snap-tackle, which simply consists of two triangles bound upon the gimp hook-link and about two inches apart. One of these triangles is placed carefully through the root of the dorsal fin, while the other is fixed at the root of the pectoral. Another advantage gained arises from the fact that here there is no waiting for the fish to run to his nook, and then gorge the bait. The instant the float disappears one can make ready to strike, and when the line becomes taut and the angler feels his fish he can do so with the certainty, in nine cases out of ten, of securing the aggressor. Pike, as is well known, take their prey sideways; thus it is clear that if a fish seizes the bait attached to snap-tackle, the triangle must be within his jaws, and the probability is that he is safe, due skill being observed on the angler's part when he is hooked. There is not the least necessity to strike heavily, a smart handstroke is amply sufficient; indeed, where the line is taut, as it should be, a simple pull on the fish when running fixes the hook firmly. A point that may be mentioned is the likelihood of an inexperienced hand mistaking the efforts of a bait to escape the murderous jaws of a big pike, for "a run." It is astonishing what an amount of strength is shown by an active, lively dace, when he sees, as he doubtless does, the fish poke his shark-like head out from a weed patch or the covet of a bank, before making his fatal rush. I have seen a large float go clean down out of sight; and where the water has been very clear, have traced the white top for some little distance, as the dace shot down-stream. A jack usually leaves little doubt on the subject: down goes the float clean away, and the water frequently eddies and surges round, showing where our friend "Johnnie" has shot out from cover.

Paternostering, another class of live-bait fishing, is a method of which I am excessively fond. It is carried out as follows:—Attached to the running line by means of a loop is a yard of good stout gut, the rounder it is the better, with a further loop at the other end. A paternoster lead, not heavier than is absolutely necessary, shaped like a pear, and with an eye of brass wire, is next fastened to the bottom loop, by simply slipping the loop through the eye and over the extremity of the lead, and then drawing it tight. Personally I prefer a silk loop attached to the end of the gut, and this loop to be put through the eye of the lead. A foot or a foot and a half above the lead a single hook (on gimp) is fastened, and a small dace or gudgeon is lip-hooked as the attraction. Drawing a sufficient quantity of line from the reel, the angler casts out in the most likely place where jack harbour, round the edge of rush-beds and reeds, or in deep still pools; the lead upon reaching the bottom communicates a distinct jar through the silk, which is easily distinguished. The line, held in the left hand, is then slowly worked in towards the bank or punt, from whichever stand-point the piscator is throwing, the lead being clearly felt as it scrapes along the bottom. I have found it much the better plan, instead of coiling the line at one's feet, to gather it backwards and forwards in the palm of the left hand, and with a good line, free from knots and kinks, this, after a little practice, is easily done. Those proficient in the use of the Nottingham winch throw from the winch itself, thus have no slack, and work in with the handle, a method, for those who care to overcome its no slight difficulties, far in advance of the other style. Much diversity of opinion exists among anglers adopting the paternoster in jack-fishing as to the correct moment at which to strike when the bite is felt. As a matter of course fish feed differently, and hardly ever two days alike. One day they are ravenous, and prepared to gulp down everything, the next dainty, and wonderfully hard to please; but I have always found that if small baits are used—and these are more killing than large ones, although the latter are possibly more attractive —few mistakes will be made in striking if one feels a good fair pull, and particularly if momentarily afterwards the fish begins to move off. It should be recollected that supposing a small dace, say of three or four inches long, is on the hook, a jack has a rare width of jaws, and an enormous power of expansion, and with such a cherry, will scarcely make two bites, but gulp it in at once. Thus the hook is very likely to nick him, and once hooked, show no mercy, but reel up at once. Always avoid having more loose line than is really required, and kill your fish, whenever practicable, with the reel, and not with the hand. If a large bait is in use it is advisable to give him more time, but if they are feeding freely and the bait is taken while the fish is moving off at the same instant, it is only reasonable to suppose that he has turned the bait as he ran, and so the "strike" may be attempted. In places where it is weedy, it will be found a better plan rather to dip down from the point of the rod, into all likely looking "shops," and abstain from working the bait on the bottom at all, from the likelihood of getting "hung up" in the weeds, and a consequent smash of tackle ensuing. Very much, however, depends upon the characteristics of the place when at the river side, and the intelligent angler will be greatly guided by circumstances. Nine times out of ten when paternoster fishing, the fish will be found hooked at the edge, or just outside the lip, and no difficulty will be experienced in extracting the hook. Beware, however, at all times of putting fingers near a pike's teeth; he'll bite like a crocodile if he has half a chance, and even a chance scratch is unpleasant. It is far better therefore first to land heavily on his cranium with the toe of your boot, and then—if the hook is gorged, and it is not easily got at with the disgorger—of slipping the hook off the trace altogether, than stand the chance of getting your fingers well scored with his grinders, which, to say the least of it, is not a pleasant process, and especially on a cold day. I speak from experience, and therefore feelingly.

PERCH FISHING.

A gloriously handsome fish, perch, when in condition, afford excellent sport, and they are deservedly favourites with each and every fisherman, let him be young or old. One of the very first fish I ever caught in my life was a perch, and to this day I recollect my pride and exultation when I effected his capture. He had located himself near the sluice-gates at the head of a mill-stream, hard by my native vale of Derwent, and day after day I caught sight of him and looked wistfully and longingly, trying him with wasp grubs and brandlings—alas! in vain. One day I met a man chubbing, using shrimps for bait, and watched him roving without float or shot under the high banks of the stream, letting the current carry his bait where it would. Thinks I,— "Shrimps will catch that perch," and so they did, for going to tea an evening or two afterwards I found the clergyman's superior moiety was expected, and amongst other delicacies shrimps were on the festive board. I "went for" that plate, and quick as thought a handful was transferred from it, and during the whole of that warm evening lovingly reposed in my trousers pocket, amongst, I doubt not, alley-taws, peg-tops, bits of string, a broken-bladed knife, a jew's-harp and a paper of eel hooks. Break of day found me on the sluice-gates, and ten minutes afterwards that perch was on the bank among the dewy grass. What man is bold enough to say that my boy's heart exulted not, and that my blood coursed not rapidly in my veins, even as the deer stalker's who sees the Monarch of the Glen totter and fall to the crack of his trusty grooved barrel? Pennant, an excellent authority, thus describes the fish under notice :—" The body is deep, the scales very rough, the back much arched, and the side line approaches near to it ; the irides are golden, the teeth small, disposed in the jaws and on the roof of the mouth, which is large ; the edges of the covers of the gills are serrated, and on the lowest end of the largest is a sharp spine." So far as colour is concerned, our friend is perhaps as brilliant an inhabitant of our lakes and rivers as we have, his back being a rich olive-green, deepest in shade at the ridge, and growing gradually lighter in hue as it approaches the belly, which is white, with a faint green tinge; transverse broad black bars, pointing downwards, mark his shapely sides, while the ventral fins are a glowing scarlet, the tail and anal fins being of a like colour, though a shade paler." The distinguishing characteristic of the perch is his formidable dorsal fin, and armed as it is with very long and spinous rays, it makes him at all times an antagonist well capable of taking care of himself. It would be just as well, if an angler is fortunate enough to get hold of a big, lusty fellow, to see that this saw-like fin is carefully smoothed down before gripping him to take the hook out, for I have known instances where a man's hand has been badly cut through incautious handling, and it is sometimes difficult to heal. They are thoroughly gregarious in their habits, herding together, and remaining for a long time, unless disturbed, in the same situation. I have watched them repeatedly when the water has been clear in a deep hole, and the larger fish always seem to claim and keep precedence over the smaller. Where such a hole is found, if the tenants thereof are in a feeding humour, it is just as likely that if the angler is wary and noiseless, and hooks and lands them, he may take every fish out of it. Prick, and hold one for an instant, and then let him escape, the probabilities are that every one of the shoal will follow their frightened fellow—then, one may just as well try somewhere else.

Perch are found nearly everywhere, all our English rivers containing them—Thames, Trent, Severn and Wye alike holding plenty of this game fish, while the Loddon is famous for bouncers, and nearly all the great inland waters of Britain, meres and lakes, are well stocked. Instances have been quoted to show that they have attained a large size, it being said that a perch of 9 lb. was taken out of the Serpentine in Hyde Park, and another of 8 lb. from Dagenham Reach. The best that I ever saw was one that weighed 4 lb., full weight; he was a splendid fish, and was caught by a lad with a sixpenny rod, a stout gut-line and a hook baited with worm, from one of the pools of the little Brent at Hanwell. I was a boy at the time, and remember offering him a threepenny bit and my dinner for it; he didn't see it, and perhaps it was just as well, for I should have assuredly deceived my worthy sire as to who caught it. Deep, quiet water, where there is a gentle eddy, under hollow banks, holes where the roots of trees run down and their pendant branches shade the retreat from the fierce heat of the sun, the piles of locks and sluice-gates, and the back-water of millstreams, are all favourite perch haunts. In navigable rivers and canals he seeks the deeper parts, where barges lie, and about floats of timber, always choosing, if obtainable, a "habitat" where the bottom is sandy and pebbly. I have found it a good plan in wandering about the banks of an unknown river in quest of perch to note where the small fry of dace, roach, &c., most do congregate. Such a place will be a sandy bank at the edge of a bed of sedge and rushes, and where the current forms a little eddy; here the youngsters get out of the force of the main stream, and if the angler remains quiet, and unobserved by the fish—meanwhile observant himself—it is any odds that he will notice ere long the rush from the deeps, of a perch, with his bristling back fin erect and menacing, and a scatter of the small fry for the shelter of the sedges. Try here, then—it is sure to be good ground and likely to be remunerative.

Now for the tackle to be used. Select a nice light cane rod, 12 ft. or 14 ft., with standing rings, and not too pliable;

indeed, the rod previously described for legering will do admirably. Use a Nottingham winch, with fine running tackle, and first try the paternoster; this should be a gut length of a yard, round, and good in quality, and mounted with two hooks, the bottom one not more than five or six inches from the lead, the top a foot and a half above it. The lead itself need not be any heavier than is absolutely necessary to find the bottom, and withstand the current; if there is little or none of the latter, use as small a one as possible. I have seen advocated the desirability of using three or four hooks to the paternoster, but I am inclined to think that all practical men will agree with me in saying that two are ample; indeed with more, when one is using minnows, it would be found that a large supply of bait would be necessary, from the frequency with which they are jerked off the hook at the moment of striking. Don't use too large a hook—"No. 7's" are large enough—and hook the minnows through the side of the lip, it is easier than through the extremity of the nose, and it should be remembered that they are a delicate little fish, and won't bear much pulling about. At a likely-looking place, particularly at a spot where one may see the aforesaid small fry, drop the paternoster quietly in, and keep the line taut from the winch the moment the bottom is felt; then move it gently along the bottom, lifting it now and again from the point of the rod, until the spot chosen has been thoroughly searched. If they are there, and in a feeding humour, the angler will not be long before he knows it, and at the sharp "tug-tug," indicating the attack, one should strike without loss of time—instantaneously, in fact—and if the fish be hooked, as he will be nine times out of ten, and proves a big one, keep the line taut; be in no hurry with him; and after the first few desperate plunges are over, he is, with ordinary care, your own; then get him to the bank as soon as you can, into your landing net—and mind his fin. It is a curious fact, but nevertheless an indisputable one, that perch will frequently refuse a minnow on the paternoster, and yet take it greedily if put on to a hook, attached to a shotted and floated line; so that it may be always wisely remembered that if they refuse the one, the other method may be tried with advantage. Small gudgeon are a capital bait for large fish, and if they persistently refuse the paternoster, a light spinning flight may be rigged up and tried, with a possible chance of success. Stone loach will also kill perch, and in waters that are brackish and subject to tidal influences, live shrimps are a killing lure. They are best kept in an open basket in wet sand, and care should be taken that they are never packed close together. Caddis worms, wasp grubs, and occasionally gentles, attract the notice of our striped friend; but having, done with the subject of live-baits as applied to fish, nothing will be found of greater killing power than the old and well-known bait, the worm of various classes, and first in order I take the lob. No perch angler should be without worms, for it frequently happens, and particularly in the autumn, and a little later on, that they will take worms freely, when minnow and gudgeon are totally disregarded. Worms cannot be too bright and tough, or too well scoured for perch-fishing, and lobs want a week at least in moss, and well looked after, if the weather is warm, before being fit for the hook. If they are wanted for immediate use, put them in a pot of tea-leaves squeezed dry, and let them remain for a few hours; it will be found that the tannin, presumably, has had a miraculous effect. In waters where there are deep, slow eddies, with little or no stream, some of the largest perch, and now and again a chub or two, are captured by using a gut bottom, of a yard in length, attached to a running line of the finest Nottingham or Derby silk. Before attaching the bottom, fit up a long cork float on the silk line, with a small well-drilled bullet below it—the hole through the bullet being sufficiently large for the line to run easily and freely. Then, having tied on the gut bottom, a split shot is fixed on the silk, just above the loop, so as to prevent the bullet running over the bow of the silk line. Selecting the place of operation, the float must be so arranged that the bullet just touches the bottom, and the proper depth being thus obtained, select a flat, silvery lob from amongst the stock, and note those with a red vein running down to the tail are the best for the hook, and put the hook point in an inch below the head. Threadle the worm until the shank of the hook is just covered. Worms put on in this manner show far better than when looped up on the hook, or entirely "threadled," and hence must be a more attractive bait. Then cast out, and draw the bullet, when it is found to have reached the bottom, towards the point angled from, until the gut length is likely to lie straight on the bed of the river. If there is any current, the float, after righting itself, must be "held back" from the point of the rod, the light silk line being clear of the water; and do not be in a hurry if a dip of the float indicates that a fish is attacking the worm. Recollect that it is likely to be a big one, and, as a consequence, a far more cautious gentleman than the smaller of the tribe; wait then, until after the first preliminary dip or two, the float goes down clean out of sight, then strike, not too hard, however, and look out for storms and a long and strong pull at the top joint. Brandlings found in old rotten manure, and red worms, sometimes kill as well as anything, but I must confess to a great fancy for the lob for nearly all big fish—the others are more suitable for the paternoster. If the water is very bright, and the fish are "dead off," take away the float previously mentioned, and, substituting a smaller bullet as a sinker, throw out the lob, across, and up and down the water with a motion similar to that of spinning; a brace of fish may be taken in this way when they are very dainty.

CARP FISHING.

The carp is perhaps as handsome a fish as British waters can boast of as a resident, and is without any exception one that will try an angler's skill and resources to the utmost. In colour, a bronze or yellowish olive, deeper in shade towards the back; and with, when in condition, a splendid burnished sheen diffused over his sides, and great round scales, he looks, when freshly caught, a very noble and handsome fellow. The fins are brown, with a faint violet or purple tinge, the dorsal, in particular, large and well developed, and continued in its rays for some distance down the slope of the back; he has a large head, but by no means an unsightly one, a small round mouth, tough and leathery to a degree, with two small cirri or beards on either side; the tail, but little forked, is set firmly on, and denotes great strength, and he is, when large, a deep and thick-set fish. Carp are extremely prolific, and in suitable waters increase and multiply to an enormous extent; indeed it has been stated upon good authority that the weight of the roe taken from a single female fish exceeded the weight of the despoiled carcase when the two have been weighed the one against the other. A good deal of uncertainty seems to exist as to when carp were first introduced into England; but we get evidence from the 'Boke of St. Albans' published in 1496 that they were known then at any rate, while other ancient writers dealing with him establish his place in our native lakes and rivers somewhere about the same period. They attain a vast age, Buffon telling us that he has seen at Pontchartrain fish of this species which were known to be 150 years old; how this age was arrived at is not very clear, but well authenticated accounts have been from time to time brought forward, proving that they are, under suitable conditions, an extremely long-lived fish. In Prussia and Germany they are cultivated carefully, and there carp of 25 lb. and 30 lb. weight is not of unfrequent occurrence, while in warm climates, India to wit, fish of this species grow to an enormous size, specimens of the family being taken in the tanks and lagoons of 40 lb. to 60 lb. Fancy, brother angler, getting a fellow of this size on a fine gut bottom! Here, a fish of 10 lb. or 12 lb. is accounted a good one, but there is little doubt that in some of the deep inland meres and lakes they grow to a much larger size. I have myself seen in an extensive sheet of water that I had the opportunity of fishing in Hampshire some years ago, fish basking in the weeds on a hot summer's day, that I have little doubt would have run from 15 lb. to 20 lb., and once or twice got hold of one, but never was able to hold him, for he pulled like a donkey, and went straight for the nearest weed-bed, and quietly smashed me up. The rod to be used should not be too long, 12 feet is ample; when it is longer it does but make it more tiring to the man using it, who, I need hardly say, should avoid laying it on the bank as much as possible, particularly when it is remembered that he is on the trail of the "water fox," as old anglers delighted to call our golden friend. This perhaps is the situation. One's arm gets a bit cramped, and one puts the rod down—tired, perhaps, of a long spell with no signs of a fish—and carelessly, of course, with the handle of the winch on the grass; then, just as one is putting the vesuvian into the bowl of one's pipe, comes a tug at the top joint; one goes with a dash at the rod, and waits eagerly for the expected pull. No go'; the golden moment is gone, and the chance of a golden prize into the bargain. The finer the running line the better, consistent with the proper degree of strength that is required, supposing a "bonser" is hooked. When baiting with paste or gentles, triangle hooks, not too large, should be used, and the lead, having the hole through it well bored out, so that the line runs very easily, should work on the silk running line or better still a very fine piece of gimp, in preference to the gut bottom, so that friction of the gut is avoided, as well as any possible obstruction from a knot. Carp will sometimes take worms freely; large red worms, thoroughly cleansed and toughened in moss, being almost a standing dish, and a bright silver lob is another very attractive bait. Wasp grubs, and the larvæ of the insect in an immature state, are another killing lure. I have taken them with green peas, and I have heard of them taking cherries; but of all the baits that I have ever tried, commend me to a yellow waxy potato, fairly well boiled, but not so as to be too soft, of course, and with a plentiful ground-baiting of the hole where one intends operating, for a day or two previously, with boiled potatoes and bran, well kneaded and worked up, so that when formed into balls about the size of a billiard ball, they sink at once. The potato should be cut into an oval shape, of the size of a thrush's egg, the gut drawn through its centre by means of a fine baiting needle, and the points of the triangle pushed into the bait until they are fairly embedded. Now cast out a yard or two beyond where your baited spot is situated, and, when the lead has reached the bottom, draw it towards you, so that the hooks lie clear of the lead and line, and straight from the point of the rod. Then hold the rod, with the top joint pointed directly to where your hooks lie, and lower the point, that the line may be straight through the rings (which, of course, should be standing rings), and directly in a line with the thumb and forefinger of the left hand. By adopting these means, one avoids the fish feeling the pull on the top, which must be felt when the rod is at an angle, and if the line is held very delicately between the fingers, the least motion can be detected. The first indication of a nibble, in nine cases out of ten, will be a tremulous movement, that will, I warrant, send a thrill through the angler's frame; hold the line as you would a gossamer thread. Niggle, niggle, niggle, again it comes; then a little pull, and at last the line begins to sneak through one's fingers. Now's the [time! Strike smartly, not too hard, and if you find that you're home, give him another little tug, just to send the hooks well into his leathery mouth; keep a taut line, and humour him nicely for a little, until you find out the calibre of the game you have to kill. Bear this in mind, however, that you have no cowardly foe to conquer. A large carp is a gallant fellow, and will resent any untimely indignity in the shape of early " pully-haulings," by a terrible rush, that may very likely upset all your previous calculations, and free himself at the same moment. Do not, therefore, be in a hurry to get him out—always reflect that, so long as your line is tight, and the hooks hold, he is as much your prisoner as though he were on the bank. If possible, get him away from the hole where you hook him, and play and land him lower down, so as to avoid disturbing others that may be lying in the same locality, and always keep, from first to last, well out of sight of the water. In pond or lake fishing, much the same tactics may be adopted, except that one may use a much lighter leger lead where there is no stream, and indeed I would not use a lead at all if it were possible to get the line out without it. If float-fishing be the order of the day, the float cannot be too light, and a small quill carrying three or four shot only is to be preferred. The bait should always be well on the bottom. I fish with the baited hook at least six inches on the bottom—and the shot may be placed on the hook-link of gut so that they too rest on the ground, and thus there is nothing of a foreign nature to catch the wary eye of the fish that may be prowling about. Even the gut may be dyed green or of a bluish tint, so as to assimilate as nearly as possible with the tinge of the water. The rod used should be a longer one than the one previously mentioned, for it is a time-honoured maxim in angling for some classes of fish; to "fish fine and far out;" and the carp is one of them where this maxim should be observed. A good plan, when float fishing, is to have an iron rod rest, or a forked stick, stuck in the ground, so that the rod, in this case, unlike when legering, may be placed in the rest or cleft stick. Throw well out, and, particularly when the water is clear and bright, have no more of the rod than is absolutely necessary projecting over the bank, then sit well away from the water; don't move the rod if you see a bit of a nibble, but if the float, after a preliminary cautious dip or two, sails slowly away and out of sight, then get your line taut, and strike, not two hard, however. The remarks I have just made apply more directly to worm fishing, and it is useless to strike when operating with this bait unless the float begins to slide off, for carp suck the bait in very artfully, and if he is not given time to gulp the whole of the worm, the chances are that you lose your fish, from the fact that by striking too hurriedly you may have only allowed him to get hold of the tail end. When fishing with paste or gentles, and using triangle hooks, I should strike immediately if the float dipped fairly down; for these fish are so crafty and wary that they will suck the whole of the bolus of paste away from the hook, and that being effected quietly sail off. Strike gently, however, and should you not succeed in hooking the fish, let the bait drop quietly again, when it is possible, if he is in a feeding humour, he may have another try. Various grubs and caterpillars, caddis and turnip worms, beetles, and a hook baited with a red worm and tipped with a gentle have been from time to time recommended as super-excellent lures; my experience, however, tells me that if carp will not take potatoes, well-scoured lobs, red worms, or a lively bunch of gentles, they won't take anything, and one might just as well go home and have a rubber of whist and a pipe.

Chub Fishing.

The chub, another member of the numerous carp family, attracts no inconsiderable share of the angler's attention, and particularly numbering amongst his followers that section who delight in getting hold of something that pulls. Amongst the number is my humble self. I know of no fish that I have had at the end of my line that goes with such a devil of a rattle as a big chub, and as he usually when pricked by a hook bolts with the speed of a rocket for the first stronghold he can get to—sunken roots of trees, or pendant boughs overhanging hollow banks—it requires no little skill to keep the line and tackle out of danger. His first rush over, however, he is pretty safe, and, unlike the barbel, who fights with dogged pertinacity to the last, quickly succumbs, and with ordinary care is soon come-atable. Common in most of the English rivers, and growing to a large size, the chub, or cheven, affords endless amusement, for he feeds well at times when other fish refuse a bait. In the summer large flies and beetles of various kinds tempt him; while in autumn and winter, cheese, greaves, lobs, pith from the vertebræ of the bullock, as well as live bait, such as minnows and small gudgeon, attract his attention. It has always been the fashion to speak of him as "the loggerheaded chub," and well-known angling writers have described him as having an ugly misshapen head, but I utterly fail to see this, and, indeed, consider him, when in condition, an exceptionally handsome fish, with a longer body than the carp, large silvery scales, his back of a deep olive green, the belly white, the irides of the eye a shining silver, pectoral fins, large and well developed, of a dusky, yellow hue, ventral and anal fins a pale salmon red, while the tail, slightly forked, is brown, with a distinct bluish line at the extremity. They are frequently taken both in the Thames and Lea, from three to four pounds in weight, it being asserted that specimens from the former river have come to bank of far greater calibre; while upon the authority of Dr. Bloch, we are told that fish of 8 lb. and 9 lb. is no uncommon size in some of the continental waters. The Loddon and Mole hold gigantic fish; from the latter river came the best chub I ever saw in my life. It was taken by my friend, Mr. Callen, of East Molesey—was tempted by a couple of shrimps, and, weighed by myself, bumped down the scale at $7\frac{1}{2}$ lb. Chub usually spawn in the latter end of March, if the weather is open and fine, or in April, and are again in full vigour in June.

No more cautious, timid fish swims than your chub, and I have frequently seen a shoal of them lying near the top of the water, sink slowly down and out of sight, the only thing that I could discover as likely to alarm them being a crow or two winging their way across the stream. Hence the chub-fisher cannot be too cautious and subtle in his operations.

Chub in the summer resort to the deeps, and large still pools overhung by foliage; here they lie, day after day, if undisturbed, watching for grubs and insects dropping from the sheltering trees; and at such places the dibber, with his humble bee in the day-time, or large moth in the evening, kills his fish. In the winter they seek places where high marly banks form the sides of the stream, or deep holes, with a sandy or clayey bottom, afford them good harbourage; and in nooks where this fish are known to resort, they are found at the proper season, year after year. Hence the saying among anglers, "once a chub hole, always a chub hole." They are a restless fish, however, and shift about in the autumn and winter months, when insect diet has failed them, continually seeking fresh ground. It is advisable, therefore, never to stay long in one spot— ten minutes or a quarter of an hour is enough—for if there are fish there and they mean feeding, they will do so at once, or not at all.

For legering for this, and indeed for all other fish, a rod of 12 ft. in length is fully long enough. I don't believe in long rods for general use, and feel assured that if an angler, with a short one, pits his own brains and resources against the craft of the fish he is trying for, he will in the long run succeed. Long rods are cumbersome and tedious to the wielder, and it is only in roach fishing from the bank in a river like the Lea, for instance, where they are practically of any use—for angling in such a water, and for this specified class of fish they are of course indispensable. I recollect, many years ago now, when my passion for the river-side and the "contemplative man's occupation" was just as keen, if not more so than now, I had an impression, and I find that young anglers of the present day indulge in the same idea, that fish can only be found in the middle of a river or pond, or so near thereto as one could throw out. Thus I used to perch myself on the extreme edge of the bank, completely forgetting that fish could see me when I could not see them. As a consequence the bag was nearly always lighter at night than in the morning. Now it is different, simply because I reflect, and reflection and the caution that naturally accrues, is in my view the great secret of success. To return to the rod: let it be of cane, light and handy, 12 feet in length and fitted with upright rings, moderately stiff and well balanced. Always avoid a rod that is top-heavy. The winch—and one can hardly improve upon the Nottingham reel for "reel work"— should be capable of holding sixty or seventy yards of fine plaited Derby silk line; some prefer a twist line, I don't, while the finer the better if the operator has a light hand, and can hold a "big 'un" tenderly. Besides which, a fine line requires a far less heavy bullet than a stout one—another advantage—and these requisites obtained, one is ready, so far as rod and line are concerned. Now for the leger bottom; this is an important item, for upon it much of the desired success is likely to attend. Choose it of the finest and roundest natural gut, a yard in length at least (I use them a yard and a half), and always have a length of gimp fitted to them for the bullet to work upon. Other accessories are entirely unnecessary, and the less foreign matter one has, the better. At any of the first-class tackle shops, these bottoms are to be obtained, stained to any desired shade ; it is therefore obvious that, if an angler is fishing a river where the bottom is composed of deep-coloured marly oose or clay, a length of gut assimilating as nearly as possible with the ground on which the wary chub are lying, is far preferable to a shiny piece of white gut, which moves about as the stream catches the line and bullet, and can certainly not look like a piece of weed. Look your gut well over before commencing, and reject a bottom that has cracks or flaws. Far better to be particular in the tackle than stand a chance of losing a fish that, if landed and "set up," may, in its case "be a thing of beauty and a joy for ever." If lob worms are the order of the day, use hooks whereon, in lieu of the ordinary length of gut, a small loop of silk is whipped ; they are easily attached to the leger bottom, and do away with the chance of the hook links of gut being stronger or weaker than the remainder of the gut in use. Some have a morsel of bristle whipped on the reverse way from the hook's point ; this certainly prevents the worm from slipping or wriggling down the shank of the hook, and is possibly an advantage, but if chub mean business, they will bolt one's lob before it has the chance of slipping very far down. Being on the bank, keep well out of sight, and avoid shuffling about, or moving unnecessarily. Every movement of the feet causes a certain amount of vibration ; and, rely upon it, chub will bolt if they fancy anything is wrong. If you have plenty of lobs, and the stream is not too heavy, throw them in whole, and some little distance above where you are fishing. Cast in down-stream and make sure that your gut bottom lies straight on the bed of the river, by drawing the bullet towards the place where you are sitting. The chub, when he feeds, is nothing like so distrustful as the carp, therefore the same intent watch is not absolutely needful, and the rod may be placed in the rest or on the bank so long as the line is fairly taut. Given a bit of a tug, up with it instanter, and strike at once, for it is most likely that the fish has taken the bait and gulped it down his capacious throttle. The same tackle may be used in baiting with cheese or greaves, save that the hook should be a triangle, and that of fair size. In fishing with cheese, two or three holes may be baited the night before angling, with some of the most rotten old cheese that can be got at. Samples outside the cheesemongers' shops, smelling strong, full of animal life, and at about $3d.$ a pound, is the correct thing; and a couple of pounds of this aromatic variety worked up roughly with some soaked bread makes a highly seasoned dish of a surety likely to please the palate of the loggerhead, wherever he may be, and keep him hanging about the baited place. Once let him get the full flavour of the sunken mess, there he'll stick until every atom is gone. Touching and concerning the paste for the hook, this cannot be too carefully made, for as cheese having a tendency to harden in the water, it is obvious that the material should be thoroughly softened and incorporated, so as to do away with this as much as possible. Select rich old Cheshire, oily, and full of unctuous quality, pare away the rind, not too sparingly, so as to get rid of the harder portions, then with a bottle, or a rolling-pin, crush the cheese thoroughly upon a table or flat piece of stone, breaking up every hard bit; when completely rolled out and soft, get a piece of stale crumb of bread—a piece the size of an egg will be sufficient for a good quarter of a pound of cheese—and moisten it thoroughly, then squeeze dry, and with the hands work and mix it up with the cheese—it will take a good half hour to do well; when finished, put it in a damp cloth for use. At the water-side it will want working up now and again so as to keep it soft and pliable, and when baiting the hook, take a piece of cheese a little bigger than a thrush's egg—the chub has a capacious gullet, and will easily negotiate this—and make a hole in it with the thumb, inserting the triangle; then pinch it close round the gut, covering the hook completely. By this method the hook lies encased simply by a shell of cheese, which will break with the strike, when the fish takes the bait. If the paste is moulded round the hook in a mass it becomes very shortly a solid body, hard as a bullet, and the chances are that a fish is lost by the bait being pulled out of his mouth, the hooks being unable to break through the bait and penetrate his leathery muzzle. Strike instantly and sharply when a bite is felt; if the fish is not hooked, drop the bait; he may try it again, if hungry. If hooked, keep him away from roots and submerged boughs, for once let him get among them, all the king's horses and all the king's men won't save the tackle unless one is very lucky, and if the hooked fish is lost it is all up with that hole for a time, and one might just as well seek fresh pastures.

Shrimps are another bait that at certain times kill chub well, and I prefer the pink to the brown. I always shell them, saving husks, heads and tails, and putting them with a few whole shrimps into some clay for ground bait; and then three or four of the shelled crustaceans neatly on a small triangle, casting into likely places. Greaves also are better on a triangle than a single hook, and the whitest and softest pieces should be selected. In preparing greaves the cake should be broken up and put in any old vessel with just water enough to cover the contents, and into a slow oven to simmer and stew until the compound is soft.

Never throw much greaves in as ground bait, fish soon sicken of it, so that it should be used sparingly.

A baby frog is the grandest bait in the world for a big chub, just at that doubtful period of his existence when even his mother might feel some pardonable uncertainty as to whether he belonged to her family or not; but it would occupy too much space to dilate impartially upon frogs and black-beetles, cockchafers and slugs, and the beauties of Nottingham fishing with pith and brains under the boughs; so that I must even leave all I would say unsaid.

Tench Fishing.

With regard to angling for tench there is really little to be said. They are so seldom met with in rivers, and are so uncertain in their biting moods, that it would be simply waste of time for an angler to devote much, if any, of his leisure to angling specially for them. One hears every now and then of a good fish that has fallen to a skilled rodster, both in the Thames and Lea. But it usually turns out upon investigation that the capture has been one purely of a chance nature, and that the fish has been taken either by a banksman who was roach-fishing, or, in the Thames more particularly, by some angler who is bream or barbel-fishing, and who gets a cautious preliminary nibble or two, puzzling him for a moment from its being utterly unlike any other bite he has had, and who upon striking when he finds his float sailing off, finds that "the doctor" has taken a fancy to his lobworm. Where, however, it is known that tench have chosen some slow, heavy water, and their habitation is a part of a river, I would always advise those who may have a sufficient stock of patience to devote part of their time in pursuit of them, to see that their tackle is of good quality and without flaws, for a river tench of any size, and who being hooked gets into anything like a strong current, will try the tackle as much, perhaps, as a barbel, and that is saying a good deal for his fighting powers. Far and away more likely places will be old clay pits, deep ponds, fleets and meres, and the large ornamental sheets of water that are found in many of our large landed proprietors' domains, and where a request for a day's angling rarely meets with refusal if properly preferred. In such a situation, and supposing the water to be fairly free from weeds, or with large open spaces between the weed-grown places, I would recommend that before fishing, the place should be plentifully ground-baited for a night or two previously. If it is intended to angle with worms, chopped lobs should form the attraction, first selecting from the stock gathered, the flat, silvery and medium-sized worms for the hook. Never bait the hook with those dull, leaden-coloured worms, with a red band running round them, and an orange-coloured belly. I don't mean to say that a tench would never take one if offered him, and nicely put on the hook; but I think the other worm will kill in the proportion of four to one—at least such has been my experience, therefore I think it proves which of the two is the better. If float fishing is preferred it should be as light as possible, for the tench is a shy feeder, and would infallibly leave the bait if he found that he was dragging at a big cork float on the surface. A small swan or porcupine quill is as good as any; the gut should be fine yet good, the hook No. 7 or 8, fairly long in the shank and round in the bend, the running line of fine yet strong silk—plaited for choice—while the rod need not be longer than is necessary to reach the place selected. If the water be very weedy and the clear places small and confined, then perhaps a long rod would be serviceable, dispensing with the running line altogether, but taking care that the gut bottom and line at the top-joint be additionally strong. In such a cramped position, should the fish feed and a big one be struck, it will be simply a case of testing the fish and his strength against the tackle; all I can say is, keep him away from the weed-beds, he'll bolt for them like a ferret after a bunny, and if he gets among them—good-bye. The bait should, if possible, touch the bottom, but inasmuch as tench retreats are usually muddy in the extreme—which fact is easily ascertainable by the plummet—it would be useless to put a lively lob well on the bottom, because he would very soon become part and parcel of the mud itself. I have found it a good plan when, as I have said, there are plenty of clear open spaces, and the bottom is sound and hard, to dispense with float, etc., altogether, and first baiting the hook with a picked lob, draw from the reel a sufficient quantity of line to reach the desired spot, and then, coiling this line, let it lie on the bank free and clear of all obstructions. Lay the rod as well on the bank, and take the baited hook in the thumb and fingers of the right hand, cast it out from the hand with a gentle swing, and the line, if sufficiently light and fine (and what big fish can be killed on a fine line if one only knows how to use it), will fly out after the baited hook, which sinks from its own specific weight and that of the worm combined; give it time to find the bottom and then reel up any slack line there may be. Keep the rod down upon the bank, with the winch handles (and the winch for this work must be a Nottingham with perfectly free action) uppermost, and clear of any twigs or other things likely to impede it, and then take a seat well away from the water, keep perfectly still and motionless, and await events. A bite is first indicated by a trembling of the line ; give him plenty of time, and presently, if master tench means business, the winch handles begin to slowly revolve and the line to sneak away yard after yard ; then strike, not too hard, for he has a leathery mouth, and the hooks are sure to hold, and the probability is that if he is a good fish there will ensue a "leetle fight" before he caves in. Never be in a hurry when tench-fishing, and the float indicates some hidden attentions—this fish will mumble and suck at your worm or gentles for a long time in some cases, before he finally makes up his mind to do or die— then the float either goes slowly down, and out of sight, or it may rise up, and seem half inclined to topple over, and then move along the surface, or it may be raised up, and laid flat on the water, indicating that a fish has taken the bait, and has risen to the surface—either are critical moments, and one is warranted in striking at once. Sweet paste, made from stale bread-crumb, and judiciously blended with honey, kills tench well at times, at others they won't look at it. Wasp grubs are another good bait, and caddis worms occasionally make their mark, while gentles are at times taken greedily. Worms, however, clean and well scoured, seem at all times to be the most favourite lure, and although I am aware that many anglers will disagree with me, I prefer the lobworm to any, even to the red worm, or brilliantly striped brandling. Bright, clean and tough, I am inclined to think that nothing beats the lob for big fish, and the bigger the inhabitants of the pool are, the more they seem to like it.

Bream Fishing.

The fish under notice is tolerably well known to anglers, and yet merits a passing word or two in the matter of description. He grows to a large size, and as he increases in weight becomes a very handsome fellow, requiring no little skill on the part of a fisher to successfully make a large bag. With a high arched back, and deep belly, he is somewhat of a rhomboidal form, his sides being, unless very well nourished, extremely flat in comparison with his great depth. His head is small, with the nose pointed and tapering down to the mouth, which is void of teeth, and not by any means a large one. The eyes are large and full, the irides of a silvery hue, the fins, the dorsal in particular, are small sized, the anal extending from the vent to the root of the tail, which is large, powerful and deeply forked. In colour, bream vary considerably; and there seems to be two distinct classes of the same species, although both inhabit similar localities. The one called the golden, or carp bream, attains a far larger size than his relative, the white bream, the latter never carrying the brilliant bronze tint of his big brother. The golden bream has his back coloured with a deep olive bronze tint, the sides gradually growing lighter in hue as they approach the belly, which is a shining silvery white, the fins of a dusky grey, tinged at the root with the predominant golden cast; the scales in both species are large, round and well developed. Bream are thoroughly gregarious in their habits, herding together in large shoals, and generally seeking the deepest and widest part of a river, where the stream is slow and heavy, and the sides are fringed with beds of reed and rushes. Such situations are always looked upon as likely habitats for the "flat, unwieldy bream," but it does not follow that there he will be invariably found, for some of the largest fish of this tribe are taken in the Thames immediately in the boil and rapid water of a heavy weir fall. The river just mentioned, the Thames, holds plenty of bream at certain places, and there can be little doubt that the fish attain a very large size. I have taken them myself close upon 6 lbs., and I have heard of them being landed considerably heavier. Halliford, Shepperton, Weybridge and Penton Hook, of the higher sections, and Teddington and Kingston of the lower parts of the river, are all famous bream waters. The Mole again, from its rise to the point where it empties itself into the Thames, nearly opposite Hampton Court Palace, and the Wey, are both celebrated for their abundant supply, while the Medway, at many of its stations, gives the bottom fisher plenty of sport with large specimens of this class. Then further afield, the Ouse, throughout its entire length, is full of them; and the Yare, and the contiguous "broads" of Norfolk literally swarm with bream; while the Trent, at some places, produces large supplies for the Birmingham and Sheffield Angler's delectation. Close home, the Lea holds a few fish in its waters, but they are rarely angled for properly, and hence rarely caught; three fish, however, may be seen at Mr. Benningfield's house, the Crown, at Broxbourne, which were taken by Mr. Bradlaugh at Carthagena Weir—fruits of philosophy and good angling combined; these three specimen fish weighing together 21 lbs. Then, quite recently, a gentleman, whose name I at the moment forget, but who is, or was, attached to the Conservancy Board of the Lea, caught a splendid bream close upon 9 lbs.; so that it proves that if they are not as plentiful as blackberries in this river, they run large at any rate. The Surrey and Commercial Docks, formerly open to the hard-working London angler, but now unhappily tabooed, unless at a terribly high price for a season ticket—£5 I am told—holds plenty of them; and the Welsh Harp and Dagenham fishery lakes as well, usually returns a take of these fish to one who knows the peculiarities of each spot, and studying them, takes the trouble to fish with caution, suitable bait and fine tackle. Very much depends upon the water to be fished, upon the method adopted and the description of tackle employed. In the Thames, except at one or two places, where the bank fisher may command one or other of the deep holes which are known to be bream haunts with the leger, it is simply labour in vain to attempt to fish for them from the bank with any chance of making a good catch. They are shy and crafty in the extreme, and take good care to keep well away from the sides of the river—and out in the more fancied security of the deeps; so that even if the bank-man can throw his leger into the hole, his only chance of success would be at the very earliest peep of "early morn" or at the close of "dewy eve;" and these two periods of the day may be taken, from first to last, as the best times to endeavour to seduce our slimy friend into appreciating the flavour of a well scoured lob, or, indeed, any other bait with which one may choose to tempt him. In Thames fishing, then, for bream, it is absolutely necessary to fish from a punt or boat, and for this method of angling a Nottingham rod, with two tops, of 12 or 14 feet in length, is the best that can be used; they are wonderfully light, and one may fish all day with one of these rods without tiring the arm, no small desideratum in a long day's work. These rods are besides so nicely adjusted that the change of tops makes a complete change in the character of the rod—with the long and somewhat flexible top, one gets a rod with the most perfect action for either long corking or the sliding float ; affixing the shorter, and consequently much stiffer top, one gets a tool the very *beau idéal* of what is required for either paternostering or legering ; and, after that, I think I need hardly say more in praise of my favourite, the Nottingham weapon. If the place selected has a bottom tolerably uniform in depth, there is no method more killing than "tight corking," i.e., using a bottom of the finest natural gut, with the shot equally placed along its entire length ; by adopting this method of placing the shot it will be obvious that the line hangs much more true and straight in the water from the extremity of the float than if they were placed all together. The running line, and there should be from 60 to 100 yards on a reel, cannot well be too fine, while the reel itself should be perfectly smooth and easy in its action—in point of fact, so nicely made and regulated that the mere action of the stream on the float, and the weight of the float itself, is sufficient to cause the reel to revolve easily, and without the least stopping or scraping. If the reel acts properly, and the line is sufficiently light, it can be held perfectly taut and straight from the cap of the float to the point of the rod, no matter how long, in reason, the swim may be, and the fish can be struck with almost as great a certainty as the roach fisherman hooks his fish with half a line only of strike line from float to top joint. Five-and-twenty, thirty, or forty yards is no uncommon distance for a swim down from the punt, and the fun that ensues when a three or four pounder is hooked on fine tackle at this distance is no little, rely on't ! The hook used for bream should be size No. 7 or 8, round in the bend, and, if for worm-fishing, long in the shank, so that the worm may be drawn neatly up the shank of the hook, and not hang in loops. Supposing then that suitable tackle has been rigged up, we will now proceed to the fishing itself. Ground-baiting, whether in river or pond, is essentially necessary for this fish; for as they frequently shift their locale and rove about in search of food, it is obvious that they are likely to be kept together where they find a supply of palatable rations. Now there is nothing that your river bream takes so kindly to as a diet of worms, and where the fish run large, lobs well scoured are a very attractive bait ; indeed I don't know anything to beat them for big fish. The hole, or run that is intended to operate upon, should therefore be well baited one or two nights before fishing with a plentiful supply of lobs, either chopped up or thrown in whole ? of the two I think the latter is far preferable, and saves a somewhat unpleasant operation. One thing should, however, be borne in mind, that if there is no clay used when ground-baiting, and it is better without it, the worms should be taken sufficiently above the hole, and the set of the current studied to ensure them sinking, and not being swept away from the chosen place. It is an extraordinary fact, yet none the less certain, that these fish will sometimes refuse to have anything to do with a worm that travels down the stream, no matter how neatly or showily put upon the hook, when the self-same bait, stationary upon leger tackle, kills him instantly; and again they frequently reverse their tactics, declining the leger business altogether, yet attacking the moving bait the instant it reaches the bottom. The bream-fisher, bearing this in mind, should, then, never despair of filling his basket if the fish seem at first to be "dead off," but try other methods, and by offering them a suitable bait, he will usually succeed in killing a brace or two of fish, and perhaps a good many more, when, if he had stuck to his original style, he would in all probability have gone home with a very light basket. In legering much the same tackle may be used as that described in carp-fishing—a fine gut bottom, a bullet no larger than is absolutely necessary to find and hold the ground against the stream, the hook the same as that previously described, allowing the fish a fair time if the bait is a large one, before striking him. A capital bait at times for a bream is a bolus of plain bread paste, made from the crumb of stale, yet perfectly sweet and white bread, just dipped into water, and worked up with scrupulously clean hands until it attains a tough and stiff consistency. This may sometimes be sweetened with a little honey to advantage, although I have usually found that when they are in a paste-feeding humour, the plain kills just as well as the sweet. Paste will not stand a heavy current long, so that the hook should be frequently looked at, and a small triangle will be found more serviceable than a single hook, holding the paste much better together. Gentles, again, sometimes exercise a powerful attraction; they are best used on a diminutive triangle, ground-baiting with plenty of "carrion," and using liver gentles for the hook. Bream seek the deep secluded parts of ponds and lakes, and thrive amazingly in favourable waters, such as have a bottom of an oozy, sandy nature, and where the sides have an edging of weed-beds, lilies and water-flags. Here, in the hot weather, they will be found rolling and tumbling about in the weeds, to which they resort for shade and shelter during the heat of the day. In some waters that can be fished only from the side, a long rod is really needful, so as to clear the weeds. At all times, however, cumbersome and heavy, a long rod, where running tackle is employed, becomes an abominable nuisance, from the difficulty in unshipping a joint to allow landing the fish. I should, then, always advise, whenever practicable, the use of a short one—of, say 12 or 14 feet, with strong yet fine-running tackle of plaited silk. When the proper depth has been obtained, a sufficient quantity of line to ensure reaching the desired spot may be drawn from the reel and taken out in a loop from the bottom ring of the rod and the reel itself. It may then, when drawn fairly taut, be hitched over a tiny twig, or a blade of stout grass projecting from the ground, and the piscator, taking up the rod and giving the float and the shotted line a swing in the desired direction, will find that the light line flies easily through the rings after the weighted portion, and, with a little practice, almost any part of a pond may be easily reached. In a gastronomic point of view the bream has always been held up to execration. Here is a recipe for cooking a river fish of, say 3 or 4 pound weight :—Cleanse him and lay him in salt and water one hour; stuff with a rich veal stuffing and bake him—plentifully anointed with good butter—in a slow oven, until the meat comes easily from the bones. Serve him up, hot and hot, with cayenne pepper and lemon juice. Carpers may say—I don't mean carp-eaters or carp-fishers —that the veal-stuffing, lemon juice and butter, are the only parts of the dish worth going in for; it may be so, but I have found the fish very toothsome.

DACE FISHING.

Dace are found in most of our English rivers, streams and brooks, and will thrive well in either swiftly running water, or in slower streams, so long as there is a fresh supply coming from the head or from the feeders running into it. To the beginner in fly-fishing, we have no fish indigenous to our waters that gives such good practice to the learner as the one under notice, for during the spring and summer months the dace rises greedily at small flies and insects of various kinds, and is besides so brave and dashing in his attempts to escape when hooked upon fine tackle, that he gets the pupil's hand well in for higher and nobler game. He is an extremely handsome fish, and elegantly shaped, the head small, with the irides of the eyes a pale yellow, the body lengthy and the tail well forked ; the scales are much smaller than those of the roach, and have a brilliant silvery gloss predominating over a cast of yellowish green ; the back is of a dusky green tint, the belly white, the ventral, anal and caudal fins of a pale reddish hue. In the Thames they are seldom taken of any great size, but in the Lea, and particularly above Ware and Hertford, they run much larger ; while in the Lark and Linnet—the former a tributary of the Ouse, of Suffolk and Cambridge, the latter another tributary stream joining the Lark near Bury—it is said that they attain a pound or more in weight. Personally, however, I have never seen anything approaching this size, and shall be inclined to take such statements *cum grano*, although Pennant gives an account of one that weighed a pound and a half, and Linnæus says that it grows to a foot and a half in some countries. The most likely localities in which to find these fish is in the vicinity of rapid currents, sharps and eddies ; the point of junction between two streams is another habitat, while mill-races and the tail of a mill-run are nearly always sure finds, and here they will work up among the sharpest streams, and in the froth and foam of the most turbulent looking water. In cold and stormy weather they leave their favourite gravelly scours, and seek deeper and more subtle water, where the bottom is marly or clayey in character, and here they are more likely to be taken by means of bottom fishing. Spawning somewhere about the middle of March, or the beginning of April, it is a wonderful sight to watch a school of these fish upon the spawning beds, working and burrowing amongst the sand and gravel, in active preparation for the deposition of their ova, and upon favourable ground, countless thousands may be frequently noticed by the attentive observer; while so intent are the little fellows upon the object at issue, that they seemingly take not the slightest notice of lookers on. Always provided they keep tolerably quiet, and don't throw brickbats among them—a little amusement I saw practised some few years ago on the Maidenhead shallows, by some of the thoughtless men who make camping out an amusement upon the banks of the Thames as soon as the sun has fairly made his appearance for the summer season. In bottom fishing for dace, there is little, if any, difference to that practised in roach-fishing; at any rate the same tackle will kill equally well. It is, however, in the autumn months that the best sport can be obtained, when they, like the roach, have retired to the deeper portions of the river. In the earlier periods of the year dace will feed greedily, occasionally upon worms of all kinds, and the little red worm in particular, as well as the larvæ of beetles, grubs, wasps and caddis worms. In the hotter months, such as June, July and August, if the angler chooses to try for them on the bottom, no bait is so killing as gentles, well scoured and cleansed in sand, and thus rendered tough and lasting on the hook. Some pieces of greaves, of which dace are extravagantly fond, are another excellent bait for them, and many an anathema has this fish to put up with from the barbel-fisher when legering with this substance, in return for the multitude of sharp tugging bites—very different, however, to that of a barbel—that he favours the angler with at such times. A capital plan for their capture when they come upon a barbel swim, is to fit up a small hook upon a length of gut, and so affixed to the leger bottom that it hangs close to the larger lump of greaves destined for the bigger fish— thus, when these little pests, at such times, rush at the big piece of greaves, one or other of their number is certain to swallow the small bit, and come to bag, where one might strike all day at their sharp tugs at the larger baits, without once hooking one of them. It is always a good sign when dace on a sudden cease biting on a barbel swim. Rely upon it, that larger fish have hustled the little thieves away, and that the probabilities are that while barbel or chub are on the bottom inspecting your bait, preparatory to a final smack at it, the dace have risen over them as a flight of wood pigeons will watch a hawk. During the summer, supposing the angler to be bottom fishing, it is always advisable to fish rather off than on the bottom for dace; for, unlike the roach, they seek the swifter runs of water, such as the angle of two sharp streams, or the races of mill-wheels, and there, stemming the current, lie poised and waiting for chance food that may come down. In such a place, where eddies and back currents whirl the waters back and forth in tortuous fashion, drop in the plummet, and set the bait four or five inches from the ground. A light, handy rod is required, a little springy in its action, fine running tackle and a fair sized cork or quill float, well shotted, and yet of such buoyancy as to resist the suction and swirl of the heavy stream; then let the stream take the baited hook—and the lure may be caddis, red worm, or gentles—right down away among the sharpest whirls and eddies. Here lie the dace, and the instant the bait reaches them away goes the float, and good sport ensues at once, for dace fight hard and pluckily, and upon such fine tackle as this, and in such a boil of water, will not yield till they've had a sharp fight for victory. For its size nothing plunges more violently at first, and proper care should always be taken in striking a fish at such a place, from the extreme probability that a trout or two may be lying there, and that one of the spotted beauties may have bolted your worm, or bunch of caddis or gentles. In ground baiting for dace I know of nothing better than plenty of carrion gentles, obtained from bone boilers' and crushers' places of business. These, mixed with coarse pollard or bran, and put loosely into balls of clay, will be found as useful as anything; but care should be exercised in the quantity given, as dace are greedy feeders at all times, and if they get thoroughly gorged with food, will cease biting at the baited hook, as a matter of course.

As I have already said, no better practice for the embryo trout-fisher can be obtained than fly-fishing for dace. An ordinary trouting rod will do as well as any; the cast should be of the finest gut, and two or three flies may be used tied on hooks of small pattern: when, however, a beginner in the graceful art of fly-fishing is desirous of obtaining instruction and accuracy in throwing a fly, one only is sufficient. Small black and red palmers and black gnats are good and staple flies for dace whipping, and occasionally, if the black flies have a gentle put upon the tip of the hook's point, it seems to possess extraordinary attractive qualities, and the fish will dash at it madly. In lieu of gentles, supposing them to be unattainable, a bit of wash-leather with the point of the hook pushed through it will be found an efficient substitute. The best method of fishing the Thames shallows is to throw from a boat, having a heavy stone, or, better still, a small anchor, so as to effectually moor the craft whenever a likely spot is reached. The flies may then be cast straight down the stream and to the right and left, and it will be soon apparent to the angler whether dace are on the shallows or no, for if there they will likely enough come with a rush at the flies at once, provided the weather is at all favourable ; if they are not there, or none are taken after ten minutes' time, try elsewhere.

Capital sport as is obtained with the artificial, I must confess that I think the practice of blow line fishing will beat it hollow, and, at the risk of repetition, I will suggest that whenever shallows and likely looking scours can be reached from the bank, they should be fished in the following manner:—Use a lengthy, light and stiff rod, with a long line of floss silk, which can be obtained at any of the tackle shops for this particular purpose, and should be two yards at least beyond the length of the rod ; then, with a small hook placed carefully between the shoulders of a bluebottle—at all times a most deadly lure—get the wind at your back, and, sheltered from view by a bit of rising ground, a bush, or the old stump of a tree, let the breeze carry the light floss until it bellies out, clear of the uplifted rod. With the baited hook held between the thumb and finger of the left hand, raise the point of the rod, and at the instant a puff of wind comes, release the fly, gradually lowering the rod until it drops gently and naturally upon the surface of the stream. It sometimes happens, from some unaccountable reason, that dace will not take the fly when upon the surface. Supposing that this occurs and few fish are observed rising over ground where they are known to lie, and those which do rise refuse to take the fly thrown, perhaps, directly over them, put on the hook-link of gut or hair a single shot, and let the insect sink, gently drawing it backwards and forwards to the surface of the water; by these means many fish may be captured that otherwise would have gone untouched. The ant fly, a winged insect found in the interior of the anthills, is a splendid natural bait for dace, and Walton thus gives instructions for their capture and subsequent keeping. He says :—" Gather them alive with both their wings, and put them into a glass that will hold a quart or pottle; first put into the glass a handful or more of the moist earth out of which you gather them, and as much of the roots of the grass of the said hillock, and then put in the flies, gently, that they lose not their wings; lay a clod of earth over it, and then so many as are put into the glass without bruising will live there a month or more, and be always in readiness for you to fish with. But if you would have them keep longer, then get any great earthen pot or barrel, or three or four gallons, which is better, then wash your barrel with water and honey, and having put into it a quantity of earth and grass roots, then put in your flies, and they will cover it, and will live a quarter of a year—these in any stream and clear water are a deadly bait for roach or dace, or for a chub." So far as culinary properties are concerned, the "silvery dace" has little, if anything, to recommend him, although when fried, crisp and brown, in good oil or lard, and eaten in lieu of anything better, with the appetite engendered by a long ramble, rod in hand, by the brink of some sparkling streamlet, he is not to be despised; and I can well recollect on one occasion, when cold, wet, and hungry, I got back to a little village "pub.," at which I had engaged a bed for the night, I was met with the comforting assurance, that save some rusty bacon, and cheese like soap, there was nothing eatable in the house. I had, however, some three dozen splendid dace, and these were forthwith consigned to the kitchen for my supper; presently they appeared, crisp and hot, and with brown bread and butter, pepper, and salt, they made an appetising and savoury meal—better than sprats, at any rate. Carefully wiped dry, and placed in methylated spirits in an air-tight jar, they will keep wonderfully well and make grand baits for winter jack spinning. I will now close my paper upon Freshwater Fishing, thanking not only my Lord Abinger for his courtesy in presiding, but you, gentlemen, for the attention with which you have listened to me.

DISCUSSION.

Mr. WILMOT said he must say a word with regard to the somewhat notorious black bass of Canada as his name had been mentioned. Mr. Wheeldon had rather misunderstood his feeling towards the black bass, which was not a favourite of his by any means; and on two or three occasions he had expressed the opinion that it was unadvisable to introduce it into Great Britain, unless it was into waters where there were no other fish of a superior kind. The black bass was a fish of good feeding quality; not a bad fish to eat; but not a favourite of his. He fished more for trout and salmon, and a man who was in the habit of doing so, would not fish for bass or any inferior fish. Black bass were a very voracious, greedy fish, and invariably cleaned out any other fish in the same waters, unless it was perch, which sometimes would hold their own, being of a somewhat similar character. Fishing in Canada was quite different to what it was in Great Britain. There they did not have barbel, dace, and roach, nor any fish of that kind. There might be some descriptions of fish of that class; but at present the sluggish streams had chub, pike shiners, and coarse fish of that sort. These fish were evidently of a low order, because they fed at the bottom of the rivers as a rule, and were therefore not to be compared with those of a higher order, such as trout, which rose to the surface for their food ; in fact you did not find trout in streams which were not limpid and clear, because they must see their food at the top of the water. He could readily understand why in a country like England, and in a city like London, so many people were fond of fish. It was very fortunate that the Thames gave the people residing in London so many opportunities of fishing, even although the fish might be of an inferior order. It was a pleasant healthy pastime, and if they got only one or two fish to eat for their day's labour, it was very pleasant when they came home to sit down and tell the tale of the day's sport. He thought, therefore, that angling in every possible way should be encouraged, because it could never seriously diminish or destroy the fish in any stream as netting would. If more encouragement were given to anglers, it would be beneficial to fisheries as a rule. In Canada no one was allowed to fish for salmon with bait ; the law was very distinct, that it should only be fly surface fishing. The belief there was that salmon did not take food in the rivers at all ; and the government was so particular with regard to the protection of salmon when they passed all the nets and other engines which might be set at the estuaries, the fish having got past those, were only to be caught by the fly. He would suggest that if a law—something of that sort—were passed in England, it would be beneficial, and encourage a higher order of angling than catching salmon with bait. He begged to propose a vote of thanks to Mr. Wheeldon for the instructive lecture he had given.

Doctor HONEYMAN, in seconding the motion, said [he did not know much about angling himself; but he so much admired the enthusiasm of Mr. Wheeldon on the subject that he was very much inclined to wish he was an angler himself.

The CHAIRMAN, in putting the motion, said he should have been very glad to have heard some further remarks from Mr. Wheeldon more in the constructive line. It appeared to him that his able lecture dealt very much with modes of destroying fish; but his love for fish was so great that his interest was almost greater in the methods of protecting and propagating fish, and he should have been glad to have heard from Mr. Wheeldon something on that point. For many years, whilst England was a Roman Catholic country, the habits of the fish were doubtless much better known, for it was impossible to go through the country and see all the ruins of ancient Abbeys without being struck with the stews and fish-ponds which were always to be found in connection with them. There was no doubt those brethren, though they lived and died in the odour of sanctity, were perfectly well aware of the odour of a good fish on Friday; but since the habits had changed, and fasting was no longer the fashion, the knowledge of breeding and rearing the fish had sunk to a very low ebb. Latterly, he saw indications amongst many noblemen and gentlemen of a great desire to cultivate this art, and he had no doubt, in the course of time, a great increase in the food of the people would be obtained from this source.

The motion having been carried,

Mr. WHEELDON, in responding, said he was quite sure when the exhibition was over they would all reflect very keenly on the loss they sustained by the absence of their American visitors, who had thoroughly endeared them-

selves to all they met by their kindly disposition and
courtesy of manner. He begged to propose a hearty vote
of thanks to Lord Abinger for presiding on this occasion.

Admiral BERNABÊ seconded the motion. He thought
there was no doubt that these Papers and discussions would
be of great benefit, not only to England but to the world at
large, inasmuch as they conveyed a large amount of useful
information. They would tend to improvement in the
modes of fishing, which would increase the food for the
people and also ameliorate the condition of that hardy
element of humanity called fishermen.

The motion having been carried,

The CHAIRMAN said it gave him a great deal of pleasure
to attend the present conference, and only regretted for
the sake of the lecturer and the public that there was
not a larger attendance. It always gave him pleasure
when he saw a good work in hand like the Fisheries
Exhibition to put his own shoulder to the wheel if possible
and help it forward.

International Fisheries Exhibition
LONDON, 1883

ANGLING CLUBS

AND

PRESERVATION SOCIETIES

OF

LONDON AND THE PROVINCES

BY

J. P. WHEELDON

LATE ANGLING EDITOR OF "BELL'S LIFE"

LONDON
WILLIAM CLOWES AND SONS, Limited
INTERNATIONAL FISHERIES EXHIBITION
AND 13 CHARING CROSS, S.W.

1883

THE

ANGLING CLUBS AND PRESERVATION SOCIETIES OF LONDON AND THE PROVINCES.

INTRODUCTION.

IN writing this handbook it was my original intention to give something like a short history of the formation and present position of some, at any rate, of the chief Angling Societies of the metropolis. Considering that there are certainly over 150 of these societies in London alone, I well knew that I had set myself no light task. Mapping the matter over in my own mind, I came to the conclusion that the only course for me to adopt was to seek the co-operation of the societies themselves, asking through their various secretaries for information as to their origin, and also what, if any, good work they were doing in the present. With this view a letter was sent to the secretaries of the various metropolitan clubs, apprising them of my design and intention. I have to thank a small proportion of these gentlemen, and I regret to say a very small one, for the courtesy of a reply. The larger number evidently considered the matter beneath their valuable notice, and so ignored it altogether. The situation hardly requires further comment.

With regard to the provincial societies, the line adopted has been entirely different—not in so far as I personally was concerned, because the same letter was addressed to each and all, but in the matter of politeness and courteous consideration towards myself. The result leaves me little room for doubt that the gentlenesses of modern society are cultivated far more abroad than they are at home. Many gentlemen have taken considerable trouble in affording me especially valuable information; to all such I tender my warmest and heartiest thanks—not so much perhaps for the knowledge conveyed in their letters, as for the kindly sentiments which accompanied it.

Thus much by way of introduction. For the reason stated, I regret very much that my little book does not contain fuller and more concise information. I leave it, however, to the tender mercies of my readers.

It would probably be very difficult for the angler of to-day to realise what the Thames and the Lea were like some fifty years ago. Those are the two great home rivers, centres of all the persevering efforts made day by day, week by week, and month after month, by the London angler, whose great aim it is to catch a big fish of some sort—it matters very little what—and have his name go down to posterity, decked with emblematic laurels as the "champion" in such and such a class of fishing. Such happy fate may be preserved for all time—until at any rate the record is beaten—upon the tablets of fame connected with some small local angling club.

But fifty years ago—and what a paradise for sportsmen the Thames must have been then!—swans were kept within bounds, and at that time it was not necessary to employ bands of men, as it is in the present day, to drive these handsome but terribly destructive birds from the line of weed-fringed roots dependent from stubbly pollards lining the bank, and upon which spawning perch have deposited their riband-like strings of ova, nor from " the hills" in the weir streams, where the great and bonny mother trout has frequented during that time when she was simply obeying Nature's urgent laws.

Steam launches, probably the greatest of all great curses to him who, following the example of a writer of other days, would fain—

> "Live harmlessly, and by the brink
> Of Thames or Avon have a dwelling place,
> Where I may see my quill or cork down sink
> With eager bite of perch or bleak or dace,
> And on the world and my Creator think,

were then absolutely unknown. In any event, there were none of those thrice detestable " puffers," with silent engines and dull moaning whistle, which daily and hourly tear through the water at the rate of 12 to 20 miles an hour, doing direful and deadly injury every yard they go. It may be said that this language is excessive in its strength, and overstrained in its application. Not a whit, take my word for it. I have seen more damage done to the ova of spawning fish in one season, and particularly perch and pike, by the everlasting swash and wash of these deadly pests, more—aye, far more than an army of poachers and fishermen could do in five years, had they even combined their forces, without absolutely netting the river wholesale every day, and harried every fish to death that came within their ken.

At the first glance this would seem to be an overwhelming

statement, hastily and rashly made. One moment's consideration will suffice to impress any thoughtful man's mind with an assurance of its truth. A pike wirer, it is true, may kill a female fish, ripe and full of ova, and hence many thousands of future pike are lost to the fair fisher. But where he kills one or two fish without detection, the steam launches are perpetually and everlastingly ploughing through the water, not only washing away the ova deposited upon the weeds and sheltering roots, but destroying thousands upon thousands of tiny just-hatched fry, which would otherwise have probably grown up, and made in time mature fish, the source and foundation of good sport to the fair fishermen.

In those far-off days of the past there were such delightful and fishful nooks as one misses nowadays. Comparatively speaking the Thames was a great stretch of maiden water, where the unharried fish dwelt in a sense of the most perfect security. Their chief enemy was then, probably, the village poacher, with his rude, yet none the less dangerous, ash pole and bit of dangling copper wire. Lazy and idle—as indeed some few perhaps of the village loungers of to-day may be—this worthy would stroll down to the river side, where mayhap, amongst bonny sweet-smelling hay-fields lined with meadow-sweet, and where glorious purple loosestrife bounds the river's marge, he met not a solitary living soul the whole summer's day. Here he would pry about, until he might haply descry, basking amongst the water weeds, a big pike, with the tip of his nose and tail clear of the water, or the dorsal fin of a great lumbering carp. Then the fatal noose would be brought into play, and towards night, when reeling home from "The Haymakers," the gloriously happy fellow might possibly reflect, and withal possessed of an infinite sense of satisfaction, that he was a very lucky dog indeed to be able to get such a skinful of good old ale with so little real trouble.

But the injury done to the fisheries of a river in such a case—and examples of it are now happily almost extinct—is increased a millionfold every year by that wrought by the terrible rate at which traffic up and down the stream is permitted. I have seen, for instance, the wave raised by a fast launch or heavy steam-tug rushing along the bank nearly a yard high, sweep up some little inland bay where the water perhaps shallowed from a foot or so at its mouth to only a few inches in depth in its interior. That little bay, and all such like it, is full to this day, I hope, of tiny mites of baby fish. I have seen, as I have said, the wave sweep across it, and as it receded it left hundreds, possibly thousands, of little fish to die amongst the pebbles and rank grass growing along the shore. Talk about the destruction effected by a pair of otters, talk about the war waged by the idle village lout upon the finny inhabitants of a river—why, the argument falls flat and becomes both baseless and ridiculous as opposed to the terrible havoc wreaked by these puffing pests, determined enemies as they are to good sport, peace, and quietude.

It may be in the recollection of some few of the readers of this little book that I have for years waged war, with both voice and pen, for the suppression of what I cannot help seeing is the chief enemy to the fisheries of the river. My work has borne at least some little fruit, inasmuch as a Bill for the better regulation of steam traffic upon the river has gone through a select Committee of the Commons, and is now before the House of Lords; and all good anglers will, I am convinced, say amen to my prayer for its success. But suppose it passes and becomes law, as I earnestly hope it may do, it will still be an abortive and useless measure, unless the "Angling Clubs of London"—and here I strike the key-note of my book—help it by their united support and assistance. It is useless for Tom to wait while Jack or Harry strikes, in the event of any outrage upon propriety. Tom, being the spectator of an abuse of the existing law, should strike at once, and then perhaps others will follow his example, so that in the event of any breach of law in the future, the result, affecting, recollect, the angler's dearest and nearest interests in connection with his sport, rests with the angler himself. As there are twenty "clubmen" fishing the Thames to one unassociated with any such body, this warning, and it is a very grave one, is addressed particularly to them.

Practically, I think, or at any rate to any great extent, poaching on the fisheries of the Thames is very nearly extinct. Now and again there is a raid made, it is true, by some of those determined spirits always to be found in villages and large towns, and who would, every man-Jack of them, infinitely prefer one poached hare or pheasant, obtained at the price of a little adventure and devilry, to a brace got by fair means ; but I hardly fancy that the extent of the mischief done is very great. The reason lies in the fact that a very large proportion of the river is now protected either by the keepers and officers of the Thames Angling Preservation Society or by the officials of some one or other of the local associations, all of whom are in reality offshoots from the parent-tree just named. There can be little doubt that the growth of the angling clubs of London has been largely fostered by the efforts made by the "Thames Angling Preservation Society" in the conservation and preservation of its fisheries. In tracing, therefore, an imperfect history of the growth of the angling clubs, due credit should be given to the leading Preservation body, which exercises such an important control over the interests of the great home river. It may therefore, at this point, be a fair opportunity for a short description of establishment and progress up to the present time.

The Thames Angling Preservation Society was, I believe, first established in the year 1838. Somewhere about that time, a report was certainly promulgated to the effect that "the Fisheries of the River Thames had of late afforded so little sport, owing to incessant poaching and the destruction of the young brood and spawn during the fence seasons, that it was almost useless to attempt angling in certain districts at all." Fortunately, that report found its way to a sympathetic quarter, and it occurred to those into whose hands it fell that if a proper representation of the facts were made to the Lord Mayor of London (then Sir John Cowan) he might probably be induced, in his official capacity as Conservator of the River Thames, to help those early pioneers of fish preservation in the course they were endeavouring to take for the good alike of anglers and the river itself. Acting upon this view, a meeting was convened on the 17th of March, 1838, and was afterwards held at the "Bell Inn," Hampton. It was attended by the following good anglers, most of whom, I am afraid, have gone to that shadowy bourne, from which no angler, however good he may have been, ever returns—Mr. Henry Jephson, Mr. C. C. Clarke, Mr. Henry Perkins, Mr. W. H. Whitebread, Mr. Edward Jesse, Mr. Richard Kerry, and Mr. David Crole. These gentlemen having met, fully discussed the important issues brought before them, and that meeting was the groundwork upon which the present important work of the Thames Angling Preservation Society was founded.

They therefore resolved themselves into a Society for "the protection of fish from poachers;" and one of the earliest steps taken was the appointment of a staff of river-keepers, selected principally from amongst the professional fishermen who gained a livelihood upon the Thames. The valuable action of this small preservative body was from the outset fully recognised by the Lord Mayor, and warrants were then granted to the river-keepers to act as water-bailiffs, while certain bye-laws were framed for the better protection of the fisheries of the river. Under these by-laws the position and power of the river-keepers is thus defined:— They are empowered "to enter any boat, vessel, or craft of any fisherman or dredgerman, or other person or persons fishing or taking fish or endeavouring to take fish, and there to search for, take and seize all spawn, fish, brood of fish, and unsizable, unwholesome, or unseasonable fish, and also all unlawful nets, engines, and instruments for taking or destroying fish as shall then be in any such boat, vessel, or craft in and upon the river, and to take and seize on shore or shores adjoining to the said river all such spawn, fish, and also all unlawful nets, engines, and instruments for taking and destroying fish as shall there be found."

The extent of water taken under control was from Richmond to the City Stone at Staines, and immediately efforts were made to preserve the various deeps in the course indicated, thus making them "harbours of refuge" for the fish. The position of such preserves may be shortly pointed out as follows.

Richmond.—The preserve is westward of the bridge to the Duke of Buccleuch's, 700 yards. Twickenham.—The preserve is the west end of lawn, Pope's Villa, to the ait, 400 yards. Kingston.—The preserve is from the Lower Malthouse at Hampton Wick to the east end of Mr. J. C.

Park's lawn at Teddington, including the back-water known as the Crolock, 1060 yards. Thames Ditton and Long Ditton.—The preserve is from Lord Henry Fitzgerald's, running eastwards, 512 yards. Hampton.—The preserve is from the west end of Garrick's Lawn, including the Tantling Bay, to the lower end pile below Moulsey Lock, 1514 yards. Sunbury.—The preserve is from the weir westward to the east end pile of breakwater, 683 yards. Walton.—The preserve is at the east end of Tankerville and west of Horse Bridge, called Walton Sale, 250 yards. Shepperton.—The preserve is, Upper Deep, 200 yards; Old Deep, east of the creek rails, 240 yards; Lower Deep, east of the drain, 200 yards. Weybridge.—The preserve is from the weir to Shepperton Lock, 830 yards. Chertsey. —The preserve is the weir to 80 yards eastward of the bridge, 445 yards. Laleham and Penton Hook.—The preserve at Penton Hook is from the guard piles eastward round the Hook to the east end of the lock. Staines.—The preserve is the City boundary stone to 210 yards eastward of the bridge.

From time to time these preserves have been rendered more efficient by the sinking of old punts, brick burrs, and by driving stakes into the river bed, as a protection against netting operations. The last of such established preserves was that at Kingston, which was made in the year 1857. Upon application being made to the Lord Mayor, the movement was opposed by some of the professional fishermen, but such opposition was overruled, and the following is a list of the obstacles sunk:—" Five old punts, two iron waggons, 7 feet 3 inches in length by 4 inches, and 2 feet 6 inches in height, open at one end; 450 stakes driven; six 2-horse loads of large brick burrs; twenty egg chests with tenter hooks; fifty large flint stones; ten tar-barrels, tenter-hooked; two large sugar casks, tenter-hooked; two punt loads of old iron gas lamps and other useful things; and three sacks of tin cuttings for the landing-places along the shore."

In December 1857 the Board of Thames Conservancy became invested with fuller powers in its government, and an application made by the Thames Angling Preservation Society for a continuance of the powers vested in their bailiffs or water-keepers was at once granted. The next step taken for the further preservation of the fisheries of the Thames was in 1869, when an application was made for the whole abolition of netting between Richmond Bridge and the City Stone at Staines. This was supported by the entire body of Thames fishermen, and in consequence of the Conservancy Board acceding to the application the following notice was inserted in several of the London papers:—

"Be it ordered and established that the 16th item of the rules, orders, and ordinances for the fisheries in the Thames and Medway, made on the 4th day of October, 1785, be repealed, and that henceforth no person shall use any net for the purpose of catching fish in the River Thames between Richmond Bridge and the 'City Stone' at Staines, except a small net for the purpose of taking bait only, of the following dimensions—namely, not exceeding 13 feet in circumference, and an angler's landing net, under penalty to forfeit and pay £5 for every such offence. The seal of the Conservators of the River Thames was this 23rd day of January, 1860, affixed by order."

But the most important work, after all, effected by the Thames Angling Preservation Society was perhaps the abolition of snatching and laying night lines. It is absolutely impossible to overestimate the destruction effected amongst spawning fish, or to others flocking to certain places where a sewage discharge induced them to harbour, than was effected by the detestable and unsportsmanlike practice of snatching. The sewer at the foot of Richmond Bridge was a noted place where the so-called angler was in the habit of exercising his unworthy craft. The *modus operandi* was very much as follows: an angler —heaven save the mark!—perhaps pretended to be fishing for dace, and attached to his tackle he had a dozen stout hooks set at intervals on his line, some of them baited— others with not even that shallow pretence—with a fragmentary portion of worm. All day long these delightful gentry kept dropping a heavily shotted line into the swim, and instantly jerking it upwards again with a powerful stroke. Thus many a great carp has been impaled, many a lusty bream dragged *nolens volens* from his watery home. The same kind of thing was done openly and in broad daylight, along the parade at Kingston, and the operators pretended they were fishing—legitimately fishing! Now and again a bold sportsman, rendered hardy and brave with impunity, disdained to use the shallow artifice of the bit of worm at all, and boldly lowered amongst the gathering shoals of bream or dace a cruel implement of sport, consisting of a bunch of bare triangles weighted with a sinker. It may well be in the recollection of a great many disgusted spectators, even as the memory is likely to abide with me for all time, of the shameful and detestable scenes that were wont to be enacted day after day at many of the accessible weirs, when the dace were heading up. I have seen them slaughtered in scores, and scores of hundreds; and this little game went on day after day, for weeks. It was stopped at last, and high time too. The only wonder

I have, thinking back upon such scenes, is this : How was it that many a good angler, who must have shuddered with indignation at the cruel, shameful waste of life, the pain inflicted upon the hapless fish, escaped trial for manslaughter at the Old Bailey, consequent upon trying to effect the death by drowning of one or other of the manly and noble crew ? I know not.

As to the practice of laying night lines, its results were all too palpably apparent to him who reads by the wayside as he runs. Many and many a grand Thames trout, the pride and crown jewel of some deep reach, has met his death ignobly at the end of a night line, ostensibly laid for the capture of eels. Then it was that the lucky captor would knock his prize on the head, and straightway take it up to the village house of a well-to-do and worthy inhabitant, who had probably tried a round dozen of times to effect his capture legitimately. Some such scene and dialogue as this then followed :—

A trim and natty servant-maid appearing at the door, honest old Bill Boozler, the hard and horny-handed, who never told an untruth in his life, or pretended to bait a barbel swim when he had not had a worm near his premises for a month, rush basket in hand, thus addresses her :—

"Mornin', Mary, my dear. Why, Lard a mussy, what cheeks them is o' yourn, surelie. Redder 'n the best Ribson pippen as I ever seen. Lard, ef I'd only bin a younger man."

"Go along with you ; a married man and all. You oughter bin ashamed o' yourself," is naturally red-cheeked Mary's retort.

"Well, so 'tis, Mary. Mortal 'shamed of myself I is, and so I don't deceive you. Muster Fubsy in? But, theer, I needn't arst. Aint them his brekfus' things agoin' in? Course they is; new laid heggs there is, which they're werry good at times, and a leetle bit o' bacon frezzled crisp. Tray bung, as the Frenchmen says, and now, Mary, my dear, will you be so good as to give Muster Fubsy ole Bill Boozler's compliments, and say he's sorry to say as that theer trout has a-come to a huntimely hend at larst."

The natty one, having delivered her message, is nearly upset by the anxious Fubsy, who rushes out, spectacles on nose, the *Times* in one hand, and loosely arrayed in his dressing-gown. He opens upon William at once.

"William—William Boozler, you don't mean to say that you've er—er—caught that trout, after all the number of times I've been out with you, and the pounds and pounds I've spent?"

"Suttenly not," cries the worthy William, with an air of mingled grief and astonishment. "No, sir, suttenly not. But this blessid mornin' as ever was, I'se a goin' down to Bunkin's Ait in the little skiff, to see about the eel barskits, and I hears a floppin' and prancin' about in my old punt—that one what the *Westa*, confound her! stoved in—and so I sculls across softly, thinkin' it was rats. Soap me never, marster, I was that knocked-a-cock as I could ha' drunk arf-a-pint o' ole ale quick, just as I could at this heer minnit, fur theer lay that theer loverlly trout, a nine-pounder ef he weighs a hounce, wi' just a kick and no more left in him; and I takes him in my two hands tenderly as ef I was a lefting a babby, and 'olds his 'ed up stream. But it worn't a mossel 'o use, he was stone gone; and I says to myself, I does, 'Bill, this punt is yourn'—which it is, cause why, my own brother's sister's husband built her, best pine deal and oak stretchers, which well it is beknown down at the bridge, and at the ferry; but, 'Bill,' says I, 'this trout ain't yourn, and for why, cause Muster Fubsy bin a fishin' wi' you, Bill, off and on, a matter of a score o' times, ole days and arf uns'—though I never was the man to arst for a ole day's pay for a arf un—'and that theer trout, Bill,' says I, 'is Muster Fubsy's fish by rights'; and so I brings him straight up to you, sir, and theer he lays—a beauty as he is—wi' spots on him as big as a crown piece, werry nigh."

"But, in the name of fate, William," cries Fubsy, carefully putting his spectacles on the bridge of his nose, "how did the trout get into your punt?"

"Chucked hisself in, sir—chucked hisself in, which it is well known they will do arter a bait, or else a leaping out o' the water arter a butterfly or what not, and so the pore creater hadn't the sense to chuck hisself back again, and theer he is. Blessed if I ain't as dry as bones, a-talking so much."

"William, you're a very worthy and honest fellow—a very worthy fellow indeed, William. There's a sovereign for you, and I'm much obliged to you, while Mary will draw you a jug of ale. Good morning, William. Good morning."

The end draws nigh. William at any time during that day may be discovered at the bar of the "Angler's Rest," where for the hundredth time, at least, he tells the story of "that theer trout a-chucking hisself high and dry into the old punt." The trout goes to Cooper, and when it comes home, at the expiration say, of six to twelve months, it may perhaps bear an inscription to this effect: "Thames Trout caught by A. J. Fubsy, spinning. Weight, nine pounds."

In my own opinion the abolition of night-lining is the

sole and only reason for the immense increase in late years of the stock of trout in the river.

The new by-laws as to snatching and night-lining were approved by Her Majesty at the Court of Balmoral on the 28th of October, 1879. They are as follows :

"Snatching of fish.—It shall not be lawful for any person to fish for, or to take, or attempt to take, any fish by using a wire, or snare, or hooks (baited or unbaited), or any other engine for the purpose of foul hooking, commonly called 'snatching or snaring.'

"Night lines.—It shall not be lawful for any person to lay night hooks or night lines of any description whatever between the 'City Stone' at Staines and Kew Bridge ; and any person laying fixed lines of hooks by night or day (commonly called night lines), or taking, or attempting to take, eels or fish of any description by such means, shall be deemed as committing a breach of this by-law."

The Thames Angling Preservation Society continues its jurisdiction as far as Staines, and at that point the first of the local associations for the preservation of the river commences its work. This is the Windsor and Eton Society, which is supposed to look after something like about twelve miles of water extending from Staines Bridge to Monkey Island. Throughout that stretch, some of the finest water in the Thames is to be found, and if this society were more thoroughly supported by the public, it is probable that no similar length of water would be more splendidly productive. It is the fashion, however, to rail at the promoters and managers of any incorporated body whose objects may not appear to be carried out well and to the point. It escapes probably the notice of those who gibe and speak harshly about the work done by the Windsor and Eton, that it is simply impossible for the

Society to keep going unless the angling public provides the sinews of war. This section of the public will know in an instant whether they have done so or not.

It is at once an injustice and a wrong to brand a body of men with shortcomings in their work, when the very work itself is dependent upon the help which a local association like the Windsor and Eton receives from the public who fish its waters. I venture to think that few, if any, of the hundreds of men who yearly go to Windsor and its charming environs from London, sometimes taking good bags of fish home with them, ever subscribe, or ever did subscribe, one single penny to its funds.

The Maidenhead, Cookham, and Bray Angling Society, whose headquarters are at Skindle's Hotel, and whose excellent secretary is Mr. W. G. Day, takes up the work of preservation at Monkey Island, continuing their operations over an important section of the Thames. There is probably none other of the local associations which has done such wonderfully good work. But then the reason is not far to seek ; they are not only supported fairly by the local gentry and inhabitants, many of whom are themselves keen lovers of angling, but also by a considerable number of London anglers, principally members of the leading clubs. That just makes all the difference, and although I do not pretend to say that the Windsor and Eton has not done all in its power with the funds which it had at command, the Maidenhead and Cookham sets such a brilliant example, by stocking their waters with splendid Wycombe trout, and that too in the most liberal manner, that their example possibly commanded the support they have unquestionably received to a certain extent from a small section of the angling public.

I say a small section advisedly, because where a society,

like that under notice, proves that it is doing a valuable and extensive work, it ought to be recognised, in no matter how small a degree, by every angler who fishes its waters.

Now is this the case, or anything approaching to it? I say no—emphatically no. I have seen scores and hundreds of men, during the many years which I have fished the Thames, pursuing their sport on the Maidenhead waters, and but very few of them ever contribute a single farthing.

If this state of things were confined solely to the coarse fish of this or any other section of the river, it would not possibly matter so much—but then it is not. Trout fishers come and take fish—not confining themselves in some instances very strictly to size—and those very trout represent so much hard cash deducted from the Society's income. Still the Society goes on its way quietly, and year by year does good and worthy work. They are assisted by an excellent body of keepers, under the command of Harry Wilder, who is himself a rare good fisherman, and year after year show an admirable return for their labours.

In justice to Harry Wilder and Captain A Styan, one of the early founders of this Association, it should be added that they were really the first to start the Society. Wilder informs me that he originated the idea of stocking this part of the river with Wycombe trout, and that he and Captain Styan raised a subscription for that purpose. Such a subscription was raised, and in the year before the Association was really started over 50 brace of fine Wycombe trout were turned into the river opposite the Ray Mead Hotel.

It may now be interesting to trace the absolute history of the Society itself.

The Maidenhead, Cookham and Bray Thames Angling Association was started so recently as 1874. The objects in view were, generally speaking, to preserve and improve the fishing from the Shrubbery to Monkey Island, that is to say, the water between the Great Marlow and the Windsor and Eton Districts.

Prior to their establishment poaching and illegal fishing were rampant in this district; and I am informed, by those who speak from personal knowledge, that netting on the meadows adjacent to the river during flood time was carried on wholesale, and large quantities of all kinds of river fish, the greater part undersized, were captured and sold. Wiring fish in the ditches, where they had retreated for spawning operations, was also a very common practice.

Ten years ago trout had become, comparatively speaking, a very rare fish in these parts, and a young trout of greater rarity still. Angling was almost at a standstill, and anglers were seeking other waters which promised greater success.

Several gentlemen belonging to London, and to the locality of Maidenhead, feeling that a great deal could be effected in the way of improvements at a comparatively small cost, if a good system were pursued, took the matter in hand. Support was solicited from the various classes of the community interested in the results, and it ended in this Association being formed.

Their first step, after forming a good working committee, was to make arrangements with the several riparian owners in the districts, by which the Society obtained the rights to drag their ditches and prosecute poachers, and I am pleased to say that they found little difficulty in obtaining these powers.

The Society then took into its service several of the fishermen of the district, and at their request the Thames Conservancy granted deputations for each, by which they were empowered to enter boats to search for fish unlawfully taken, and seize any unlawful net, &c. The Society also had an understanding with its water-bailiffs, that they were to net the ditches adjacent to the river immediately after floods, and that they were to be constantly on the watch for any infringement of the Thames Conservancy By-laws.

During the nine years which have elapsed since their establishment, a number of prosecutions have resulted from the vigilance of their officers, and several convictions have been obtained. The Society has also, after floods, dragged the ditches in their district, from whence large quantities of fish have been returned to the river. The water-bailiffs have also taken a number of night-lines at different times, and I feel, I may say without fear of contradiction, that the Thames Conservancy By-laws are now far more respected in this district than they ever were before.

With a view to improve the fishing, the Society turned in, by way of experiment, a large quantity of golden bream, which were kindly placed at their disposal by the Bedford Angling Association, but the fish appear to have left this locality altogether, probably because the water, except in certain places, was entirely unsuitable to their habits.

From time to time a large quantity of good sized Wycombe trout have been turned in, running from half to five pounds in weight. I should mention that this Society wisely recognised from the first that it was worse than useless to turn in fish below half a pound in weight; and if one may judge from the quantity of trout of that breed now taken, and the numbers of young fish seen in the Maidenhead waters, the Society has been successful in that branch of their undertaking, or at any rate so far as the limited means at their disposal would permit.

The difficulty experienced in purchasing trout of the

right sort and size induced the Society, some time since, to obtain competent advice as to the practicability of breeding and rearing them. With this view one of the vice-presidents, Mr. W. H. Grenfell, of Taplow Court, who has always shown a lively interest in the success of the Society's undertaking, expressed his willingness to place at their disposal a likely place for the purpose. In every respect but one it was pronounced suitable, but it was soon found that the constantly recurring floods would render attempts at breeding useless, and hence the scheme was not prosecuted farther.

The Great Marlow Thames Angling Association does capital work, and is thoroughly well officered. The honorary secretary is Major Simpson Carson, who most efficiently helps the Society in their efforts for the general good of the river. Here again a large share of the Society's income is laudably spent in the purchase of trout of excellent size from the Wycombe waters, which are turned into the Thames at an age, and when they have attained such a size, as enables them to take care of themselves.

The Reading and District Angling Society comes next, and in the hands of its worthy and efficient secretary, Mr. Arthur Butler, of Zinzan Street, Reading, prospers exceedingly. This Society has made the most strenuous efforts to re-stock that portion of the river more immediately under their own control, and I have little doubt that their efforts have met with the success they deserved. It was only a few years ago that the fisheries of the Reading district bore a most unenviable reputation from the extent of netting going on. To my certain knowledge now there is no section of the river which is better looked after and where I think less netting or poaching is prosecuted. Much of this happy state of things is due to Mr. Butler, who is not only a hard practical worker, but a man, moreover, who never walks about the world with his eyes shut. Such a man is bound to do good, and Mr. Butler does it without stint.

This flourishing Thames Preservation Society—one of the most useful and influential on the river—was formed in December, 1877, at a meeting at the Queen's Hotel, Reading, at which upwards of 100 gentlemen of position were present. The intention at first was to protect and improve the fishing in the fine stretch of water between Mapledurham and Sonning—then so denuded of fish that even the poachers let it alone. Henry John Simonds, Esq., J.P., was appointed the first president; Charles Stephens, Esq., J.P., treasurer; and Mr. Arthur Butler—the originator of the movement —honorary secretary, an office he still holds. Mr. Stephens still acts as treasurer. It was soon found desirable to extend the operations of the association both up and down stream, and its district now reaches from Goring Lock to Shiplake Lock. The first president resigned in February 1881, and James Simonds, Esq., J.P., who still occupies the position, was chosen in his stead.

The association has done a really great work for the public, and all its operations have been attended with success. Since its formation about 60,000 trout have been turned in, a large proportion having been reared in a stream belonging to the association; and, as a result, trout fishing has vastly improved. Six years ago the trout were very "few and far between;" this season at least 150, ranging from two to nine pounds in weight, have been landed in the immediate neighbourhood of Reading. Coarse fish have by no means been neglected. Tens of thousands of pike, perch, roach, dace, &c., have been recovered from the ditches after floods, &c., and restored to the river; and several reservoirs and lakes have from time to time been netted, by the kind permission of the owners, and great numbers of perch, carp, tench, rudd, &c., thus added to the stock.

Coarse fish culture has this year been undertaken with surprising success. Two large "Lund" hatching-boxes—stocked with fine Kennet perch—have been filled with spawn, all of which hatched out; and since the perch fry were liberated, a great quantity of carp spawn has been hatched.

No less than eleven bailiffs are employed by the committee, and their work has been so effectual that illegal practices have been, practically, entirely stamped out. It is gratifying to be able to state that every prosecution undertaken by the committee has resulted in a conviction.

Extensive private rights of fishing have lately been acquired for the members (an annual extra charge of five shillings being made). From these waters, fish may not be taken under the following sizes: trout 2lbs., pike 3lbs., tench 2lbs., perch ½lb., barbel 3lbs., carp 3lbs.—a sportsmanlike standard, which the committee recommend for observance also in the public fisheries.

The minimum subscription to the association is 10s. 6d.; but subscribers of £1 1s. and upwards have the privilege of cheap railway tickets to 28 fishing stations. There are at present 117 subscribers (elected by ballot) on the books. Last year's income was £109 19s. 7d., and the expenditure £84 5s. 11d.

The Henley and District Thames Angling Association does no doubt excellent service, and certainly not before it was wanted in that much be-poached district.

The honour of originating this Society belongs to the late honorary secretary, Charles H. Cook, Esq., whose bad health unfortunately compelled him to retire. They preserve the Thames between Temple and Hurley Locks, and have turned into the river considerable numbers of trout. Hardly is this a very satisfactory district, I am afraid, but certainly the improvement made in the fisheries of the neighbourhood redounds very much to the credit of the Association. The president of the Association is the Right Hon. W. H. Smith, M.P., while the present secretary is Mr. J. W. Knight.

The Wycombe Angling and Preservation Society is another body of, shall I say, private conservators, from whom the Thames itself derives a very large amount of good. All the splendid trout which have been turned into the river at Maidenhead, Marlow, and other places, come from the water under the control of this association, and the following short particulars embody nearly all that is necessary to say about a Society whose reputation as trout preservers is a very great one. It has been in existence for nearly four years. It originally commenced with about one hundred members, who paid a low annual fee, but it was found necessary to gradually reduce their number and raise the subscriptions. At present it consists of 30 members who each pay an annual fee of from three to five guineas. This number also includes six artisan members at a nominal subscription. The club preserves a mile and a half of the Wycombe stream, and possesses a magnificent stock of trout. The president is the Rt. Hon. Lord Carrington; honorary secretary and treasurer, J. Thurlow, Esq.

The last of the Preservation Societies of which I shall have occasion to speak in connection with the Home District is the Newbury and District Angling Association. The following short history of its position at the present time is full of interest to anglers frequenting the lovely Kennet Valley, over which this Association has jurisdiction.

This very young association was started on the 18th of June, 1878, with the object of protecting the rivers in and about Newbury—putting a stop to poaching which had been going on for years, and also the practice of taking fish out of season, which was very rife.

After considerable trouble on the part of its chairman and committee it succeeded in obtaining leave to exercise its protective right over the whole of the waters under the control of the Mayor and Corporation of Newbury, also more than seven miles of the Kennet and Avon Canal; and it also rents on a long lease about one mile of the river Lambourne, abounding with trout, and on which stream only the fly is allowed.

The streams over which this association exercises control are the Kennet and many of its back streams, the Lambourne, and the Kennet and Avon Canal.

The fish found in these streams are all very fine, and comprise trout, pike, perch, chub, barbel, roach, dace, carp, tench, eels, gudgeon and—last, but by no means least—very famous crayfish. Indeed, not many miles up the stream there is an old saying concerning them, running as follows—

> "Hungerford crayfish,
> Catch me if ye can;
> There's no such crawlers,
> In the o-ce-an."

In a short sketch like this it is impossible to do more than glance at one or two of the notable fish for which this neighbourhood is celebrated.

Its trout are beaten *nowhere*, having been taken up to 20 lbs. While Pope pleasantly says of its eels—

> "The Kennet swift,
> For silver eels renowned."

And travellers of a nearly bygone age in the old

coaching days could tell of the great gastronomic attractions of the Kennet eel,

"At the house below the hill."

There it was that, in the days when the "Pelican" did flourish, seventy coaches in the day and night passed through the good old town.

But I must pass to the present time and the working of the Association. Well, from small beginnings it has grown so much that at the meeting previous to the next angling season this question will have to come to the fore —either the Committee must raise the price of the tickets or place a restriction upon the number of the members.

It may be as well to add that no profit whatever is made out of the Association, as it is only in existence to preserve the water and improve sport, and all its Committee of Management wish to see is enough to pay the outgoing expenses. They are of necessity large, when consideration is given to keeping up a stock of fish, by turning in hundreds at the proper season, the pay of the keepers all the year, and the constant supervision that is required.

Many fine specimens of Kennet fish may be seen in the Western Quadrant of the Fisheries Exhibition now open at South Kensington.

It only remains to add that all particulars may be obtained of the worthy chairman of the Association, Mr. John Packer, 87 Northbrook Street, Newbury, who will forward rules and all needed information upon application, and from whom *alone* tickets can be had.

There is yet another Society doing good work upon the Thames, called the Oxford Angling Association, but I regret that I received no particulars as to its constitution until too late for insertion in this book.

Finding it to be a matter of exceeding difficulty to

obtain reliable information as to the origin and growth of the various preservation societies scattered about the country, I was compelled to fall back, either upon the horns of a dilemma, or upon the charity of my very good friend, Mr. R. B. Marston, the editor of the *Fishery Gazette* who has very kindly placed at my disposal "The British Fisheries Directory," a valuable little book of reference, dedicated to Mr. Birkbeck, the Chairman of the Executive Committee of the International Exhibition. From that little volume I extract much of the following information with regard to the London and Provincial Preservation and Angling Societies of this country.

METROPOLITAN AND DISTRICT ANGLING CLUBS AND FISHERY ASSOCIATIONS.

The Fisheries Preservation Association, 22 Lower Seymour Street, Portman Square, London.

The National Fish Culture Association of Great Britain and Ireland, Royal Courts Chambers, 2 Chancery Lane.

Thames Angling Preservation Association. Thomas Spreckley, *president;* W. H. Brougham, *secretary.* Office, 7 Ironmonger Lane, E. C.

Thames Rights Defence Association, Francis Francis, *chairman;* J. M. R. Francis, *hon. sec.* Office, 11 Old Jewry Chambers, E.C.

United London Angling Associations Fisheries Society, *Star and Garter*, St. Martin's Lane, Charing Cross, W.C.

West Central Association of London and Provincial Angling Societies, P. Geen, *president;* T. Hoole, *hon. sec.* Club-House—*The Portman Arms*, Great Quebec Street.

LONDON CLUBS.

Albert	The Crown Coffee House, Coronet Street, Old Street.
Alliance	Clerkenwell Tavern, Farringdon Rd., E.C.
Alexandra	Crown and Anchor, Cheshire St., Bethnal Green.

SOCIETIES OF LONDON AND THE PROVINCES. 29

Amicable Brothers . .	Bald Faced Stag, Worship St., Finsbury.
Amicable Waltonians .	Horse and Groom, St. John's Street, Clerkenwell.
Angler's Pride . .	Five Bells, Bermondsey Square, S.E.
Acton Piscatorial Society	George and Dragon, High St., Acton, W.
Albert Edward . .	Tile Kiln, Tullerie Street, Hackney Road.
Anchor and Hope . .	William the Fourth, Canal Bridge, Old Kent Road.
Act on the Square . .	The Ferry Boat, Tottenham.
Admiral Brothers . .	Admiral Hotel, Francis Street, Woolwich.
Acorn	Duke of York, Gloucester St., Clerkenwell.
Acme	Weaver's Arms, Drysdale Street, Kingsland Road.
Bostonian . . .	Dalby Tavern, Prince of Wales Road, Kentish Town.
Battersea Friendly . .	Queen's Hotel, Queen's Road, Battersea.
Bloomsbury Brothers .	Rose and Crown, Broad St., Bloomsbury.
Bermondsey Brothers .	Alscot Arms, Alscot Road, Grange Road, Bermondsey.
Brothers Well Met . .	Berkeley Castle, Rahere St., Goswell Rd.
Beresford . . .	Grove House Tavern, Camberwell Grove.
Burdett	Joiners' Arms, 118 Hackney Road.
Bridgewater Brothers .	Three Tuns, Bridgewater Gardens, Barbican.
Brunswick . . .	Brunswick Arms, Stamford St., Blackfriars.
Brentford . . .	Angel Inn, Brentford End, Brentford.
Buckland . . .	Middlesex Arms, Clerkenwell Green.
Barbican . . .	White Bear, St. John Street, Clerkenwell.
Battersea Piscatorials .	Queen's Head, York Road, Battersea.
Cadogan . . .	Prince of Wales, Exeter Street, Sloane Street, S.W,
City of London . .	Codger's Hall, Bride Lane, Fleet Street.
Cavendish . . .	Duke of York, Wenlock Street, Hoxton.
Clerkenwell Amateurs .	George and Dragon, St. John Street Road.
Convivial . . .	Bull and Bell, Ropemakers' Street, Moorfields, E.C.
Carlisle	Hall of Science Club and Institute, Old Street, E.C.
Clapham Junction . .	Lord Ranelagh, Verona Street, Clapham Junction.

Canonbury	Monmouth Arms, Haberdasher Street, Hoxton.
Cambridge Friendly	Rent Day, Cambridge Street, Hyde Park Square.
Cobden	Cobden Club, Landseer Terrace, Westbourne Park.
Clerkenwell Piscatorials	Horse Shoe, Clerkenwell Close.
Crescent	Giraffe Tavern, Newington Crescent, Kennington Park Road.
Critchfield	Myddleton Arms, Queen's Rd., Dalston.
Crown	Crown and Sceptre, Friendly St., Deptford.
Crown Piscatorials	Crown Tavern, Clerkenwell Green.
Dalston	Hope, Holles Street, Dalston.
De Beauvoir	Lord Raglan, Southgate Road, Islington.
Duke of Cornwall	Duke of Cornwall, Lissmore Circus, Haverstock Hill.
Duke of Norfolk	Ledbury Arms, Ledbury Road, Bayswater.
Ealing Dean	Green Man, Ealing Dean, W.
Excelsior	The Hope, Bird Street, Kennington.
Excelsior	Palmerston, Well Street, Hackney.
Eustonian	King's Head, Swinton St., Gray's Inn Rd.
Edmonton and Tottenham	Three Horse Shoes, Silver St., Edmonton.
Friendly Anglers	Albion Tavern, Albion St., Hyde Park.
Foxley	Foxley Arms, Elliot Road, Brixton.
Golden Tench	Somers Arms, Ossulton St., Euston Rd.
Golden Barbel	York Minster, Foley Street, Portland Rd.
Good Intent	Crown Inn, Church Street, Shoreditch.
Grafton	King's Arms, Strutton Ground, Wesminster.
Grange	Grange Club and Institute, Bermondsey, S.E.
Great Northern Brothers	Robin Hood, Southampton Street, Pentonville.
Globe	Bank of Friendship, Blackstock Road, Highbury Vale.
Gresham	Mason's Hall Tavern, Basinghall St., E.C.
Hammersmith Club	Grove House, Hammersmith Broadway.
Hammersmith United	Builders' Arms, Bridge Road, Hammersmith.
Hearts of Oak	Dolphin, Church Street, Shoreditch.

SOCIETIES OF LONDON AND THE PROVINCES. 31

Highbury	Plimsoll Arms, St. Thomas's Road, Finsbury Park.
Hoxton Brothers	Cherry Tree, Kingsland Road, Shoreditch.
Hampstead	Cock and Crown, High Street, Hampstead.
Isledon Piscatorials	Crown and Anchor, Cross St., Islington.
Izaak Walton	Old King John's Head, Mansfield Street, Kingsland Road.
Jovial	Jolly Anglers, Whitecross Row, Richmond, Surrey.
Junior Piscatorial	Duke of Cornwall, South Island Place, Clapham Road.
Jolly Piscatorials	Sugar Loaf, Great Queen Street, W.C.
Kentish Perseverance	Corner Pin, Cold Bath, Greenwich.
Kenningtonian	The Clayton Arms, Kennington Oval.
Knights of Knightsbridge	Grove Tavern, Grove Place, Brompton Road, S.W.
King's Cross United	Prince Albert, Wharfdale Road, King's Cross.
Kingfishers	Oliver Arms, Westbourne Terrace, Harrow Road.
Kentish Brothers	George and Dragon, Blackheath Hill.
L. & S. W. Railway	Brunswick House, Nine Elms.
Larkhall	The Larkhall, Larkhall Lane, Clapham.
Limehouse Brothers	Dunlop Lodge, 70 Samuel St., Limehouse.
Little Independent	Russell Arms, Bedford Street, Ampthill Square.
Metropolitan	The Rose, Old Bailey.
Marylebone	Prince Albert, Sherbourne Street, Blandford Square, W.
Nautilus	British Lion, Central Street, St. Luke's.
Norfolk	Norfolk Arms, Burwood Place, Edgware Road.
North London	Prince Albert, Hollingsworth St., Holloway.
North Eastern	Shepherd and Flock, Little Bell Alley, Moorfields.
North Western	Lord Southampton, Southampton Road, Haverstock Hill.
New Globe	Albion, Bridge Road, Stratford.
Never Frets	Crown and Shuttle, High St., Shoreditch.

Nelson	Nelson Working Men's Club, 90 Dean St., Soho.
Odds and Evens	Albion, East Road, Hoxton, N.
Original Clerkenwell	White Hart, Aylesbury St., Clerkenwell.
Original Alexandra	Duke of Wellington, Three Colt Lane, Bethnal Green.
Peckham Perseverance	Eagle, 118 Trafalgar Road, Camberwell.
Pictorial	King's Arms, Tottenham Court Road.
Penge	Lord Palmerston, Maple Road, Penge.
Phœnix	Tavistock Arms, Wellington St., Oakley Square.
Prince of Wales	Victory, Newnham Street, John Street, Edgware Road.
Portsmouth Waltonian	Golden Fleece, High Street, Landport.
Peckham Brothers	Prince Albert, East Surrey Grove, Peckham.
Princess of Wales	Prince of Wales, Gt. Barlow St., Manchester Square, W.
Perseverance	The Perseverance, Pritchard's Row, Hackney Road.
Pike and Anchor	Pike and Anchor, Ponder's End.
Queen's	Queen's Arms, Bomore Road, Notting Hill, W.
Reform	Jolly Coopers, Clerkenwell Close.
Royal George	Hope Tavern, Tottenham St., Tottenham Court Road.
Richmond Piscatorial	Station Hotel, Richmond.
Royal Piscatorial	Foxley Tavern, Elliott Road, Brixton.
Rodney	Albion, Rodney Road, Walworth, S.E.
Second Surrey	Queen's Head, Brandon St., Walworth.
South Essex	The Elms, Leytonstone, E.
Sportsman	Lady Owen Arms, Goswell Road.
Suffolk	Suffolk Arms, Boston St., Hackney Rd.
South Essex	Victoria Dock Tavern, Canning Town, E.
St. John's	Three Compasses, Cow Cross Street, Farringdon Street.
Savoy Brothers	Green Man, St. Martin's Lane.
Silver Trout	Star and Garter Hotel, St. Martin's Lane, W.C.
St. Alban's	Royal George, Great New St., Kennington Park Road.

SOCIETIES OF LONDON AND THE PROVINCES. 33

Sir Hugh Myddleton	Empress of Russia, St. John Street Road, Clerkenwell.
South London.	George and Dragon, 235 Camberwell Rd.
St. Pancras Club	2 Crescent Place, Burton Crescent.
Stanley Anglers	The Lord Stanley, Camden Park Road Camden Town.
Star	King's Arms, Charles Street, City Road.
Stepney	Beehive, Rhodeswell Road, Stepney.
South Belgravia	Telegraph, Regency Street, S.W.
Surrey Piscatorial	St. Paul's Tavern, Westmoreland Road S.E.
South Eastern.	Prince Arthur, Stamford Street, S.E.
Sussex	Sussex Arms, Grove Road, Holloway.
Sociable Brothers	Princess, 237 Cambridge Rd., Mile-End.
Social Brothers	Prince Regent, Dulwich Rd., Herne Hill.
St. James's and Soho	39 Gerrard Street, Soho, W.
Stoke Newington	Myddleton Arms, Mansfield St., Kingsland Road.
St. John's Wood	Queen's Arms, Lower William Street, St. John's Wood.
Society of Caxtonians	Falcon Tavern, Gough Square, E.C.
The Piscatorial	Ashley's Hotel, Henrietta Street, Covent Garden.
Trafalgar	Star and Garter, Green Street, Leicester Square.
True Waltonians	White Horse, 80 Liverpool Rd., Islington.
Three Pigeons	Three Pigeons, Lower Richmond Road, S.W.
United Brothers	Druid's Head Tavern, Broadway, Deptford.
United Essex	Dorset Arms, Leyton Rd., Stratford New Town.
United Society of Anglers	Duke of Wellington, Shoreditch.
United Marlboro' Brothers	Hercules' Pillars, 7 Greek Street, Soho.
Woolwich Piscatorials	Cricketer's Arms, Sand Street, Woolwich.
West Ham Brothers	Queen's Head, West Ham Lane, E.
Woolwich Invicta	Golden Marine, Francis St., Woolwich.
Waltonians	Jew's Harp, Redhill St., Regent's Park.
Walton and Cotton	Crown and Woolpack, St. John's Street, Clerkenwell.
Walworth Waltonians	St. Paul's, Westmoreland Rd., Walworth.

D

West Central . . . Cross Keys, Theobald's Road, High Holborn.
Woolwich Brothers . . Prince Regent, King Street, Woolwich.
Westbourne Park . . Pelican, All Saints' Road, Westbourne Park, W.
Walthamstow . . . Common Gate, Markhouse Road, Walthamstow.
West London . . . Windsor Castle, King St., Hammersmith.
Watford . . . . Leathersellers' Arms, Watford, Herts.
Wellington . . . Prince Regent, Beresford St., Walworth.

ENGLAND.

BEDFORDSHIRE.

Bedford Angling Society, Bedford.

Blunham Angling Association—C. Forge, 11 and 12 Addle Street, Wood Street, *secretary*.

BERKSHIRE.

Maidenhead, Cookham, and Bray Thames Angling Association— W. G. Day, *secretary*. Club-House—*Skindle's Hotel*.

Newbury and District Angling Association—J. Smith, 62 Northbrook Street, Newbury, *secretary*.

Reading and District Angling Association—Arthur C. Butler, *hon. sec.* Club-House—*Great Western Hotel*, Reading.

Windsor and Eton Angling Club. Club-House—*Royal Oak Hotel*, Windsor.

Windsor and Eton Angling Preservation Association—Rev. E. James, Eton, *secretary*.

BUCKINGHAMSHIRE.

Great Marlow Thames Angling Association—Major Simpson Carson, Great Marlow, *hon. secretary*.

High Wycombe Angling Association, High Wycombe.

Marlow Angling Association—A. Maskell, Great Marlow, *secretary*.

CAMBRIDGESHIRE.

Cambridge and Ely Angling Society—W. Purchas, *secretary*. Club-House—*Lion Hotel*, Cambridge.

CHESHIRE.

No. 1 Crewe Angling Society—John Dickens, *secretary*. Club-House—*Dog and Partridge Inn*, High Street, Crewe.

CUMBERLAND.

Carlisle Angling Association—J. B. Slater, Carlisle, *secretary*.

DERBYSHIRE.

Aquarium Angling Society—T. Winfield, *secretary*. Club-House—*The Three Crowns*, Bridge Street, Derby.

Burton-on-Trent Angling Association—Sir M. A. Bass, Bart., M.P., *president;* John C. Perfect, *hon. sec.* Club-House—*Midland Hotel*, Burton-on-Trent.

Castle Fields Angling Club, Messrs. Beden's Factory, London St., Derby—M. Bland, *secretary*.

Chatsworth Angling Club, Chatsworth.

Chesterfield Angling Association—G. R. Hornstock, 26 Durrant Road, Chesterfield, *secretary*.

Excelsior Angling Club—J. Hibbert, *secretary*. Club-House—*Lamb Inn*, Park Street, Derby.

Mazeppa Angling Club, Traffic Street, Derby—F. Bond, *secretary*.

Melancthon's Head Angling Club, Park Street, Derby—W. Peet, *secretary*.

Pride of Derby Angling Club—W. Tunnicliff, *secretary*. Club-House, *Old English Gentleman*, Normanton Road, Derby.

Red Lion Angling Association, Bridge Street, Derby—Joseph Selvey, *secretary*.

DEVONSHIRE.

Avon and Erme Fishery Association, Plymouth.

Culm Fishery Association—C. J. Upcott, Shortlands, Cullompton, *secretary*.

Exe Landowners' Salmon Fishing Association—Mr. Whippell, Rudway, Silverton, *secretary*.

Exe Occupiers' Trouting Association—W. C. James, Thorverton, *secretary*.

Lower Exe United Fishing Association, Exeter.

Tiverton Angling Association, Tiverton.

Upper Culm Fishery Association, Exeter.

Upper Exe Angling Society, Exeter.

GLOUCESTERSHIRE.

Avon and Tributaries Angling Association—E. B. Villiers, 26 Bath Street, Bristol, *hon. secretary*.

Bristol Golden Carp Angling Association—Lewis Wride, Digby House, Barton Hill, Bristol, *secretary*.

Bristol United Anglers' Association—R. D. Frost, 48 Victoria St., Bristol, *secretary*.

Cheltenham Angling Society—W. H. Davis, 7 Priory Terrace, Cheltenham, *secretary*.

City of Bristol Angling Association—H. Lewis, Morton House, Barton Hill, Bristol, *secretary*.

HAMPSHIRE.

Portsmouth Waltonian Society—F. Tranter, *secretary*. Club-House —*Golden Fleece*, Commercial Road, Portsea.

Stockbridge Angling Club, Stockbridge.

Titchfield Angling Club—E. Goble, solicitor, Titchfield, *secretary*.

HEREFORDSHIRE.

Bodenham Angling Club, Bodenham.

Leominster Angling Club—V. W. Holmes, National Provincial Bank, Leominster, *secretary*.

HERTFORDSHIRE.

Harefield Valley Fishery, Rickmansworth.

Watfield Piscatorial Society—H. A. Vincent, *hon. sec.* Club-House—*The Leathersellers' Arms*, Watford.

KENT.

Maidstone Angling and Medway Preservation Society—David Pine, Maidstone, *hon. secretary*.

Stour Fishery Association—Club House—*Fordwich Arms*.

Tonbridge Angling Association—Edwin Hollomby, *secretary*. Club-House—*Bull Hotel*, High Street, Tonbridge.

LANCASHIRE.

City of Liverpool Angling Association, 19 West Derby Road, Liverpool.

Liverpool Angling Association—Richard Woolfall, *hon. sec.* Club-House—*Strawberry Hotel*, West Derby Road, Liverpool.

Liverpool Central Angling Association, 181 Dale Street.

Manchester Anglers' Association—Abel Heywood, jun., *hon. sec.*

Manchester and District Anglers' Association—J. Procter, *president*; Edwin Hicks, 6 Belmont Street, Eggington Street, Rochdale Road, *secretary*. The Association comprises sixty-six different Clubs.

Stalybridge Anlging Society—J. B. Udale, *secretary*. Club-House —*The Q. Inn*, Stalybridge.

Stamford and Warrington Angling Club. Club House—*Guide Post Tavern*, Stalybridge.

Wigan and District Amalgamated Anglers' Association—Levi Booth, *president;* John Stones, *secretary*. This Association consists of twenty-six different Clubs.

LEICESTERSHIRE.

Leicester Jolly Anglers' Club. Club-House—*The Earl of Leicester, Inn*, Infirmary Square, Leicester.

North Britons' Angling Association. Club-house—*The York Castle*, Northgate Street, Leicester.

LINCOLNSHIRE.

Boston Angling Association—Mr. Day, Boston, *secretary*.

Great Grimsby Angling Association. Club-House—*Masons' Arms Hotel*, Great Grimsby.

Market Deeping Angling Association—S. B. Sharpe, Market Deeping, *hon. secretary*.

MONMOUTHSHIRE.

Abergavenny Fishing Association —C. J. Daniel, Cross St., Abergavenny, *treasurer*.

Usk Fishery Association—Charles R. Lyne, Tredegar Place, Newport, *secretary*.

NORFOLK.

Bure Preservation Society—C. J. Greene, London St., Norwich, *secretary*.

East Anglian Piscatorial Society—R. Palmer, Great Eastern Wine Vaults, Norwich, *secretary*.

Great Yarmouth Piscatorial Society—James Lark, St. George's Tavern, 162 King St., Great Yarmouth, *secretary*.

King's Lynn Angling Association—Frederick Ludby, *president;* H. Bradfield, *hon. secretary*.

Norwich Angling Club—R. Moll, *hon. sec.* Club-House—*Walnut Tree Shades*, Old Post-Office Yard, Norwich.

Norwich Central Fishing Club. Club-House—*Old Oak Shades*, Lower Goat Lane, Norwich.

Norwich Champion Angling Club—G. Daniels, *president*.

Norwich Piscatorial Society—Mr. Capon, *secretary*. Club-House—*Walnut Tree Shades*, Old Post-Office Yard, Norwich.

Wensum Preservation Association—E. H. Horsley, Fakenham, *hon. secretary*.

Yare Preservation and Anglers' Society—C. J. Greene, London St., Norwich, *secretary*.

NORTHAMPTONSHIRE.

Northampton Working Men's Angling Club. Club-House—Bridge Street, Northampton.

Wellingborough and Higham Ferrers Angling Club—E. Brummitt, Wellingborough, *secretary*.

NOTTINGHAMSHIRE.

Lenton Anglers' Association—George Tilley, *hon. sec.* Club-House —*Black's Head Inn*, Lenton, Nottingham.

Newark Piscatorial Society. Club-House—*Horse and Gears Inn*, Portland St., Newark.

Nottingham and Notts Anglers' Preservation Association—Mr. Clarke, *secretary*. Club-House—*The Minstrel Tavern*, Market St., Nottingham.

Wellington Angling Association—Club-house—*Wellington Hotel*, Station St., Nottingham.

OXFORDSHIRE.

Henley and District Thames Angling Association—Mr. Cooke, Henley, *secretary*.

Oxford Angling Society. Club-house—*The Pheasant Inn*, St. Giles, Oxford.

Oxford Thames Angling Preservation Society—W. T. Mayo, 13 Cornmarket Street, Oxford, *hon. secretary*.

RUTLANDSHIRE.

Oakham Angling Society, Oakham.

SHROPSHIRE.

Plowden Fishing Association (River Onny)—A. B. George, Dodington, Whitchurch, *hon. treasurer*.

Shrewsbury Severn Angling Society—F. H. Morgan, *hon. sec.* Club-House—57 Mardol, Shrewsbury.

SOMERSETSHIRE.

Kingswood and District Angling Association, Kingswood.

STAFFORDSHIRE.

Cobridge Angling Society. Club-House—*Wedgewood Hotel*, Waterloo Rd., Burslem.

Isaac Walton Angling Club—William Gregory, *secretary*. Club-House—*Coach and Horses*, Stafford St., Longton.

Isaac Walton Angling Club—Frederick Higginson, *secretary*. Club-House—*Dresden Inn*, near Longton.

Longton Excelsior Angling Club—Thomas Morris, *secretary*. Club-House—*Crown and Anchor*, Longton.

Stoke-upon-Trent Angling Society—J. Hollins, *hon. sec.* Club-House—*Pike Hotel*, Copeland Street.

SUFFOLK.

Gipping Angling Preservation Association—George Josselyn, *president;* W. C. S. Edgecombe, National Provincial Bank, Ipswich, *hon. secretary.*

Norfolk and Suffolk Fish Acclimatisation Society—Edward Birkbeck, M.P., *president;* W. Oldham Chambers, Lowestoft, *hon. sec.*

SURREY.

Godalming Angling Society—F. Dowse, High Street, *hon. sec.* Club-House—*Sun Inn*, Godalming.

Richmond Piscatorial Society—F. Gaunt, *secretary*. Club-House—*Station Hotel*, Richmond.

SUSSEX.

Brighton Anglers' Association, Brighton.

Chichester Angling Society—W. Cooke, *secretary*. Club-House—*Globe Hotel*, Chichester.

Ouse Angling Preservation Society—Hector Essex, Hillside, Lewes, *hon. secretary.*

Rother Fishery Association—D. N. Olney, Blenheim House, Robertsbridge, *secretary.*

WARWICKSHIRE.

Birmingham and Midland Piscatorial Association—James Gregory, 39, Vyse St., *hon. secretary.*

WESTMORELAND.

Kent Angling Association—G. Fisher, Kendal, *hon. secretary.*

Milnthorpe Angling Society—W. Tattersall, Milnthorpe, *secretary.*

WILTSHIRE.

Bradford-on-Avon Angling Association.
Sarum Angling Club—H. Selby Davison, 40 King St., London, E.C., *secretary*.

WORCESTERSHIRE.

Evesham Angling Club, Evesham.
Isaac Walton Angling Society—Club-House, *Plough Inn*, Silver St., Worcester.
Teme Angling Club—W. Norris, Worcester, *secretary*.

YORKSHIRE.

Aire Fishing Club—T. H. Dewhurst, Whin Field, Skipton, *secretary*.
Burnsall, Appletrewick, and Barden Angling Club—T. J. Critchley, Brook St., Ilkley, *secretary*.
Costa Anglers' Club—J. H. Phillips, 22 Albemarle Crescent, Scarborough, *secretary*.
Derwent Anglers' Club. Address—Mr. Patrick, gunmaker, Scarborough.
Hawes and High Abbotside Angling Association—B. Thompson-Hawes, *secretary*.
Knaresborough Star Angling Club. Club-House—C. M'Nichols, Knaresborough.
Marquis of Granby Angling Society—T. H. Settle, *hon. sec.* Club-House—*The Marquis of Granby*, Leeds.
Middleham Angling Association—J. E. Miller, Middleham, *secretary*.
Otley Angling Club—Mr. Pratt, Otley, *secretary*.
Rockingham Angling Society—E. F. Atkinson, *president*. Club-House—*The Fox*, Leeds.
Ryedale Angling Club, Hovingham.
Sheffield Anglers' Association—Charles Styring, *president*; Messrs. Baker, Gill, Greaves, Guest, Jenkinson, Leonard, Sheldon, Stuart, Swinden, Thompson, Unwin, and White, *committee;* Thomas Walker, 24 Blue Boy St., Sheffield, *secretary*. This Association comprises 232 Clubs in Sheffield and district.
Wilkinson Angling Association, Hull.

ANGLING CLUBS AND FISHING ASSOCIATIONS IN SCOTLAND.

ABERDEENSHIRE.

Dee Salmon Fishing Improvement Association—William Milne, C.A., 147 Union St., *secretary*.

BERWICKSHIRE.

Berwick Anglers' Club—Robert Weddell, solicitor, Berwick, *secretary*.

Coldstream Angling Club—John Tait, High St., Coldstream, *secretary*.

Ellen Fishing Club, Duns—The Hon. Edward Marjoribanks, *president*; G. Turnbull, 58 Frederick St., Edinburgh, *secretary*.

Greenlaw Fishing Club—David Leitch, Greenlaw, *secretary*.

DUMFRIESSHIRE.

Esk and Liddle Fisheries Association—The Duke of Buccleuch, K.G., *president*; Robert M' George, writer, Langholm, *secretary*.

EDINBURGSHIRE.

Cockburn Angling Association—George E. Y. Muir, 1 West Crosscauseway, Edinburgh, *secretary*.

Edinburgh Angling Club—William Menzies, 18 Picardy Place, *secretary*.

Edinburgh Amateur Angling Club—J. Gordon Mason, S.S.C., *secretary*.

Midlothian Angling Club—Joseph A. Cowan, 53 Rose St., *secretary*.

Penicuik Angling Club—James Foulis, clothier, Penicuik, *secretary*.

St. Andrew Angling Club—Professor Williams, *president*; J. Young Guthrie, S.S.C., 29 Hanover St., Edinburgh, *secretary*.

Walton Angling Club—Professor Williams, *president*; James Grant, S.S.C., 12 Howard Place, Edinburgh, *secretary*.

Waverley Angling Club—John M'Dougal, 3 Rutland Place, Edinburgh, *secretary*.

FIFESHIRE.

Dunfermline Angling Club—James Mathewson, Dunfermline, *secretary*.

Kirkcaldy Angling Club—Patrick Don Swan of Springfield, *president;* Thomas Johnston, solicitor, Kirkcaldy, *secretary*.

FORFARSHIRE.

Alyth Angling Club—Major Japp, *president;* James D. Murdoch, Alyth, *secretary*.

Arbroath Angling Club—David A. Wilson, Kirk Wynd, Arbroath, *secretary*.

Brechin Angling Club—James B. Hodge, 2 Swan St., Brechin, *secretary*.

Canmore (Forfar) Angling Club—David Maxwell, 16 Watt St., Forfar, *secretary*.

Dundee Angling Club—David Ireland, Calcutta Buildings, Dundee, *secretary*.

Dundee West End Angling Club—Alexander Mitchell, Roseangle, Dundee, *secretary*.

Dundee Walton Club—W. Mudie, 3 Athole Terrace, Maryfield, Dundee, *secretary*.

Forfar Angling Club—James Dall, joiner, Market Place, Forfar, *sec.*

Strathmore (Forfar) Angling Club—James Paton, 10 Arbroath Road, Forfar, *secretary*.

HADDINGTONSHIRE.

East Linton Angling Club—The Rev. Thomas Stirling Marjoribanks, Prestonkirk, *president;* George Smellie, East Linton, *secretary*.

Haddington Fishing Club—Captain Houston of Clerkington, *president;* George Angus, 35 Court St., Haddington, *secretary*.

KINROSS-SHIRE.

Kinross-shire Fishing Club—Thomas Steedman, Clydesdale Bank, Kinross, *secretary*.

Loch Leven Angling Association (Limited)—Sir J. R. Gibson-Maitland, Bart. of Craigend, *president;* George Bogie, solicitor, Kinross, *secretary*.

LANARKSHIRE.

Abington Angling Club—David Oswald, teacher, Abington, *sec.*

Buckland Angling Club—William Cross, 41 York St., Glasgow, *secretary*.

SOCIETIES OF LONDON AND THE PROVINCES.

Coatbridge Angling Club—David Girdwood, Langloan, Coatbridge, secretary.

Echaig Angling Club—John Clark, 17 Royal Exchange Square, Glasgow, secretary.

Glasgow Dodgers.

Glasgow Junior Angling Club.

Lanark Amateur Angling Association—David Gourlay, Bannatyne Street, Lanark, secretary.

Lanarkshire United Anglers' Protective Association—Crawford Brown, 110 Garthland Drive, Glasgow, secretary. (Nine associated Clubs.)

Loch Lomond Angling Improvement Association—Alfred Brown, 163 West George Street, Glasgow, secretary.

Motherwell Star Angling Club—James Brown, Braidhurst Colliery, Motherwell, secretary.

Stonehouse Angling Club—A. Hamilton, Stonehouse, secretary.

St. Mungo Angling Club—W. Craig Ramsay, writer, Glasgow, secretary.

Trout Preservation Association—David B. Macgregor, 51 West Regent Street, Glasgow, secretary.

West of Scotland Angling Club—David B. Macgregor, 51 West Regent Street, Glasgow, secretary.

Western Angling Club—John Wilson, 59 St. Vincent Street, Glasgow, secretary.

LINLITHGOWSHIRE.

Armadale Angling Club—Robert Kerr, South Street, Armadale, secretary.

Avon Conservancy Association—W. Horn Henderson, Linlithgow, secretary.

Bathgate Angling Club—Robert Bryce, Bridgend, Bathgate, sec.

PEEBLESHIRE.

Peebles Vigilance Trout Protection Association—Charles Tennant, M.P., The Glen, president; James Anderson, Peebles, secretary.

Peebles Angling Association—James Wolfe Murray of Cringletie, president; Alexander Pairman, grocer, Peebles, secretary.

St. Ronan's Angling Club—James Cossar, Innerleithen, secretary.

PERTHSHIRE.

Aberfeldy Club—James Forbes, Chapel Street, Aberfeldy, secretary.

Aberfoyle Angling Club.

Blairgowrie Angling Club.

Perth Anglers' Club—P. D. Malloch, 209 High Street, Perth, *secretary*.

Perthshire Fishing Club—Robert Keay, City Chambers, Perth, *sec.*

ROXBURGHSHIRE.

Kelso Angling Association—Sir G. H. S. Douglas, Bart., of Springwood Park, *president;* Archibald Steel, Bridge Street, Kelso, *secretary*.

Upper Teviotdale Fisheries Association—The Duke of Buccleuch, K.G., *president*; Walter Haddon, Royal Bank of Scotland, Hawick, *secretary*.

SELKIRKSHIRE.

Caddonfoot Fishings—H. W. Cornillon, S.S.C., 139 George Street, Edinburgh, *secretary*.

Gala Angling Association—Robert Hall, 131 High Street, Galashiels, *secretary*.

Selkirk Angling Association—John Anderson, Elm Row, Selkirk, *secretary*.

STIRLINGSHIRE.

Bonnybridge Angling Club—Alexander Mitchell, Greenbank Cottage, Bonnybridge, *secretary*.

Callander Angling Club—D. Melrose, Callander, *secretary*.

Denny and Dudipace Angling Club—Robert Shearer, Well Strand, Denny, *secretary*.

Dollar Angling Club.

Dollar and Devondale Angling Club—Peter Cousins, Dollar, *sec.*

Doune Angling Club—W. H. Hogg, Lanrick Castle, Doune, *sec.*

East Stirlingshire Association of Anglers—John Hogg, writer, Larbert, *secretary*.

Falkirk Angling Club—J. A. Miller, 144 High St., Falkirk, *secretary*.

Forth Angling Club, Stirling.

Haggs Angling Club—George Mirk, Haggs, by Denny, *secretary*.

Muiravonside and Polmont Angling Club—A. Campbell, Blackbraes, Falkirk, *secretary*.

Sauchie and Whins of Milton Angling Club—Sir J. R. Gibson-Maitland, Bart., of Craigend, *president;* Wm. Reid, Whins of Milton, by Stirling, *secretary*.

Skinflatts Angling Club—William Russell, Skinflatts, by Falkirk, *secretary*.

Stirling Forth and Teith Angling Association—Alexander Moffat, Clydesdale Bank, Stirling, *secretary*.

Stirling Fishing Club—Sir J. R. Gibson-Maitland, Bart., of Craigend, *president;* Robert M'Luckie, Stirling, *secretary*.

The following short descriptions of some of the most prominent Angling and Preservation Societies of the Provinces are compiled mainly from the information kindly supplied by the secretaries of each Association. They are placed as nearly as may be in alphabetical order, the particulars being summarised as much as possible, so as to come within the scope of this little book.

AIRE FISHING CLUB.

This club, which has been in existence some [forty-five years, was founded and fostered by J. R. Tennant, Esq., of Kildwick Hall, Skipton. It consists of twenty members, paying an entrance fee of ten guineas, and an annual subscription of the like amount, who preserve the river from Cargrave to Eastburn Brook. It has also a number of subscribers, limited to thirty, paying an annual subscription of thirty shillings, who are allowed to fish the river from Carleton Stone Bridge to Eastburn Brook. The Hon. Secretary is T. H. Dewhurst, Esq., of Whinfield, Skipton, while the President is J. R. Tennant, Esq.

ABERGAVENNY FISHING ASSOCIATION.

This Association was founded in 1860, and has been carried on from that time with fairly good success. The number of salmon and trout season tickets is limited to 20, the holders of such tickets in the previous years having the option of renewing them. Five of these tickets are reserved for persons living twenty miles from the town.

Rule 6 provides: That the price of salmon and trout season tickets be 40/-, except to persons who, in the judgment of the committee, are professional fishermen, who will be charged £10; season tickets for trout, 20/-, to admit the use of fly, worm, minnow, or gentle; season tickets for trout, if fly only be used, 10/-. Day tickets for salmon and trout, 5/-, to be restricted to persons residing 10 miles or more from the town; day tickets for trout, fly only to be used, 2/6; or 5/- to admit the use of worm, minnow, or gentle. None of these tickets are transferable, except as provided for in Rule 8. Also that tickets for clodding for eels shall be issued at 5/-; and that tickets for dace fishing during the trout closed season shall be 5/-; or to include both eels and dace, 10/-, such fishermen to be subject to Rule 10, as to time of fishing. Ladies may be allowed to fish on the payment of half the price of any of these tickets.

The Association has about two miles of water, most of which can be fished from both banks. The Marquis of Abergavenny gives the right of fishing from his property on the left bank, while the Association rents the right bank from a local landowner.

The Birdsgrove Fly-fishing Club, Mayfield, Ashbourne.

This club, which is limited to twenty members paying an annual subscription of five pounds each, was formed by J. H. Villiers, Esq., and fishes four miles of the river Dove situate about a mile from Ashbourne, and lying between the Okeover and Norbury Fishing Clubs. The river abounds in trout and grayling, and runs through some very fine scenery.

The members at present consist of eighteen gentlemen, thus showing a vacancy for two more rods.

BRADFORD-ON-AVON FISHING ASSOCIATION.

This Association was formed about ten years ago with the object of putting a stop to the poaching, netting and pollution which was then going on in the Avon. The principal supporters of it were W. Stevine, Esq., of Warleigh, the Rev. George Baker, of Manor House, Freshford, and Captain Sainsbury, of Bathford. It preserves the river from Holt to Stoke, which distance is divided into three sections. The charge for a yearly ticket for the whole of the water is £1, and such ticket is transferable to any member of the owner's family. For half the water the cost of a ticket is 10s., and for one of the sections it is 2s. 6d. per month. In 1876 the water was handed over to an association formed at Bristol, of which Mr. E. W. B. Villiers, of 26 Bath Road, Bristol, is secretary.

BOSTON ANGLING ASSOCIATION

Was established in 1871, having for its object the prevention of the wholesale destruction, by netting, of fish in the river Witham and its tributary streams, so that good angling might be provided for the inhabitants of Boston, its visitors, and the neighbourhood. This object the Association has undoubtedly attained, and is now one of the largest and best free fisheries for coarse fish in the kingdom, being bountifully supplied with pike, perch, roach, rudd, chub, ruffe, bleak, bream (two kinds), tench and eels. Burbot are occasionally taken. It is 148 miles in extent, comprising the river Witham, and the drains in the East,

West and Wildmore Fens, under the jurisdiction of the River Witham Drainage Commissioners, and under whose by-laws the B. A. A. have power and act. At the present time it is the principal resort of the Sheffield anglers, it being nothing uncommon to witness two thousand in a single day. It is computed by competent authorities that there were not less than 30,000 visitors last season. It is regulated by a code of rules twenty in number, and supported by voluntary contributions. The officers consist of patrons, a president, vice-presidents, treasurer, secretary, and a committee of management. The officers are appointed annually by ballot, on the first Monday in July. The committee meets monthly on the second Wednesday in every month, having power to call special meetings. The quarterly meetings are held the first Monday in October, January and April.

Besides the above there is the North and South Forty-foot drains, about forty miles in extent, under the jurisdiction and management of the Black Sluice Drainage Commissioners. The latter drain is large and deep, with excellent water, and though it has only been preserved three seasons it abounds with most kinds of the fish previously mentioned, but is particularly noted for its pike and perch. There is a small annual fee of 2s. 6d. charged by the Commissioners on these waters.

BRISTOL GOLDEN CARP ANGLING ASSOCIATION.

This Association was founded in September 1879, and is limited to 200 members. The subscription for the first year is 5s., and 2s. 6d. per annum afterwards. General meetings are held the last Monday in each quarter, and committee meetings last Monday in each month.

Secretary, Lewis C. Wride, Digby House, Barton Hill, Bristol.

CARLISLE ANGLING ASSOCIATION.

This Association was formed in 1852 to preserve the River Eden and its tributaries. Up to that time a great amount of poaching had existed, there being no regular watchers on the river. In the first year of its existence the bailiffs seized thirty-two illegal nets, in most cases securing convictions. Up till 1870 they were the only preservers of the river, then, however, the Eden Board of Conservancy was formed, having a staff of ten men and an inspector, whose salaries were paid out of the funds arising from the sale of net and rod licences. The number of salmon and trout has steadily increased since the Association was formed. In 1878 the salmon disease broke out amongst the fish, and has continued more or less ever since, showing itself principally in the spring and autumn. The Eden is one of the finest trout and salmon rivers in England, abounding in fishy streams and runs with occasional rocky pools. There are netting-stations for fifteen miles from the outlet, but in spite of these salmon and grilse run up the river in large numbers. The Hon. Sec. is J. Bedwell Slater, Esq., of Chatsworth Square, Carlisle.

THE CHICHESTER ANGLING SOCIETY.

This Association was established in 1881. Its Patron is His Grace The Duke of Richmond and Gordon, while the President is W. W. Baker, Esq., and Vice-President, W. Kerwood, Esq.; Treasurer, Mr. A. Purchase; Hon. Sec., Mr. G. F. Salter. The head-quarters are at the "Globe Hotel," Chichester.

This Society numbers over 100 members, and has a fine

stretch of water within a short distance of the club-room, well stocked with carp, bream, perch, roach, and a few tench and eels. Pike are also fairly represented. The canal from the basin to the lower lock is over three miles, and since the weed clearance by the Society in 1882 is in fine angling condition.

THE COSTA ANGLERS' CLUB.

The River Costa at Keld Head runs in considerable volume at the foot of the oolitic limestone moorlands, lying north of Pickering, in the North Riding of the County of York. In many respects it is a remarkable stream. It is of high uniform temperature, rarely below 37 degrees, consequently it never freezes, and in cold winters the condensation of vapour is a striking phenomenon, rising, as it frequently does, high into the air, and may be seen for many miles.

This high temperature naturally promotes the rapid growth of weed, and is one of the annoyances which the managing committee have to contend with in being compelled to cut and keep it under so very frequently in the height of the fishing season. On the other hand, this weed forms a capital shelter for fish, and produces a vast amount of insect food, on which young fish rapidly increase in size and condition.

The club is only a youthful institution; nevertheless, the managers have already a breeding establishment in operation, and are able to turn out annually from 15,000 to 20,000 fry, consequently the stream is becoming fairly stocked with both trout and grayling. Those killed last season, and so far as this one has progressed, have been of an average weight of $1\frac{1}{2}$ to 2 lbs., and a few 3 lbs.

Each member is limited to ten brace a day, not less than

10 inches in length, and to 20 days, angling during the season, for which he pays four guineas subscription and an entrance fee of five guineas. There are 40 subscribing members, under the presidency of the Rev. J. R. Hill, of Thornton Hall, near Pickering, a thorough sportsman and a county gentleman of the truest Yorkshire type.

The Costa receives the Pickering Beck near Kirby Misterton, and two or three miles below the united waters are discharged into the Derwent. J. H. Philips, Esq., of Scarborough, is the honorary secretary, and it was mainly through his exertions that the club was re-established some four years ago.

DERWENT ANGLERS' CLUB.

This Club preserves a stretch of water extending from two miles below East and West Ayton, near Scarborough, through the celebrated Forge Valley, thence past the highly picturesque village of Hackness, the seat of Lord Derwent, to Hill's Green Bridge at the entrance of "Barnescliffe," a wild gorge of surpassing beauty, running up and forming the eastern side of the lofty "Langdale Rigg," from the summit of which there is a magnificent view of a large expanse of country. On the east the cliffs of the sea coast, with the baronial castle keep of Scarborough standing out like a sentinel to guard that ancient borough and queen of watering places—on the south are the Great Wolds, with the bold promontories of Filey Brigg and Flamborough Head forming striking objects, whilst on the west the eye stretches away to Malton and the Howardean Hills, with the Hambleton plateau in the far distance. On the north is large expanse of moorland lying in the direction of Robin Hood's Bay, and the Peak, flanked by the railway from Pickering to Whitby, emerging from Newton Dale on to the heights above. It is here on high ground, under the shadow of "Lilla's Cross," that the "Derwent" takes its rise; and, descending in a meandering form, with many a pretty waterfall, it traverses the monotonous expanse of moor in a south-easterly course until it meets at the foot of the upper end of Langdale Pike the "Luggerhowe" stream coming from Harwood Dale, and unitedly they enter the Barnescliffe Valley. From this point to Hill's Green Bridge is a nice stretch of stream, full of small yet toothsome trout, of which Lord Derwent is the owner, and who liberally grants permission to honest anglers. That portion of the Derwent which is preserved by the club is a pleasant fishable stream, with abundance of trout and a few grayling, though neither of them are of large size, averaging about three to the pound. The stream may be briefly described as one of alternate pool, with here and there gravelly streams, fringed on both sides with trees and bushes where trout love to hide and dwell and to watch for their daily ephemeral food. Through the Forge Valley the stream runs deep and sluggishly, but many a lusty trout lies there in ambush, only to be interviewed when there is a wind blowing up or down the valley. A practical hand then may readily fill his pannier.

Lord Derwent and Lord Londesborough are the chief proprietors, and are the liberal patrons of the Club, though there are other riparian owners, all of whom generously place their respective waters at the disposal of the members. The Derwent being at such a convenient distance from Scarborough and easily accessible by rail, are great facilities for the members reaching the stream. The Club was formed upwards of forty years ago, namely in 1839, and, from its many surroundings, has always been a popular one, especially with the gentry residing in Scarborough. The managers have a breeding establishment at the Forge Cottages, and for many years past have turned out from 10,000 to 20,000 fry, so that the stream is kept constantly replenished with an abundant stock of fish, to supply diversion for its many members, who occasionally jostle each other —as for instance in the Mayfly season, when every one is anxious for the fray and to secure a basket. If, however, the angler should fall on an untoward day, when trout decline conclusions with his " gentle art," he has before him magnificent scenery which will well repay him for his outing, though he may have to return home with an empty creel. T. B. Etty, Esq., of Scarborough—a relative of the distinguished painter—is the acting and obliging honorary secretary of the Club, which consists of 40 members, subscribing two guineas each annually and three guineas entrance.

THE DART DISTRICT FISHERY BOARD

Exercises certain powers of control over a defined district, the limits of which were settled by a certificate from the Secretary of State dated 26th of March, 1866, under the powers conferred by the Salmon Fishery Acts; and under the same powers the members of the Board are appointed by the Magistrates at Quarter Sessions. The Board has the power to issue licences, without which no person (not excepting owners of property) can fish. The Chairman is Jeffrey Michelmore, Esq., of Totnes, while the Hon. Secretary is Anthony Pike, Esq., of the same place.

DERWENT VALLEY ANGLING ASSOCIATION.

At a public meeting held at the Town Hall, Shotley Bridge, on Tuesday, March 9th, 1865, to consider the propriety of forming an association for the protection of fish in the River Derwent, the late Thos. Wilson, Esq., of Shotley Hall, in the chair, it was resolved :

I. That the above Association be formed for the above object.

II. That it be governed by a president and a committee of not less than six members, with secretary and treasurer.

III. That Mr. Wilson, of Shotley Hall, be president, and that the provisional committee to carry out the resolutions of meeting should be composed of the following gentlemen, viz : Mr. John Armandale, Mr. Thos. Ramsay, Mr. Geo. Peile, Mr. Thos. Richardson, Mr. (now Dr.) Renton, the Rev. W. Cundill, Mr. Featherstonehaugh, and Mr. Thirlwell, Mr. A. Town (Hon. Treasurer), the Rev. F. B. Thompson, and Mr. Booth (Hon. Sec.).

IV. That such committee be authorised to communicate with the landed proprietors along the bank of the river, asking their co-operation, &c., and report to future meeting, together with proposed rules and regulations for working of the association.

V. That a subscription list be now opened and subscriptions solicited towards funds of the Association.

At a public meeting held on Monday, 30th October, 1865, the report was presented and rules adopted, while it was settled that fishing should commence on the 16th of March, 1866, and close on the 1st of October. Tickets 10s. each. The first subscription amounted to £32.

Since March 1879 the tickets to new members have been 5s., to old members 2s. 6d.

From report of annual meeting held in February last I find that the Society commenced earlier, viz., on March 1st instead of 16th. Since its formation 6,000 fry (*fario* and *levenensis*) have been introduced in the river and tributaries. (Fishing in the latter is strictly prohibited.)

The subject of introducing grayling is postponed for the present.

THE EAST ANGLIAN PISCATORIAL SOCIETY.

This Society had its origin in the City of Norwich, and was founded by Mr. Alfred Palmer, the then proprietor of the Great Eastern Hotel. It was first started in the year 1879, and up to the present time has had a most successful career. The society consists of, and is limited to thirty members, besides several honorary members. Prominent amongst the latter is the name of Edward Birkbeck, Esq., M.P., as also the names of W. H. Grenfel, Esq., M.P. for Salisbury, and Edward Fanshaw Holley, Esq., of Gunyah Lodge, Norwich. The above gentlemen have taken a keen interest in the welfare of the Society.

The members meet once a month for the transaction of business, special meetings for readings, and "Social Board" meetings are held at intervals. The society has done much in prohibiting netting and other unfair fishing both in the rivers Yare and Bure.

THE EATON FISHING CLUB.

The club preserves about three miles of the rivers Lugg and Arrow, commencing a mile below the town of Leominster, Herefordshire. The water which runs through land belonging principally to the Earl of Meath is well stocked with both trout and grayling.

This society was originally formed some thirty-five years since, and is limited to fourteen members. Since then it has passed through various changes in rules and constitution, and is now managed by a committee of local gentlemen.

THE ESK FISHERY ASSOCIATION

Was founded in the year 1866, and consists of the landowners consenting to the preservation of their portion of the stream by the club, and persons who subscribe to the whole of the club waters. This Association has done good and important work in breeding salmon, having turned into the river not less than 100,000 fish. Last season more salmon were taken with the rod than sea-trout or bulltrout.

THE GRASSINGTON, THRESHFIELD AND LINTON ANGLING CLUB

Was commenced in 1855, for the purpose of preserving a length of about three miles of the river Wharfe near Grassington and between the Kilnsey and Burnsall angling waters. The fishing is almost entirely for trout and grayling.

The present subscription is 10s. for a season ticket, and 2s. 6d. for a day ticket. The Club is managed by a committee consisting of a president, secretary, and three other members of the club. Tickets may be obtained from the secretary, Mr. William Harker, Grassington, near Skipton, Yorkshire.

GREAT GRIMSBY ANGLING ASSOCIATION.

This Association was formed a short time back by Mr. Hollingsworth, "Mason's Arms Hotel," Grimsby. It now numbers 100 members, and has secured by rental a great part of the "South Navigation Canal." The society rents several fishing streams. The river Ancholme is within easy reach of the vicinity of Grimsby, and contains numbers of bream, roach, perch, pike, &c. It is the property of the "Ancholme Commissioners," who issue a season ticket at the moderate charge of 5s.; it is strictly preserved, and affords excellent sport. From the docks a stream called the "Haven" runs for miles through several adjoining villages, and contains plenty of trout and roach; it is preserved in some parts by the owners of the land through which it passes. The docks abound in roach, pike, &c., and the fishing is free. The Association is managed by a president, vice-president, secretary, treasurer, and a committee of twelve members, and is in a very flourishing condition. Their head-quarters are the "Mason's Arms Hotel," Grimsby.

KING'S LYNN ANGLING ASSOCIATION.

This society was started in December 1880—the originator being H. Bradfield, Esq. It preserves the Gaywood river, and hires the Middle Level Main Drain, the Hundred Feet river, Roxham Drain, and the Drain—Downham or St. John's Eau—the Walks rivulet, Long Pond, and Lake, the latter being provided for the fishing of the inhabitants of the borough free of charge.

The Association rears large numbers of trout fry, part of which are procured from parent fish in the neighbourhood. The greater portion of the ova is hatched in the Lynn Museum—entrance to which is free—and the operation is one of great attraction to the inhabitants. The young fry is afterwards transferred to a nursery pond. Last year 15,000 fry were hatched, and this year 20,000.

The annual subscription is 5s., honorary members £1 1s. and 10s. 6d. The Hon. Sec. is H. Bradfield, Esq., of Gaywood Road, Lynn.

LIVERPOOL ANGLING ASSOCIATION. — Head-quarters, "Strawberry Hotel," West Derby Road, Liverpool.

Some four years ago a number of anglers who were in the habit of meeting at the above hotel conceived the idea of forming an angling association, and after some difficulty succeeded in their endeavour. The number of members at first was thirteen, but this has now increased to 100, with about twelve hon. members. They had great difficulty in obtaining or renting fishing waters, but have now secured the right of fishing in the reservoir of the Ruabon Water Company, which is well stocked with trout averaging half a pound each. About 2000 Lough Neagh trout have been placed in the brook leading into the reservoir as a trial, with the intention of placing some 10,000 more there if this attempt is successful. They have also got permission from the Parks Commissioners to fish in the Park lakes. The President is James Wilkinson, Esq., while the Hon. Sec. is Mr. R. Woolfall, of 27 Troughton Road.

LOWER MONNOW FISHING CLUB.

This Club is limited to twenty-five members, paying an annual subscription of £5 each, and has the fishing for about nine miles on the lower Monnow. The trout average three to the pound; fish of three and four pounds are, however, frequently caught. There are vacancies for more members. The Hon. Secretary is R. Wrightson, Esq., Newport, Monmouth.

LOWER TEIGN FISHING ASSOCIATION.

This Association was formed in February 1876, after a public meeting held at Newton Abbot on the 24th of that month. All the principal landowners on the Teign and its tributary the Bovey gave up their fishing rights to the Society. Since then part of the Bovey has been withdrawn, and the Association right now extends for about nine miles up the Teign, and about two miles up the Bovey. Tickets are issued to the public at 10s. 6d. for the season, 5s. per month, 2s. 6d. per week, and 1s. per day; a trout licence of 2s. 6d., and a salmon licence of £1 1s., is also imposed by the board of conservators.

The Secretary is the Rev. J. Yarde, of Culver House, Chudleigh, while the Treasurer is Sidney Hacker, Esq., of Newton Abbot.

THE MARKET DEEPING ANGLING SOCIETY.

The right of fishery in the river Welland at Market Deeping extends from a point at the end of Mr. Thorpe's mill-stream to Kenulph's Stone, a distance of six miles, and formerly belonged to the Crown as Lord of the Manor of East and West Deeping. It was let until 1872 to a fisherman who netted it at all times and seasons, sparing nothing. Mr. S. B. Sharpe represented the matter to Mr. Gore, Commissioner of Her Majesty's Woods and Forests, who accordingly discharged the tenant and accepted Mr. Sharpe, in company with Mr. Holland and Mr. Molecey, of that place, as tenants. In 1875 the manor was sold, and in 1877 the right of fishery was purchased by a few local noblemen and gentlemen, consisting of the following:— Lord Kesteven, Lord Burghley, William Holland, William Beadzler Deacon, George Linnell, John Thorpe, John Molecey, Twigge Molecey, Edmund Lawlett, and Samuel Bates Sharpe, Esqs., and an angling society formed which has been eminently successful. The Welland is a very good breeding river, running over a gravel bottom, the lower parts running through low-lying lands which in winter become flooded, and form what is called Crowland Wash, a few miles below Deeping, and there the fish, especially pike, breed in great numbers. The dace in the higher waters about Deeping are very fine and rise freely to the fly; large numbers have been caught from eight to fourteen ounces. Through the efforts of the proprietors, aided by the untiring exertions of the Hon. Sec., Mr. S. B. Sharpe (who is also on the Council of the National Fish Culture Association), the river Welland at this portion literally teems with fish. The object of the Society being "the preservation of fish for legitimate sport," and that alone, the rules are extremely liberal to anglers—the annual subscription of five shillings, for example, including the head of a family and his young children.

THE MIDDLEHAM ANGLING ASSOCIATION.

This Society was founded in 1880, and preserves the fishing on the river Cover (a tributary stream of the Yore). The water contains trout and grayling, and is rented from the lord of the manor, J. Wood, Esq. The members at present number about twenty, and pay an annual subscription of £1 1s. with an entrance fee of a like amount.

The President is S. T. Scrope, Esq. of Danby Hall, Bedale; Secretary and Treasurer, J. E. Miller, Esq., Middleham, Bedale.

THE NENE ANGLING CLUB.

This Club was established in 1856, Dr. Webster being the first President and J. Hensman, Esq., Hon. Secretary. They preserve from twelve to fourteen miles of the river Nene. The water contains jack, bream, perch, carp, &c., and large bags are frequently made. A bream of 6 lbs. and a carp of 9¾ lbs. were lately taken from the water.

The annual subscriptions are £3 3s. for the whole fishery extent; from the Paper-mills to Castle Ashby, £1 1s.; and 10s. 6d. for the third fishery, from the Paper Mills to Billing; there being also an entrance fee of 10s. 6d. for the whole water, and 5s. for the £1 1s. preserve.

President, the Rev. H. Smyth, Little Houghton; Hon. Sec., H. P. Hensman, Esq.

NORWICH PISCATORIAL SOCIETY.

This Society was originated by Mr. W. Capon, of Norwich. It numbers 50 fishing and a large number of honorary members. The annual subscription is 10s., hon. members 20s. The Club gives a very fine Challenge Cup, to be won twice before becoming the property of any member.

Hon. Secretary and Treasurer, Mr. W. G. Capon, Market Street, Norwich.

THE NORTHAMPTON WORKING MEN'S ANGLING CLUB

Was formed May 22nd, 1876, and now numbers 80 members; fishes about 8 miles of private water in the Nene. Annual subscription 8s. 6d., hon. members 10s. 6d. The Society has several prize competitions during the year. Its head-quarters are at the 'Half Moon' Inn, Bridge Street. Hon. Sec., Mr. J. James, 10 Pike Lane.

NEWARK AND MUSKHAM FISHERY ASSOCIATION.

This Association was formed 1868, it has about 4½ miles of private water rented from Lord Middleton and H. Manners-Sutton, Esq. The number of members is about 70, paying a subscription of 15s. per annum for a single ticket, and £1 1s. for a family ticket. The limits of the fishery are defined as follows, and include some of the very finest lengths on the river Trent. The "Muskham Fishery" extends on the north bank of the river from the "Fir Trees" in Kelham Lane to the fence dividing the parishes of North and South Muskham, two fields below "Toder's Holt;" and on the south bank, from the fence dividing the parishes of Kelham and South Muskham, nearly opposite the aforesaid "Fir Trees," to the fence dividing the same parishes opposite the Bottom Lock. The "Dead Water" and "Muskham Fleet" are also included in the Fishery.

The Hon. Secretary of the Association is J. Neal, Esq., of Mount Schools, Newark-on-Trent.

OTLEY ANGLING CLUB.

The Otley Angling Club was formed in 1876, principally through the kindness of Ayscough Fawkes, Esq., of Farnley Hall, who gives to the Club about six miles of fishing on one side of the river Wharfe. The number of members is limited to 30, paying an annual subscription of £3 and an entrance fee of £2. The society hatches about 26,000 trout fry annually and places them in the river. The President is Ayscough Fawkes, Esq., while the Hon. Sec. is R. M. Pratt, Esq., Otley.

THE REDDITCH PISCATORIALS.

The Club was established a short time ago to meet the requirements of the working-men anglers (who are mostly engaged in the Redditch hook, &c., manufactories). So far it has been a decided success. The subscription is 1s., with 1d. for a book of rules. The Club has been greatly assisted by several of the manufacturers giving prizes to be fished for.

President, Mr. George Welch ; Secretary, John E. Wilkes, 31 Edward Street, Redditch.

RYEDALE ANGLING CLUB.

The Ryedale Angling Club was formed June 1st., 1846, and consists of 20 members paying an annual subscription of £4 4s. and £2 2s. entrance fee. They rent from Lord Feversham the length of water from Helmsley Bridge to Newton, a distance along the stream of about 4 miles ; the fishing is restricted to artificial fly and dead minnow. The river Rye is a good trout and grayling stream, and is strictly preserved both above and below the Club water. The Honorary Secretary is Bryan Ed. Cookson, Esq., of 40 Holgate Road, York.

SHREWSBURY AND SEVERN ANGLING SOCIETY.

This Angling Society was started in March, 1882, having then 70 members, which have increased to 110 at the present time. The honour of originating it belongs chiefly to T. H. Morgan, Esq. The annual subscription is 2s. 6d., with 1s. entrance fee; hon. members 10s. 6d. The Society has promoted an Act of Parliament to do away with netting in the part of the Severn within the limits of the borough.

President, James Watson, Esq., of Berwick Hall ; Hon. Sec., T. H. Morgan, Esq., Shrewsbury.

THE SPALDING ANGLING CLUB.

This Club was formed in the year 1864. The fishing exists in the Drains belonging to the Deeping Fen Drainage Trustees and extends over some 25 miles of water, the Society also has a reach of about four miles of the River Glen.

Tickets are issued to subscribers at the rate of £1 1s. for double tickets and 10s. 6d. for single.

The Hon. Secretary is J. G. Calthrop, Esq., of Spalding.

THE STOUR FISHING ASSOCIATION.

This Association was formed in January 1866, in the place of an old private club which had almost become extinct. They preserve part of the River Stour, containing some of the finest trout in England, and also breed artificially with success. The number of members is limited to 100, paying an annual subscription of £3 3s. to £5 5s. and an entrance fee of £10 10s.

Hon. Sec., Captain Lambert, Stanmore, Canterbury; Assistant Sec., Mr. F. G. Haines, 9 Watling Street, Canterbury.

ST. JOHN'S AMATEUR ANGLERS' ASSOCIATION.

This Association was formed about five years ago by several anglers residing at St. John's, Worcester, with a view to securing for themselves good fishing waters and to encourage sportsmanlike angling. The number of members is limited to 30, paying an annual subscription of 2s. 6d.

Hon. Sec., Arthur Hill, Fern Villa, St. John's, Worcester.

UPPER EXE FISHING ASSOCIATION.

This Association was formed in February, 1851, by the owners and occupiers of land on the river Exe, and was then called "The Occupier's Exe Fishing Association," but has since been altered to the above title. Cards for the season are issued at £1 1s.; monthly, 10s.; weekly, 5s.; day, 2s. 6d. The extent of fishing is about five miles up the river Exe, from Thorverton Bridge to near Beckleigh Bridge, and comprises the best fishing in that river.

The Hon. Secretary is W. C. James, Esq., Thorverton, Collumpton, Devon.

TRENT FISHERY BOARD OF CONSERVATORS.

The chief honour of the establishment of this important Board belongs unquestionably to Thomas Worthington, Esq., solicitor, of Derby, who in 1863, by means of a series of letters addressed to the *Derby Mercury*, called public attention to the fact that no proper steps had been taken, under the Salmon Fisheries Act of 1861, for the preservation of the Trent. At a public meeting which followed, Mr. Worthington and another gentleman, on the motion of the late Sir Oswald Mosley, Bart., were appointed the first conservators under the act. The movement greatly interested the then Lord Vernon and other fishery proprietors, amongst whom was Mr. Dennison, the then Speaker of the House of Commons. In June 1864 a meeting of fishery proprietors was held at Mr. Dennison's residence, when an association was formed, and called the "Trent Fishery Association." Mr. Thomas Worthington, and Major Scott, of Knaith Hall, near Gainsborough, were appointed joint honorary secretaries.

In 1865, the Salmon Fisheries Amendment Act having been passed, the Trent Fishery Association was duly formed into the "Trent Fishery Board," in pursuance of the act. Major Scott resigned the honorary secretaryship, and Colonel G. M. Hutton, of Gate Burton, Gainsborough, was appointed in his place, and still remains hon. secretary.

In December 1880 Mr. Worthington, in consequence of ill-health, was compelled to resign the hon. secretaryship, and Mr. C. K. Eddowes, solicitor, Derby, was appointed clerk and solicitor in his place.

TONBRIDGE ANGLING CLUB AND FISH PRESERVATION SOCIETY.

This Society was established at Tonbridge about eight years ago to preserve the upper reaches of the Medway, and put a stop to the continuous poaching and netting which was then going on. The Society received great assistance from the riparian proprietors, and is now in a very flourishing condition. They have recently acquired "The Ballast Pit," a lake of about six acres, which it is the intention of the association to stock with trout. The annual subscription is 10s. 6d. for the whole fishery, and 5s. for part; day tickets, 1s.

President, A. T. Beeching, Esq.; Hon. Sec., Mr. E. Hollomby, Quarry Hill, Tonbridge.

UNIVERSAL ANGLING SOCIETY.

This Society was formed in 1872, and was principally composed of the former members of the "Yorkshire and Lincolnshire Angling Association," which had ceased to exist as a club in the preceding year. The association owes a great deal of its present success to the good services and management of Mr. Thomas Maplebeck, who was for several years their president. The number of members at present is eighty, paying an annual subscription of 8s. with an entrance fee of 1s.

Secretary, Mr. W. H. Barker, High Street, Hull.

THE WATFORD PISCATORS.

This Society was established in March 1882, for the purpose of putting a stop to the poaching which was going on in the public waters of the neighbourhood, and to rent fishing for the exclusive use of its members. In May the club got under their control about half a mile of the river Colne from the railway arches to the Leathersellers' Arms, and some time afterwards secured a reach of the canal from Cassio Bridge to Beasley's Lock. The number of fishing members is limited to 50, with numerous hon. members. The annual subscription is 5*s*.

Hon. Sec., Mr. H. A. Vincent, 4 Carey Place, Watford.

LONDON ANGLING CLUBS.

I now come to an entirely distinct consideration of the "Angling Clubs" of London pure and simple. It is very likely that a certain class of unreflecting people, or people who don't know any better, may imagine that the sole aim and ambition attendant upon the formation or weekly gathering together of the members of an angling club is centred in the consumption of a good deal of fourpenny ale, unlimited grogs, and the strongest sort of tobacco.

Now and again it is possible, but they are very isolated instances, that this view of matters represents something like the facts of the case. More frequently such an ungenerous reading is as far wide of the mark as the North Pole is to California. Then, again, it may be asked 'What good do angling clubs effect? what are they really doing that is worth doing? and what might they not do? Truly three such queries open up a terrible vista of argument, and although the first question may be, and is, easy enough to answer, the two following must inevitably place the majority of the angling clubs, to speak simple truth, in a by no means complimentary or particularly enviable position.

What good do angling clubs effect? Well, by way of

answering that question I will endeavour to show the difference between angling clubs past and present.

At a date by no means very far antecedent there were, comparatively speaking, only a very few angling clubs in existence. Such as they were, they embraced all the best and longest-lived societies then in being, with some few of the now rapidly springing body of piscators, constantly resolving themselves into some new club, and which might, under proper skilled management, become in time a mighty host, powerful to do good.

Such angling societies as existed then, or many of the members at any rate, were anglers only in name. They recognised, save with rare exceptions, no fence seasons at all, and as to size, bagged every living thing in the shape of a fish that they could entice with either worm or gentle. It was no disgrace then for an angler proudly to display in the club room, as the result of his day's sport, such a collection of fish as nowadays he dare not even bring home. It was literally shocking in those degenerate days to see what baby fish were slaughtered. It was sad to think that men were amongst us calling themselves sportsmen— Heaven save the mark!—who were content to base their claim to the title upon the wretched laurels they might win by the production of such a tray of fish as would have almost disgraced the doughty deeds done in the days when the embryo angler sallied forth armed with a peastick, bent pin, some stolen cotton, and a borrowed pickle bottle. However, such were the facts, and I turn gladly to a contemplation of the picture in our own day.

That resolves itself into a totally different one. Anglers nowadays are, in the first place, restricted by most wholesome rules, which bar them from showing anything but fairly good sample fish, and in the second, I fully believe that their latent sportsmanlike feeling has been so thoroughly developed by good example, that in many cases they would not exhibit poor specimens even if they had the chance. A very strong feeling, emanating it is only right to say with the "Gresham Angling Society," has sprung up of late years against the promulgation of "gross weight competitions," and in favour rather of specimen fish. The scale of weights has been fixed in all cases at a fair size, and in many instances some of the clubs—and notably those old Societies, "The Piscatorial Society" and "The Friendly Anglers"—fix their weight at a very high standard indeed. How different from the old days, when everything in the shape of a fish was bagged, and the waters north, south, east, and west of the compass, were slowly, it is true, but not the less surely, depleted and gradually fished out.

I may ask now, What are the London Anglers doing for the common good of their brethren? and the answer, without giving offence, which I should be sorry enough to do, is one especially difficult to shape nicely.

In the first place they have established by joint effort, spread over certain districts, three institutions by means of which cheap railway facilities have been obtained from all those companies whose permanent way leads to well-known angling resorts. These are the West Central Association of London and Provincial Angling Societies, The United London Anglers' Central Committee, and the Central Association.

In the next place, they have founded what should be known as the best and most important work that the London anglers, as a body of sportsmen, have ever attempted to give root and birth to, in the shape of "The Anglers' Benevolent Association." This has for its main object the assistance of anglers who through declining years, or the working of that strange unwritten law which would seem to hamper some unfortunates with the unvariable and accursed sting of poverty, sink gradually into a pitiable state. Before its institution, and when a properly accredited member of an angling club fell into distress, there was nothing by way of relief save the "whip round" with its open declaration of distress, sometimes especially hurtful to a man's feelings, but which, to the credit of his comrades, they were never disposed to shirk. Now a distressed angler simply makes his case known to the Committee of that institution, and he is instantly relieved to the best of its ability.

But is this institution, which should be one of the first and most important, properly supported? No, I answer—emphatically no; yet the very men probably who hesitate in the time of prosperity to put their shilling into its funds are the very men who would think they were hardly dealt by if, in the hour of need, they were not offered pounds.

My friend Mr. Geen, the hard-working practical "anglers' friend," if ever man deserved the title yet, has lately written a paper, which has been read before various Angling Societies, upon "The better Organisation of the London Anglers." I had not intended to trench upon the ground he, in that admirable and sensible essay, has taken up, but he speaks so much more powerfully than my feeble pen is capable of expressing, that I shall not hesitate, with many apologies for so doing, to quote here and there his opinions, mainly as a means of strengthening my own.

Hear what he says, ye London Anglers, concerning this same "Anglers' Benevolent," and mark, learn, and inwardly digest the wisdom of his repeated warnings.

"Another fault, and not a small one, is the difficulty of getting members to join. One of the chief reasons which caused me to work for the society was the hope that begging would be done away with. I feel certain that there have been more journeys undertaken, and more earnest pleading, and eloquent speeches made to get members to join the Anglers' Benevolent than was ever made for the needy angler under the old system.

"And what does all this begging for members produce? £37 8s. 7d.—actually a smaller sum than they took out of it. No one could possibly take exception to a single item of the expenses, yet they amount to £31 3s. 4d., which is only £5 15s. less than the members' subscriptions."

The last good working of the London anglers, or at any rate its outcome, is the establishment of the "United London Fisheries Association," having for its object the renting and stocking of various waters for the use and pleasurable enjoyment of its members.

Now the business working of these five associations means simply and totally, apart from their admirable objects, a sheer waste of both time, labour, and money. Mr. Geen's great idea, and in this I fully and entirely join issue, is that all might be comprised under one general head, and that in lieu of five sets of officers, embracing three presidents, two vice-presidents, five chairmen, five treasurers, fifteen trustees, five committees of twelve each, and five secretaries, all might be well and efficiently done by one set of officers alone, and that in opposition to the ridiculous issue of three sets of privilege tickets for railway purposes, all might be easily comprised in one, saving trouble, expense, and a lot of entirely unnecessary roundabout business.

What would be the result? There would be more money at command to help the various Preservation Societies, at present greatly neglected; there would be still more to help to stock the waters, at present absolutely in the London anglers' hands, and get them more efficiently protected and watched, and there would be still more left vested, and ready when needful, to help and assist the sacred cause of charity.

I quote Mr. Geen again, because no language of my own could make the question of how is this desirable result to be obtained more clear than he does.

He first of all tells us that there are 4117 enrolled members of one or other of these split-up associations. Some belonging to one, some to another, but few to all three combined. Upon the question of ways and means he says :—

"I have left the important matter of ways and means until the last, as I thought it best you should first be informed as to the nature and extent of my other suggestions.

"At present we pay 1s. to the association of whom we get a privilege ticket, and 1s. to the Fisheries Society; so that the yearage is now 2s. Then the Benevolent steps in and asks us to voluntarily pay them 1s. Six hundred and ninety-one out of the 4117 responded to that appeal, and paid over £37 8s. 7d. How much easier, how much fairer and more satisfactory that we should all pay 3s.! I hope no one will accuse me of being unmindful of my poorer brother anglers. I would not be a party to taking a single penny unnecessarily from their pockets, and before I could bring myself to consent to make this suggestion, I had ascertained that it is the poor angler that is paying the 3s. now. I have also asked myself the question, 'What do I offer in return?' The answer is, your railway concessions shall be guarded, and, if possible, extended; your free rivers shall be protected, and private waters shall be rented for you; the needy and distressed among you shall be relieved.

"Three shillings per year means a trifle more than one halfpenny a week. Many of you must have been struck with the wonderful penny's-worth offered. Cheap travelling, good sport, pleasure and charity for one half-penny per week. Small as this sum is, it would produce £617 11s. The donations and annual subscriptions to the Benevolent amount to £65 17s. 8d., making our gross income £683 8s. 8d. Out of this sum we must pay our secretary and bailiff, vote a sum to the Benevolent committee, and provide for printing, stationery, stamps, and general expenses.

"Much will depend on our getting a good practical secretary, whose salary I fix at £150 per annum, payable monthly, not yearly £150 0 0
Head bailiff, 30s. per week 78 0 0
Benevolent vote (the amount expended last year) 50 0 0
Present amount paid for printing, stationery and stamps, £133 15s. 5d.; proposed amount, £33 15s. 5d. (This sum would be found ample, if not more than sufficient, when augmented by the numerous advertisements which a fully paid secretary could get) 33 15 5
Incidental expenses 20 0 0

Total .. £331 15 5
Which leaves us an available balance of £351 13 3

"What are we going to do with this handsome sum of money? Why, give it to the Preservation Committee, who, with the active assistance of our secretary and bailiff, and with our support and encouragement, will remove those cruel evils in our present system of preservation."

The following short particulars give some idea of the formation and history of such few of the London Angling Societies as responded to my application for them. I regret personally that they are so few, in opposition to the lengthy list of provincial societies. The regret, however keenly felt, will not unfortunately supply the deficiency.

THE PISCATORIAL SOCIETY.

In the year 1836 a few friends, who were in the habit of meeting at the "Granby Tavern," South Audley Street, Grosvenor Square, who were devoted to angling, and frequently made parties for competing in a friendly manner, resolved to form an association to take the name of "The Piscatorial Society."

This was done in October of the same year, the object of the Society being to meet their friends and associates in social conversation and harmony (religion and politics being excluded), to encourage fair angling; while a portion of the funds was to be appropriated to prizes, and forming a museum and collecting works on angling, &c. Rules were formed, and under their Secretary, the late Mr. Cotterill, the Society was launched and has sailed on progressively to the present time.

In the course of the past 47 years they have had a great many good anglers, who have contributed largely to the museum and library. The late Frank Buckland, Esq., an old member, was especially devoted to their welfare, and frequently gave a lecture on the Natural History of Fishes. He presented, in conjunction with the late H. L. Rolfe, Esq., a cast of pike, which was painted in his usual excellent manner, forming a noble and valuable angling trophy. The late Mr. Chapman, who was Hon. Secretary for several years, contributed largely to the museum and library, and his celebrated composition of the "Fine Old Jolly Angler" was also presented to the Society. A valuable album of original sketches was presented by T. H. Parker, Esq., and another, containing comic sketches of the members of the Piscatorial Society, by B. Perelli Rocco, Esq. The library now consists of over 150 volumes, with many valuable paintings and portraits.

In 1838 the Society exerted themselves in giving assistance to the formation of the Thames Angling Preservation Society, and one of the members, the late H. Dean, was for several years secretary. The Piscatorial Society have subscribed three guineas annually to that association, independently of the subscriptions of the individual members.

The museum consists of a large number of cases, and have been exhibited at the Westminster Aquarium, for which a silver medal was awarded; also at the Fisheries Exhibition, Norwich (silver medal and £15); at the Fisheries Exhibition, Edinburgh (a gold medal); and now exhibiting at the International Fisheries Exhibition, Kensington.

The Society now holds its meetings at "Ashley's Hotel," Henrietta Street, Covent Garden, on Monday evenings at 8 o'clock.

The members number 150.

THE TRUE WALTONIANS

Was established in 1830, and the number of its members is limited to 40. It seeks rather to avoid than to court publicity, and the feeling of the society is strongly opposed to prize fishing.

Quoting from its memoirs, I find that "This society was established in the year 1830 to encourage periodical meetings of its members whereat they might reason, converse or instruct with sober pleasantry and unlicentious hilarity; to promote the principles of fair angling, to vigorously oppose every description of poaching, and to cultivate and advance brotherly and true Waltonian feeling among the members of the society and anglers generally.

It also provides for the renting and preserving, for the purposes of angling, such water or waters as may be decided upon from time to time."

THE WALTONIAN ANGLING SOCIETY.

After many removals from place to place in search of suitable head-quarters this Society settled down at last at the "Jew's Harp," Redhill Street, Regent's Park, where they now number 58 members, and under the secretaryship of Mr. J. Packman are in an extremely flourishing condition.

THE SPORTSMEN'S ANGLING CLUB

Is one numbering amongst its members many who devote themselves to other pursuits than a study of the gentle art. One of them is now lion-hunting in Africa, while several other members are fishing on far off continental waters. Its head-quarters are at the "Lady Owen's Arms," Goswell Road, and its Secretary Mr. Benjamin Denny,

THE EALING DEAN CONVIVIAL ANGLING SOCIETY

Was started in October only of last year, yet already numbers 54 members. They fish for no prizes and have no subscriptions, are very rigorous as to the size of fish shown, and support the Thames Angling Preservation

Society. I care not to say more, for if their rules are novel they are at least good.

WESTBOURNE PARK PISCATORIAL SOCIETY.

This Society, started in 1876, has gradually increased until it stands now with a list of nearly seventy names. Although in existence but seven years the walls of the club-room boast of twenty-three cases of preserved specimen fish (thirteen of the cases are now being exhibited at the Fisheries Exhibition). Amongst this number may be mentioned the following: Jack weighing 26½ lbs., a Thames Trout 6 lbs., 2 Roach 4 lbs., 1 Dace 16½ ounces, and also a very pretty Jack of 16 lbs. taken from the Regent's Canal by the late Mr. Severn (in which water he recently lost his life), 1 Bream weighing 6½lbs., 1 pair Tench 9lbs., and also a pair of Carp weighing 16lbs.

I may mention that "gross weight" competitions have been entirely abolished in the Society, and none but specimen fish of the following weights are now recognised: Jack 5 lbs., Bream 3 lbs., Trout 2 lbs., Barbel 2 lbs., Chub 2 lbs., Carp 2 lbs., Tench 1½ lbs., Roach 1 lb., Rudd 1 lb. Perch 1 lb., and Dace ½ lb.

WEST LONDON ANGLING CLUB.

This Society was formed March 31, 1880, at a meeting held at the "White Bear," King Street, Hammersmith. It holds its meetings now at the "Windsor Castle," and under the secretaryship of Mr. G. S. Benham the Society is in a thoroughly sound condition.

THE HAMMERSMITH UNITED ANGLING SOCIETY

Is another excellent association of anglers possessing a splendid museum, upwards of sixty members, and under the presidency of Mr. P. Geen and the secretaryship of Mr. J. Hoole is as flourishing as need be.

THE WOOLWICH BROTHERS ANGLING SOCIETY, AND WOOLWICH PISCATORIALS.

These are two capital clubs, numbering a fair average number of members, established in the town of Woolwich.

THE ACTON PISCATORIAL SOCIETY.

This excellent Society, small in number yet high of purpose, at its start in 1881 had very few members, yet it now musters forty to fifty. Gross weight is barred, and specimen fish are entirely sought after. Its secretary is Mr. C. Simpson, and its head-quarters the "George and Dragon," High Street, Acton.

GOLDEN BARBEL ANGLING SOCIETY.

The above Society was established in the year 1872 at the "Bear and Runner," Wells Street, Mortimer Street, by Mr. Fullerton, then a fishing-tackle maker of Wells Street, W. Dixe, the late secretary, and six or seven other gentlemen.

After some two years or so the Society was removed to the "York Minster," Foley Street, Portland Street, W., where it still remains. The Society is enrolled on the "West Central Association of London and Provincial Angling Societies," at whose meetings the Society send two delegates to represent it.

The objects of the Society are to promote the interests of its members, so far as regards angling, to assist its members to preserve specimen fish. The Society gives prizes for every species of fresh-water fish, and prizes for the three first gross weights, and one for the gross weight of pike.

The Buckland Angling Society

Was formed in September, 1881, and its title taken, as may be surmised, from the name of the late Mr. F. Buckland. Its head-quarters are at the "Middlesex Arms," Clerkenwell Green, and its secretary is Mr. L. V. Delean.

The Alliance Angling Society

Holds its meeting at the "Clerkenwell Tavern," Farringdon Road. It possesses a good museum of preserved trophies, and under the secretaryship of Mr. T. J. Cundell flourishes exceedingly.

Clerkenwell Piscatorial Society.

The above Society was founded in August 1879 by the united efforts of Messrs. Stebbings, Trott and Cooper. Its head-quarters were fixed at the "White Hart," Aylesbury Street in Clerkenwell, and at the present time it has about forty members. The contribution is 12s. per annum, which sum clears all expenses. The members fish free waters only.

The Grange Angling Society.

This Society was formed in 1882, and although only in existence for little more than twelve months, is in a highly efficient state, being both well officered and well supported. Their head-quarters are at the "Earl of Derby," Grange Road, the Society having for president W. Hosken, Esq., while its hon. secretary is Mr. William Kayes.

This ends the list of the "Angling Clubs of London." If it is "cribbed, cabined, and confined," it is not the fault of J. P. W.

LONDON:
PRINTED BY WILLIAM CLOWES AND SONS, Limited,
STAMFORD STREET AND CHARING CROSS.

International Fisheries Exhibition
LONDON, 1883

ANGLING

IN

GREAT BRITAIN

BY

WILLIAM SENIOR

("*RED SPINNER*")

AUTHOR OF "WATERSIDE SKETCHES"; "BY STREAM AND SEA";
"TRAVEL AND TROUT IN THE ANTIPODES," &c.

LONDON
WILLIAM CLOWES AND SONS, Limited
INTERNATIONAL FISHERIES EXHIBITION
AND 13 CHARING CROSS, S.W.

1883

CONTENTS.

CHAP.
I. A GENERAL SURVEY
II. SPRING
III. SUMMER
IV. AUTUMN
V. WINTER

ANGLING IN GREAT BRITAIN.

CHAPTER I.

A GENERAL SURVEY.

THE opening sentence of this Handbook I should like to be the expression of a belief—to wit that, take it all in all, year in and year out, there is no better sport in the world for the angler than in Great Britain. The affected sighing after the good old times, and the gloomy apprehension that this highly favoured country is going to the dogs, with which we are all but too familiar, are shared in by him, of course, if he would live up to his privileges; nevertheless, grumbling granted, and too much cause for grumbling granted in the same breath, he has not a great deal to complain of.

At a very interesting meeting last year at the Society of Arts, when a goodly congregation of anglers met to hear and discuss a paper by Mr. Marston on the propagation of coarse fish, we were all highly amused at a speech from an eminent American pisciculturist, who dilated upon the excellent qualities of the Black Bass, and suggested the propriety of introducing that sportive fish into certain British waters. He incidentally referred to some of the angling paragraphs which appear week after week in the English sporting papers, and raised an easy laugh by dwelling upon the fuss sometimes made over infinitesimal catches of fish. Doubtless, there is an element of absurdity in the published reports of an angling contest carried out upon solemnly promulgated rules, and with all the formality of supervision and directions from a responsible committee, yet which results in the gentleman who bears away the most valuable prize winning by an interesting roachlet seven inches long, and a small eel* to make the weight more imposing. Every week, as a matter of fact, if any one cared to search for them, a dozen reports of angling might be selected to support the one-sided view that in this ancient land we are, in the matter of sport, reduced to a very sorry plight.

Since that meeting was held, I have, however, employed myself in carefully noting the corresponding literature of the United States, and I find that the angling records there, where everything is so splendidly new and gloriously big, do not materially differ from our own. Time after time have American sportsmen assured me that the piteous cry, in lamentation for rivers overfished and sport destroyed, is familiar under the Stars and Stripes, and that the American angler has continually to push out to fresh fishing grounds. In New Zealand and Tasmania, where the best trout-fishing in the world will probably be found within a few years, that plaintive wail would also be echoed but for the obvious sparsity of population, and it will be heard when there are more fishermen to worry the fish.

In the angling waters of Great Britain we may at any rate fairly assume that we know the worst. With us, there is no pushing out west until we reach the Rocky Mountain trout. Our sport is confined within a comparatively tiny

* I believe in most angling clubs eels are not recognised as weighable game. But I saw a match won in the manner described.

ring fence of island surf. It is not possible for any angler to explore and discover a new river. But let us be thankful, if we know the worst we also know the best. We know that, by careful conservation, by spread of knowledge upon matters connected with fishes and their food, and by the possibilities of applying to their homes some of the sanitary principles which we are beginning to find out ought not to be neglected by human kind, angling in Great Britain has vastly improved, and may in the future be improved to an almost indefinite extent. There are, no doubt, streams once renowned, for their sport, that have been as nearly overfished as any streams can be, and there would be room for despair but for the certainty that the evil can and will be remedied.

If a tenth portion, or a twentieth, of the sound advice given in the Papers and discussions of the International Fisheries Exhibition Conferences, and in the Handbooks published during the summer, were carried out with regard to our lakes and rivers, there would be no necessity to indulge in the unwholesome luxury of sighing after the sleepy old days of our grandmothers. And, in time, theory will have fruition in practice; rivers that are to-day polluted will sparkle clear; trout that are starved, ugly, and unhappy from causes well known *not* to be beyond control, will be as merry as the denizens of the Tennysonian brook; depleted streams will be once more dimpled with rises; and the 'prentice boys may again have the opportunity of protesting against too much salmon, and have that protective clause (purely imaginary, there is every reason to believe), of which so much has been written, inserted in their indentures.

In confirmation of the humble belief which is expressed at the beginning of this chapter, let me proceed to the recital of a few facts. A deceased statesman, who was himself extremely fond of felling his opponents with statistics, once, when such tough arguments went against him, contemptuously remarked that figures might be made to prove anything. My figures, I hope, will prove simply what they are intended to show, namely, that angling in Great Britain, up to the present moment, is anything but a played-out institution.

In the very last month of the present season some magnificent takes of salmon have been recorded from nearly all the Scotch rivers. The largest fish appears to have been taken on the Stobhall water, of the Tay, by Lord Ruthven. It weighed 54 lbs., and was of such fine proportions that it was reserved for preservation and setting up in the museum of the Perthshire Society of Natural Science. This, it is said, was not only the heaviest fish killed by the rod in the Tay during the season, but the heaviest since 1870, when a gentleman, on the Stanley Waters, killed a fish of 61 lbs. In one day upon the Stobhall water, thirty-four salmon were killed : and on the following day two rods landed two-and-twenty fish.

In the Tweed and Teviot the anglers also obtained sport, sometimes three, sometimes four, and in one instance Col. Vivian and Mr. Arkwright, on the Rutherford Water, killed nearly a dozen fish. On the Mertoun Water the Hon. H. Brougham had twelve fish, and on the Earl of Home's water (Bingham), a couple of gentlemen used their rods to some purpose, the result of a day's sport being fish of 24 lbs., 23 lbs., 23 lbs., 21 lbs., 16 lbs., 16 lbs., 11 lbs., 11 lbs., 8 lbs., and 6 lbs. In another part of the river, a day or two later, Mr. Brougham killed thirteen fish, and on the Floors' Water the Duke of Roxburghe, in one afternoon, had four—one of 22 lbs., another of 12 lbs., and two of 10 lbs. Up to the 11th November in the season of 1881 (the Tweed close time being from December 1st to January 31st), I read somewhere that one gentleman at one stand had killed 3,782 lbs. of salmon; while a few days after, 177½ lbs. fell to his rod in a single day, with nine fish. The same angler, in one day, in the next season, took nine fish weighing respectively 25 lbs., 25 lbs., 23 lbs., 19½ lbs., 16½ lbs., 16 lbs., 16 lbs., 14 lbs., 15 lbs.—total, 170 lbs.

The finest sport, probably, in this present season of 1883, was that on the Spey, which, after the removal of the nets, began to afford the rodsters a round of splendid sport. According to a report in the *Field*, from which paper I have also taken the figures of this year's Tweed fishing, General Gipps, on the 1st of October, landed seven; on the 2nd, five; on the 3rd, three; on the 4th, seven; on the 5th, five; and on the 6th three salmon. On another water, Mr. Todd killed seven fish; on the 2nd October, six; on the 3rd, six; and on the 4th, six. On the Gordon Castle Water the Duke of Richmond, the Earl of March, Lord Francis Gordon Lennox, Lady Florence Gordon Lennox, and several visitors every day made most enviable baskets. It is unnecessary to go through all the daily returns in the early part of October, but taking one day I find that the Duke of Richmond to his own rod had six salmon, weighing respectively 27 lbs., 24 lbs., 22½ lbs., 22 lbs., 20 lbs., and 19 lbs., besides a brace of grilse weighing 8 and 10 lbs. respectively. On another day His Grace got a 30 lbs. and a 20 lbs. salmon; and, on the same day, the Earl of March killed six fish—of 24 lbs., 19 lbs., 15 lbs., 21 lbs., 21 lbs., and 12½ lbs. On another day the noble earl must have been kept pretty well occupied with his seven salmon—of 15 lbs., 15 lbs., 17 lbs., 17 lbs., 16 lbs., 18 lbs., and 22 lbs., and four grilse, three of 10 lbs. and one of 9 lbs. Even a bishop who was fishing the Water (St. Alban's) got his three salmon and one grilse, while several ladies were quite as successful.

In another part of the country I read that on the Aboyne section of the Dee a gentleman, in one day, killed his eight salmon—from 8 lbs. to 37 lbs., and on the following day, with the natural minnow, he had four, the largest of which was 30 lbs. These returns are taken from one paper only, the *Field*, of October 13th, and they tell of sport that should surely satisfy the most rapacious sportsman. At the same time they convincingly indicate that while such fishing is to be had at home, there is no need to fly to foreign parts, even to try conclusions in the swarming rivers of Canada.

As to trout fishing, I do not happen to have on hand a suitable clipping from which to quote, but I can draw upon a recent experience of my own to supply all that is necessary for my argument. Within thirty miles of London, which I did not leave till eleven o'clock in the morning, I killed, mostly with a small alder fly, on one summer's day, ten brace of trout. The largest, it is true, was a very ugly fish of two pounds and a quarter, but the rest were beyond reproach, and ranged between a pound and a half and half a pound. This, I may be told by some friendly monitor, is nothing to boast about. Nor is it. But it is quite enough to satisfy my wants, and, indeed, the more modest basket of four brace and a half, which on my very last outing in August rewarded seven hours' hard whipping, made me as happy and contented as a man has a right to be in this vale of tears.

The business transacted with the Thames trout appeared in an authentic return prepared by Mr. W. H. Brougham, the Secretary of the Thames Angling Preservation Society, in the summer. He gave the following captures as representing one week's Thames trouting between Chertsey Weir and Kingston only :—Chertsey Weir, four fish, weighing respectively 7¾ lbs., 4 lbs. 14 oz., 5 lbs., and 3½ lbs. ; Shepperton Weir, four fish, weighing respectively 5¼ lbs., 4½ lbs., 3¾ lbs., and 2 lbs. ; Sunbury Weir, two fish, weighing respectively 7 lbs., and 4½ lbs. ; opposite the Waterworks Sunbury, one fish weighing 10 lbs. ; Hampton Court Weir four fish, weighing respectively 14 lbs. 10 oz., 7 lbs., 4 lbs., and 2 lbs. ; Thames Ditton, one fish, weighing 7 lbs. 2 oz. ; Kingston, one fish, weighing 7 lbs. Thus we have a total of seventeen fish, weighing together 99 lbs. 14 oz.

The coarse fish have also been kind enough to furnish me with ready examples of the quality of our English sport. Mr. Jardine, who is accepted as the most successful pike angler of the country, as the superb specimens shown by him in the western arcade at the Fisheries Exhibition will indicate, is thus spoken of in a newspaper paragraph :—" Messrs. A. Jardine and Knechtli had a magnificent catch of pike the other day, which were shown at the Gresham Angling Society. Ten fish weighed in the society's scales 135 lbs. This represented two days' fishing. This capture has no parallel in angling history, so far as London clubs are concerned, because the fish shown were only the largest, and they took thirty more, from 3 lbs. to 7 lbs."

In *Bell's Life* of January 7, 1883, I read—" We have seen or heard of some remarkable takes of pike and perch recently. One of the finest shows of pike to be seen this season was that of Mr. H. D. Hughes, jun., last Saturday. Fishing with his brother in a private lake, the united take was forty good fish. The largest, weighing 25 lbs., was caught on single gut, and was on view last Monday at Messrs. Alfred and Son's, Moorgate Street. Equally remarkable was another day's sport. Mr. Carter Milburn, fishing last week in private water (a lake), took, between eight and ten o'clock on the morning of Thursday, six pike weighing 20 lbs., 17 lbs., 15 lbs., 11 lbs., and 6 lbs. This achievement is all the more remarkable when we know that Mr. Milburn has been for years deprived of his left arm. The business was managed entirely with the snap-tackle."

Perch exist in such incredible quantities in many British waters, that we might almost pass them by, and take them, like official reports, as read. In the *Field* of August 25, however, an account appeared of the capture by two anglers, between eleven and five o'clock, in Slapton Ley, of more than 800 fish. This haul was made on a well-known piece of water which may be fished by all comers on payment of a small fee. The accuracy of the statement was questioned, but the evidence of subsequent correspondents confirmed it, one gentleman stating that he and a friend in five hours fishing took 476 perch.

What may be done amongst roach and barbel was duly set forth in the Paper on Freshwater Fishing read at one of the Exhibition conferences by Mr. Wheeldon. In the short space of five hours on a winter day, he killed, in the Hampshire Avon—a notable roach river from Ringwood upwards—75 lbs. of roach, numbers of which were considerably over a pound in weight. In another portion of his Paper he stated that he and Mr. Smurthwaite not long ago killed three hundredweight of barbel in one day, near Sonning Weir. In the tidal waters of the Thames during this present autumn, takes of dace of 35 lbs., 26 lbs., and 25 lbs. have been registered by the Richmond and Twickenham punts-men. During the month of July, according to the *Fishing Gazette*, in a lake near Swindon, open on payment to the public, Messrs. Wheatstone and Walker, of the Stanley Anglers' Club, caught 230 lbs. of tench in five days. One of these anglers, on July 9th, took with rod and line twenty-five fish, nine being over 4 lbs., nine over 3 lbs., and seven over 2 lbs.. The total weight of the days' angling was 89½ lbs.

These results, which speak for themselves, I give as they occur to me at the moment, and not by any effort at research. They fairly enough serve the purpose I have in view, and if I wished to extend the list of good baskets, the averages of the last five years, as they may be unearthed from the periodical literature devoted to the subject, would probably show as fine, and much finer sport in some of the branches of angling upon which I have casually touched.

But the rapidly increased and increasing number of anglers in Great Britain should be a continual stimulus to exertion in keeping up the stock of fresh-water fish. Such an impetus has been given to the culture of Salmonidæ of all descriptions (adding latterly to the fish indigenous to British waters, the brook trout of North America), that there is little fear that they will be neglected.

Private fish-hatching establishments have sprung up in England as well as in Scotland, from which our colonial rivers are being tenanted, and by which losses and deterioration at home may be made good at any time; and the interesting collection of fish cultural appliances at the Exhibition must have been, to hosts of observers during the summer, a serviceable object lesson that cannot fail to produce practical results in time to come.

The increase of anglers, however—and this is a point we are too apt to overlook in considering the general question

—has been chiefly amongst the classes of the population that cannot afford, either in time or money, to fish the best waters for the best fish. The anglers who devote themselves to salmon and trout can, in the main, look very well after themselves. Give them an adequate legislation that shall ensure fair play against the proprietors and occupiers to whom the netting of salmon is a business, and all other things will, without much trouble, be added unto them. They represent the higher branches of the sport of angling. They are the followers of Cotton rather than Father Izaak, the patron saint of what are termed general anglers ; and the time has gone by when the humble angler, who is content with a modest day's roach or perch-fishing, is regarded by them with contemptuous indifference. The angling-books of twenty years ago show that the fortunate individuals who could betake themselves to Norway, or across the St. George's Channel, or North of the Tweed, were given to looking down from a lofty pedestal upon their less fortunate brother sportsman, who was dubbed a Cockney, and held up, together with his floats, worms, maggots, and ground-bait, to derision. But that day is past.

If space permitted, it would be interesting to trace how the change has been brought about. Broadly speaking, it has been done by the printing-press, and during the last twenty years, not so much by angling-books, as by literature of a more unsubstantial character. The journalistic fathers in Israel are answerable primarily for the tens of thousands of members of angling clubs, who weekly obtain healthful recreation by the waterside. "Ephemera" aforetime of *Bell's Life*, Francis Francis, Greville, F., and Cholmondeley Pennell (too young to be a veteran yet, but still ancient enough as an angling writer to come within the category), by their contributions to journals and maga-

zines awakened popular interest ; and it happened that a
revolution in the means of communication had come at an
opportune time, to add to their teachings the necessary
opportunities of putting them into practice. Anglers have
now an organ of their own in the *Fishing Gazette;*
Mundella's Act was passed for the especial behoof of
bottom-fishers ; railway companies are recognizing the
brotherhood as of sufficient influence to be considered in
the granting of special privileges ; and the Fish Culture
Association, of which the Marquis of Exeter is President,
would never have been started, had not the necessity
been felt of looking after the stock of coarse-fish in rivers
frequented by the many. It must suffice, however, to
take these things for granted, and so I pass on with the
hearty wish that all societies, and all movements which
aim at assisting and encouraging the fair general angler,
may prosper abundantly. The man who is a fair fisherman, though his ambition soar no higher than a plate of
gudgeon from the well-raked gravel, has his place in the
common confraternity, and is deserving of consideration.

The general angler at the present time is not altogether
without his apprehensions. Angling Associations have
befriended him, but the awakened interest which he has
himself helped to extend, threatens to curtail his privileges.
Claims to the ownership of waters hitherto considered
public are being advanced with the view of keeping him at
a distance. As, however, the Defence Associations should
be able to prevent wrong-handed or high-handed proceed-
ings, this, though a vexatious sign of the times, is a difficulty that will be removed, one way or another, by
appeal to the law. Still, it should be mentioned in a
general survey of the English angler's present position.
I confess I see most cause for alarm in the snapping-up of

every available bit of water by societies of gentlemen who can afford to pay for it. For this there is no help. We live in a free country, and if the owner of a stream, which his forefathers permitted to be fished by his neighbours, chooses to let it at a rental, he has the right to do so. Equally have a dozen city gentlemen, who love the amusement of angling, and can, by their purses, command the means of indulging in it under agreeable conditions, the right, morally and legally, of securing it for a consideration, or without one if they have the chance. Nevertheless, the effect is to limit the waters available to the masses of anglers.

The larger rivers beloved of general anglers are open, under easy and equitable regulations. The Thames, Trent, Ouse, and others of that class, are not yet parcelled out into subscription waters, and of smaller streams, like the Lea, and portions of the Colne, it should not be forgotten that the small fee demanded for a day-ticket is more than counterbalanced by the advantages gained by watching and preservation. In the immediate vicinity of large towns, indeed, there is something to be said for the oft-heard complaint that open waters are scarcely worth fishing, unless they are under the charge of some such model guardians as the Thames Angling Preservation Society. The cutting down of ancient privileges is suffered mostly in rural or semi-rural districts, to which town anglers were wont to issue, attracted as much by the pleasures of the country surroundings, as the more direct operations of fish capture.

Of the joys of angling I have nothing at present to say, except to remark that it is a sport which, more than any other, owes much of its fascination to features that are only indirectly connected with it. Some years ago a masterly essay (by its editor) appeared in the *New Quarterly* upon trout fishing, and this sentence at once challenged my attention: "One apologist will talk of wandering amid pleasant scenery, rod in hand. The hypocrite! As if the scenery were the inducement, and not the rod, which he affects to speak of so lightly. The best of all apologies is Shakespeare's, and yet it is a poor one :—

> 'The pleasant'st angling is to see the fish
> Cut, with her golden oars, the silver stream,
> And greedily devour the treacherous bait.'"

In a couple of angling books which I had at that time cast upon the waters, I had endeavoured to remind the reader of the countless charms to be found in the lanes and hedgerows through which, on an angling excursion, we pass to the cornfield; and the objects of interest visible from the footpath amongst the waving grain; and the meadows "painted with delight" over which we brush through the grass to the river's brink; to say nothing of the harvest which the eye may gather in the intervals of fishing. Wherefore I began to hold court of justice upon myself, if haply it were true, after all, that we were indeed the hypocrites thus described. The verdict was one of "Not Guilty," and much was I comforted upon taking up the magazine, in fear and trembling as to what would follow, to find the accusing article itself flavoured with a very pretty sprinkling of poetry and sentiment. All in sweet form came the fine summer day, and the rill trickling down the remote hillside "among club rushes and the blue water-grasses, till it reaches the valley, finding its way along, a mere thread, half lost to sight at times beneath the herbage, then stagnating for a space into a little pool," &c. It was my turn now. "The hypocrite!"

mused I. "As if he climbed the hillside to catch trout in the thread-like trickle!"

The old names by which the pastime of angling is known are, it will be noticed, significant on this head. It is "The Gentle Craft," and "The Contemplative Man's Recreation." To be sure, there are plenty of anglers of all ranks who are pot-hunters pure and simple. They take their surly way to the water, doggedly settle down to slay, and are deaf and blind to the compensations which Nature, in her kindlier mood, offers against that too frequent ill-luck for which the angler in Great Britain, in Greater Britain, and all the world over, must be prepared. But the rule is otherwise; the majority of anglers in this country, at all events, *do* take appreciative note of the scenery; *do* keep a friendly eye upon bird, beast, and insect; *do* delight in the foliage of the coppice, the whispering of the sedges, and the long gay procession of flowers, even from the curious blossom of the coltsfoot, which is probably the first to greet him in the earliest spring days, to the yellow stars of the solitary ragwort, which shivers in the late October days.

It stands to reason that it should be so. Amongst out-of-door sportsmen the angler is peculiar. The deer-stalker has little to look at but barren hills misnamed a forest, or the broad sky above him; the fox-hunter has his horse and his own neck to study, and the briskness of impetuous advance to divert his thoughts; the fowler's eye has a definite duty to perform. The angler, if using a fly-rod, has frequently-recurring "waits," what time he moves from stream to stream; the bottom-fisher, too, has a superfluity of enforced leisure at his disposal. And over and above all the British angler lives in a country whose rural parts are unique in their winsomeness. Walton's famous old book savours of honeysuckles, hawthorn hedges, sycamore trees, and crystal streams. He was a typical angler, and the type remains.

We may now pass to a more practical branch of our general survey, and having glanced at some of the characteristics of the situation as concerning the angler, may take a birdseye view of the inland waters of Great Britain. I do not, however, pretend to attempt anything like a guide to the rivers, nor even to furnish a comprehensive list. *The Angler's Diary* deals in brief with all the fishing districts of the United Kingdom, and, indeed, of the world, so far as they are known, and to that useful little book shall the inquiring reader be referred. All that I am able to do is to hint at the main features of our chief angling resorts.

A bulky handbook might, for example, be written upon the one section comprising the lochs and rivers of the

"Land of brown heath and shaggy wood,
Land of the mountain and the flood."

Placing, as is but meet, the migratory Salmonidæ at the top of the list, Scotland naturally first claims our notice. To the ordinary angler, however, all but a few of the prime waters, which are a source of rich revenue to Scotland, are close boroughs. The fishings, like the shootings, are rented at enormous figures, although there are, here and there, given to the sojourner at particular hotels, the privilege of wetting his line in odd reaches of well-known salmon rivers. There is never so much difficulty in obtaining permission to fish for *Salmo fario*, or, as our Scotch friends call it, the yellow trout, and if some travellers complain of persistent refusals to applications for permission, I must personally say that I have always had reason to be grateful for ready kindness in various parts of the country.

On the whole, the angler visiting Scotland cannot do better than take his technical instructions about salmon fishing from Francis Francis's 'Book on Angling.' Perhaps no English angler has had more experience of the Scotch rivers, from the angler's point of view, than he. It is no secret to the initiated that the list of salmon and sea-trout flies, which he gives for the various rivers and lakes of Scotland, Ireland, and Wales, cost him years of labour, and that in compiling them he received the assistance of some of the most experienced of British anglers.

What the principal Scotch rivers produce I have already illustrated by figures. The Tweed is held in high esteem as an angling river, though it is not so long, and does not form so large a watershed as the Tay. The Kirkcudbrightshire Dee, the Cree, and the Luce, are small rivers in the south of Scotland, and the Annan and Nith, the former famous for its sea-trout and herling, also run into the Solway Firth. The Tay is a superb salmon river, and like the Tweed has, in its lower part, to be commanded from a boat. It yields, with its many tributaries, good spring fishing. Aberdeenshire is a famous county for the angler, for it can boast of its Dee and Don, and a number of smaller streams. Inverness, also, is a notable angling county, containing as it does the magnificent Spey. This river has peculiar characteristics for the angler, having high banks and much rough, rapid water, demanding the exercise of all his skill. In this county is also the Ness, where the public have access on given days to a portion of the water near the Highland capital. In the Beauly, some years ago, Lord Louth killed to his own rod 146 salmon in five days, and this beautiful river is still first-rate for fish.

Upon the Thurso, in the extreme north, the fishing opens earlier than in any other portion of the United Kingdom.

Argyllshire, the country of the Mac Callum More, has, in addition to its lochs, a number of small salmon rivers, such as the Awe, the Orchy, and the Leven. In Banffshire the best salmon rivers are the Deveron and Fiddich. In Berwickshire are the Blackadder and the Whitadder, two good trouting streams. The Findhorn, once a phenomenal salmon river, is in Elginshire, and it is on record that years ago 360 salmon were caught in the same pool in one day. This, however, was exceeded by another miraculous draught of fishes described by the Earl of Moray, who wrote to his countess that 1,300 salmon had been taken in a night. There is fair fishing occasionally even now in the Findhorn, but ruthless nettings below have considerably spoiled it. The Lossie, in the same county, is good for sea-trout and yellow trout. Forfarshire has the North and South Esk. The Clyde, whose falls are fatal to the ascent of salmon, is in its upper waters excellent for trout, and it is of additional interest to anglers since the experiment of introducing grayling into Scotland has there been successfully carried out. The best rivers of Perthshire are the Garry, the Tummel, the Lyon, the peerless Tay already referred to, and the Teith. Roxburghshire, besides the Tweed, which is famous for both trout and salmon, many of its casts being historical, and which has romantic historical associations with Melrose, Dryburgh, Norham, and Kelso, has also the Teviot, which, like the Ale, the Bowmont, the Jed, the Kale, the Rule, and other such minor streams, are of excellent repute for trout. Sutherlandshire, the paradise of loch fishers and the stronghold of the *Salmo ferox*, has the Brora, an early salmon river, where the fish run large; the Borgie, excellent for grilse and sea-trout; the Inver, where the wandering angler staying at Loch Inver can fish, for a daily payment; the Lexford, a short river, but that still is the second best salmon river in the county, and the Shin one of the best rivers in the Highlands.

As for the lochs, one might almost be pardoned for using the familiar expression that their name is legion. Loch Lomond, between Dumbarton and Stirlingshire; Loch Awe, in Argyllshire; Lochs Tay, Rannoch, Earn, and Katrine, in Perthshire; Lochs Ness, Lochie, and Lagan, Inverness-shire; Lochs Maree, Luichart, and Fannich, in Ross-shire, at once occur to us; while below the Grampians there are Loch Leven, with its wonderful fishing, and St. Mary's Loch in the Yarrow country. Some of these grand sheets of water contain the destructive pike, and perch, which are only less fatal to trout by reason of their smaller size. But in the hundreds of lochs which lie twinkling within the hollows of the bonny Scotch mountains there is an abundance of small trout, and heavy specimens of the *Salmo fario*, while many are inhabited by the great lake trout, the night prowler that so seldom takes a fly, and to which the name of *ferox* has been aptly given.

Ireland is not so much patronised by English anglers as Scotland, though there is more and cheaper general sport at his command. The Green Island, manifold as are its physical beauties and angling capabilities, has been not a little neglected. Of late years there has been some excuse, perhaps, for timorous tourists, though surely never was fear more ungrounded; but to the angler, for some incomprehensible reason, Ireland has never been such an attraction as Scotland, though, as I have hinted, a stranger who can only afford to expend a moderate amount of money in his amusements, and desires a variety of fishing, would do much better in Ireland than in Scotland. The largest pike in Europe, I believe, are roaming in the depths of the big lakes; it is the land *par excellence* of the white trout;

and all round the coast, from the merry but much preserved Bush, within easy hail of Giant's Causeway, to the early Lee, in county Cork, the salmon come and go with beautiful regularity. One of the most delightful angling tours I ever had was in Ireland, fishing my journey from Sligo through Connemara to Galway by easy stages, and taking whatever came in my way—perch, pike, brown trout, white trout, and salmon—with praiseworthy impartiality. Rivers, mountains, land and sea, the courteous people, even the pigs and wretched hovels—everything, in short, but the too freely weeping skies, contributed to the sum total of a pleasant holiday.

The angling in Ireland, though very good, is not what it was when the chapters of 'Wild Sports of the West' were written. The fish are, generally speaking, of the same class as those to be found in the Scotch rivers—salmon and trout everywhere, and in the larger lakes leviathan pike, and here and there bream. There are gillaroo in Lough Erne, and pollan in Lough Neagh. It goes without saying in these days, when the taste for angling has extended so much, that the free fishings are not numerous.

Still there are many bits of open salmon fishing, and lakes that are to all intents and purposes free; and the sea and brown trout fishing is plentiful enough to satisfy the most rapacious appetite. Boats are cheap and the boatmen very modest in their demands, and what is more, the latter are always satisfied with the treatment they receive, while their humorous sayings and doings are a source of continual amusement. One salmon fishing licence will do for the whole of Ireland, which is a great advantage. The open season, as elsewhere, is from February 2nd to October 31st, with the usual exceptions of special districts. The principal rivers in the south are the Blackwater, the Lee, and the Bandon, while upon the wild shores of Bantry Bay and by Glengariff there are plenty of trout streams. Close by, in county Kerry, there are the Killarney lakes, overrun during periods of the year by tourists, spoiled by the use of cross lines, but still, in early months, not hopeless for the rodster.

Continuing our way up the western coast, we come to the estuary of the magnificent river Shannon, which contains samples of most of the fish to be found in Ireland. Songs have been sung in praise of the salmon of this river, and it has obtained more prominence in the literature of sport than any other Irish river, which is but natural, seeing that it runs from Leitrim in the north, passing through a number of lakes, the last of which is the prolific fishing ground of Lough Derg. County Clare, being somewhat out of the way, and not much written or talked about, is but little frequented by anglers, but the best pike fishing in Ireland is probably to be obtained in some of its lakes.

Galway, according to its angling value, should have been mentioned first. In this county is the famous fishery of Ballynahinch, the white trout station of Glendalough, and the Galway river, in which the salmon fishery has been brought to a high pitch of perfection; it drains Corrib and Mask, in the latter of which trout of the phenomenal proportions of twenty pounds are very occasionally taken.

From Galway the angling tourist makes his way through Connemara by Westport to Ballina, a famous centre on the Moy, with Lough Conn not far distant. Mayo is the country of which Maxwell wrote, and there are privileges in connection with its fisheries that make this station the most attractive of all for the man of moderate means, though the upper portions of the Moy are strictly preserved. Lough Arrow is in the next county, Sligo, but the best fishing is in the river which runs from Lough Gill through the county town.

Still further north, in wild and beautiful Donegal, we have on the southern boundary of the county the river Erne, with the grand lough of that name stretching down by Enniskillen into Fermanagh. The short length of water between Lough Erne and Ballyshannon used to be, and, for aught I know to the contrary, now is, one of the favourite salmon reaches in the country; and hard by, in Leitrim, we have the Bundrowes river and Lough Melvin, in which some good fish, at reasonable charges, may be obtained, especially during April and May. Across, in the other corner of Ulster, there is the Bann, with Lough Neagh. These are the principal angling resorts in the sister island; but we should not forget the Blackwater, the Suir, the Slaney, and the pretty trout streams within convenient distance of Dublin. As a rule, it may be taken that the angler, more particularly the angler who will be satisfied with sea-trout, brown trout, occasionally gillaroo, and lively pike fishing, can never very well do wrong in going to Ireland.

The principality of Wales is a delightful country for the trout angler who will be as a rule content with small fish, and who can make up for the rest with the most picturesque and beautiful scenery. In North Wales the principal rivers are the Conway (good occasionally for salmon), the Dee, the Dovey, the higher waters of the Severn, the Clwyd, and the Verniew; while in South Wales, where the sewin gives spirited sport in the autumn, and the brown trout run to a larger size than in the small lakes and mountain streams of the north country, we have the Ogmore, Taff, Taw, Teme, Towy, Usk, Monnow, and Wye. The salmon fishing of the Usk is proverbial, and I have in my possession a photograph given to me by the late Mr. Crawshay, of Cyfarthfa Castle, at the close of a day's successful trout fishing, during a frosty day in the month of February a few years ago, representing nine salmon killed by him on October 22nd, 1874, with the fly; and a singular thing in connection with this day's sport was that the three largest fish, one of 22 lbs., one of 19 lbs., and one of 16 lbs., were hooked foul, the salmon being, as they too often are, in a more playful than feeding humour; yet carried their gambols too far, and were nicked accordingly—two in the pectoral fin, and a third in the side. These fish were placed upon an unhinged door, which was tilted up by a couple of men to allow Mr. Crawshay, who was a very skilful amateur photographer, to take their likenesses.

Considering the amount of poaching to which the English rivers, up to within ten or fifteen years, were subjected, and the gross neglect from which they long suffered, it is marvellous that in all parts of the country the commoner kinds of fishing should be so good as they are at the present time; and considering the number of anglers who test their value upon every available day of the year, it would not be surprising if the rule was to toil all day and catch nothing, and if the language of every English angler was that of the prophet of old, "The fishers also shall mourn, and all they that cast angle into the brooks." But, as I have remarked on a previous page, we have more to be thankful for than to complain of.

It would be invidious to single out one county as better than another, were it not that our best trouting districts are limited. There is probably no county in England that has not a trout stream of some kind; and tributary streams and brooklets known only to a few, and very naturally kept secret by them, sometimes keep up very ample stores of surreptitious trout. But the true trouting counties are comparatively few. Beginning with the south, Cornwall may be passed by with a brief reference, although all the streams trickling down from the backbone of the hills which constitute the Cornish highlands, contain more or less of trout. Devonshire is quite another matter. Its larger trout rivers are numerous, and salmon are taken in Taw and Torridge, in Exe and Tavy, while the interior is intersected in all directions with lively little streams. There are a few strictly preserved trout streams in Dorsetshire, and a good salmon river in the Stour, which joins itself with the Avon at Christchurch, the Avon itself being swelled by a famous grayling river, the Wiley, from the Salisbury Plain region.

The largest river in Great Britain, and the one to which most importance is attached by the main body of general anglers, is, of course, the Thames, with its magnificent watershed representing a basin of over six thousand miles. It is not so long as the Severn by some twenty odd miles, but it is fed by a rich array of tributaries right and left. In its higher portions, under the influence of the Cotswold hills, there are the Windrush and Coln, both capital trout streams. In the Kennet, the most important of its southern tributaries, the richest specimens to be found in England of the *Salmo fario* are taken. To all London anglers the Roden, the Lea, the Colne, Wick, and Thame are familiar, while the trout and trout fishing of the Wandle and Darenth, the one on the west and the other on the east side of southern London, but both almost within hearing of the roar of its traffic, are traditional. In the midlands there are the brilliant Derbyshire streams, which may be considered midway, in physical characteristics, between the pastoral rivers of the Hampshire lowlands (the Itchen and the Test) and the mountain burns of Wales and Scotland.

The Derbyshire streams, being for the most part open to the purchasers of day tickets, are a good deal fished, but there are plenty of respectable trout and grayling yet to be taken, and the anglers of the big cities—London in the south, and Manchester and Liverpool in the north—have in them splendid opportunities of exercising the art of fly-fishing from spring, to the close of the grayling season, when spring comes again. The Derwent, Wye, and the Dove rising in the mountains that characterise the peak country, are tributaries of the Trent, from which a few salmon are taken, and which affords everlasting sport to the Nottingham anglers, who have founded a school of their own, and whose reserves of coarse fish seem to be little affected by the contributions levied upon them. A kindred river to the Trent, though running in a southerly instead of a northerly direction, and delivering its tribute, like the Trent, into the Humber, is the Yorkshire Ouse, into which, galloping down from the Pennine chain, are delivered a succession of first-rate trout and grayling streams, the Swale, the Yore, the Nid, and the Wharfe; and on the other side, easily commanded from Scarborough, and in its earlier waters running under the north wolds, is the Yorkshire Derwent, the grayling fishing of which is not inferior to that of the Wharfe.

Lancashire, in days long since passed, was probably an excellent angling county throughout, but the Mersey and the Irwell have been years ago pressed into the service of manufacture and commerce, and we have to go into north Lancashire to the Ribble, Lune, Hodder, and the waters of Ribblesdale, before anything like adequate sport can be obtained. The lakes of Cumberland, and its fine river the

Eden, still maintain their long-established character; and on the other side of the country, the north and south Tyne have not entirely lost their salmon, and certainly not their trout. Above Newcastle, the Wansbeck, the Coquet, Breamish and Till, keep up the reputation of the border streams for trout angling. The Severn I have not passed by intentionally. But it is as much a Welsh as an English stream, having a decidedly Welsh origin, and by its tributaries watering a good deal of Welsh country. At any rate, I do not mention it last because it is least, for we have to thank the Severn for some of the unsurpassed grayling rivers of Worcestershire and Herefordshire. The Teme and the Arrow, with the Lugg, a tributary of the Wye, are not second to those of any part of England for the quality and quantity of their grayling. On the eastern coast of England, other than the trout streams of the border, there are some coarse fish rivers in Essex and Suffolk, and three particularly good general angling streams, namely, the Ouse (Bedfordshire and Huntingdonshire), which is famous for its bream and pike, the Nen, and Welland. In east Anglia there is a special description of angling, to which reference will be made in another portion of this pamphlet, while beyond the Wash there is the fen country, with the Ancholme and Witham; upon these the Sheffield anglers swoop in their hundreds, and, when fishing matches are arranged, by their thousands, during the summer season, and, spite of the rows of rods, uncommonly good baskets are occasionally taken away.

The angling of England is more prosaic, taking it as a whole, than in either of the other countries that compose the national union. Until we get considerably north of the Trent, and within measurable distance of the lakes and mountains of Cumberland, our landscape scenery is softly pleasing rather than imposingly wild and romantic. Our rivers for the most part flow tranquilly through fat meadows, upon which the mildest mannered kine graze their fill. They are at every turn brought under tribute by the millowner, sometimes becoming hopelessly demoralised as a reward for the service they render. They do not thunder through gloomy granite gorge as, in some portion of their career, do the rivers of Scotland. With impetuous torrent they do not dash around massive boulders, as do well-remembered Irish salmon streams. They *flow* to the sea, seldom leaping, or boiling, or swirling, after the manner of rivers cradled in mountain heights.

Thanks, however, to the liberally distributed tributaries, and the drainage of the hill countries, the English angler has, in the wide variety of waters from which he may take his choice when meditating a piscatorial excursion, the opportunity of forming acquaintance with many a bright, swift-running river, making music in such solitary dales as those of Derbyshire, or amongst the rocky walls and overhanging foliage characterising many of the Devonshire streams. There is, in short, some sort of angling in every part of the country. Even the Isle of Wight has a trout stream if the tourist only knew it, and the trout of the Isle of Man have certainly outlived the animal which is the sign manual of the Manxman.

In an essay of this description the writer is confronted with the difficulty of deciding how to act, without dwelling too much or too little upon any one subject. Clearly the orthodox method of dealing with the many-sided topic of angling will not answer. Space would altogether fail me to deal in detail with the various methods of angling, or with the thousand-and-one appliances which are recommended for the successful prosecution of the art, and which have of late multiplied to a bewildering extent. I have already declined the duties of guide to localities, and in the same spirit I must put aside the pleasant functions of tutor in the rudiments. Nor would such a *rôle* be necessary even if it were expedient. There is nothing new to be said about practical angling, after such past masters as Francis Francis, Stewart, Stoddart, Cholmondeley Pennell, Manley, Greville F., Keene, Foster, Alfred, Martin, and others too numerous to mention have had their say.

Easy, therefore, is my conscience in shaking off the temptations which have beset me to attempt a technical disquisition upon the best method of tying a fly, making and fitting up rod and line, handling it from bank or boat, impaling a worm, or compounding ground bait, except so far as may point a moral or adorn a tale. These are most essential subjects to study and master let no man gainsay, but I will courteously ask the reader to permit me to deal with the subject, in what space remains, in the spirit—if I may employ the expression—rather than in the letter. This, after not a little cogitation, I have resolved to do by endeavouring, so far as in me lies, to conduct the reader through the Angler's Year, making spring, summer, autumn and winter develop the essential types of angling in Great Britain.

CHAPTER II.

SPRING.

THE boundary lines between the seasons, into which we will take the liberty of separating the angler's year, must for our present purposes be somewhat more elastic than those of the calendar. At the very beginning, for example, we shall find it convenient to assume that spring begins in February, for in that month both salmon and trout anglers have a legal right to commence operations; and we are bound by all considerations of honour and tradition to deal with them in the forefront. There is no British freshwater fish absolutely out of season in February. On the contrary, some of the coarse fish—a designation which, spite of its unsatisfactory character, we may continue to use for want of a better—are at this period in good condition, more particularly if winter continues to have a firm grip upon the infant year. It sometimes, but of late rarely, happens that February is a tolerably pleasant month, and in that case general angling is prosecuted with the ardour which comes of knowing that the fence months are hurrying on apace. The coarse fish just now, however, must bide their time, and be content with swimming about in other chapters.

Besides, who would forgive the heretic who suggested a thought of the common herd, while the kings and princes of our watery realm were at hand? It is a moot point with many anglers whether salmon or trout fishing be the highest order of sport. For myself, I hold the salmon to be the king of fish, but trouting to be the choicest form of angling; in the word salmon, including all the migratory species, and by trouting meaning also fly-fishing for grayling. This predilection for the trout rod is a whim of my own, I am aware, in which few will probably give me countenance. At the same time, there are foolish folks of some experience on lake and river who take a like view, and I mention the matter here to justify the statement that the point with some is an open one. But there can be no question that salmon and trout between them represent the science, ethics, poetry, rhetoric (and all the rest) of the delicious sport of angling.

Had every salmon-fisher a record to show like some of those transcribed in the preceding chapter, he might sing everlasting anthems in praise of that phase of angling. We should then all be salmon fishers according to our opportunities. But it is weary work toiling through the day with one "fish" as a result, and as often as not with nothing to show for the pains. That day, in the first weeks of the season, will probably be cold and wet and blustering, and the play uncommonly like downright hard work. Still the big rod is plied, the long cast essayed upon every likely pool, the fly changed (changed too often by some men), and every tactic observed. The angler loves his work, and when it runs in the direction of salmon there are many special breezes that keep his zeal alive. A coterie of anglers lounging round the smoking-room fire after a day's fishing, betray in a very brief conversation why they will not stoop to any but salmon angling.

The things we do *not* know about a salmon, for instance, would make, if not a book, a pamphlet of decent dimensions. How the noble *salar* spends his time at sea, and his tastes in the item of food, if any, are discussed. Fishing men are never tired of propounding, as a sort of conundrum, the question, "Why do salmon take a fly?" And after long years echo answers, "Why?" Next comes the unpleasant subject of *Saprolegnia ferax*, and then the conversation surely drifts down to those lower proprietors who are, in their greed, ruining all the honest sport. But the talk is most animated when out-of-the-way theories are advanced about flies. All anglers who are worthy of the name have some fancy or other about tackle. Frequently it is a "fad" rather than a well-grounded fancy, and to this all fly-fishers are very prone. The salmon-fly, being not a fly, in the sense that a March brown or Alder is an imitation of a natural insect, admits only of limited debate. There remains still, however, for settlement, the matter of gaff *versus* net, and when all else fails, old battles have to be fought over again with mighty fish, and new laments uttered over that phenomenal salmon that sulked at the bottom of the pool, and sawed away against the ledge of rock until the gut parted.

The salmon angler in action should be a strong, patient man, knowing the water he works, and the tricks and natural propensities of the game he attacks. But the process does not, in any of its stages, require such delicate manipulation as the trout angler must exercise. When you begin to handle the 18-foot rod, and run the heavy eight-plaited line through the rings, and affix the strong gut cast, with its gaudy Parson or Jock Scott, it may dawn upon the beginner, who has been accustomed to brown trout angling only, that salmon fishing, though an art, is scarcely a fine art. The downward casts, and the rough jerking movement of the fly worked through the water, do not tend to remove this impression from the mind of the angler who has been used to difficult trout fishing. The impression, in many such instances, is never wholly removed, though the capture of a few heavy fish has a wonderful effect towards creating an enthusiasm that shall abide.

But there is a majesty in a salmon river that helps to put the sportsman on terms with himself. All is movement. Born in the snow-covered mountains, the streamlet has bounded from rock to rock, whitening into cascades, broadening out into foam-flecked pools, streaming abroad over shallows and scours, gathering force down the headlong rapids, sweeping, in mature river-like dimensions, under lofty crags, eddying past dark masses of wood, and anon gently lapping yellow strands, in whose tiny wavelets children may play. Some day will come the roar of the spate, and the dark-tinted waters which call the angler to be doubly on the alert, with by-and-bye, in the dog-days, low bright streams, when his highest skill is requisite for even a small modicum of success.

February brings the opening day upon rivers such as these, with varying chances in this capricious climate—tempest to-day, north-easters, with driving sleet, and snow, and dirty water, to-morrow; but who cares if, with the fight with the elements there come at last mortal tussles with clean-run fish, though, intermingled, be the profitless hooking of foul, hungry kelts, which, be they never so well mended, must be returned to gain convalescence in the sea? Upon the banks of the Thurso, Tweed and Teviot, Tay, Lyon and Tummel; by Spey, Dee, and Don; on the turbulent surface of Loch Tay, with the shoulders of the surrounding mountains kept warm by their white mantles, the Scotch anglers ply their rods in the second month of the year, while in Ireland the lure is simultaneously cast upon the Lee and Blackwater in County Cork, the Suir above Clonmel, the Moy and lakes at Ballina, the Ballynahinch pools, the streams and lakes of County Donegal, and all kindred salmon haunts.

The trout angler who stands up for the superiority of his favourite amusement must, spite of his prejudices, admit that the capture of a salmon, upon legitimate terms, is the most exciting of all feats of piscatorial prowess. Afar off, as he fishes fruitlessly down the river bank, strewed with smooth-washed boulders, he espies the movement of a fish; not the dainty rise that scarcely attracts observation, but a heavy roll over. He has been long looking for some such token; has honestly worked every inch of the water, from the falls to the rapids, and from the rapids to this darksome pool. He has tried short casts and long casts; has humoured the fly slowly, now on the top, now sunken, and has jerked it with energy; has tried all the flies approved and recommended, small and large, and to no avail. Here at last is his chance. But nothing less than 20 yards will bring him to that unmistakable fish.

Now let him pause awhile, and run his fingers down the cast to the fly, making sure that unawares to him the tackle has not been frayed by the trial it has already undergone. Let everything be done leisurely and in order. The salmon will not move far from where the angler saw him gambolling. What he has chiefly to do is to take things quietly. He must not bother himself—I am assuming that he is not an old hand at the salmon business—by recalling all the advice he has heard and read as to the regulation conduct at this supreme moment, nor allow his attendant to disturb him with *his* advice. Let him take his own course. He has to dispatch his fly so that it shall introduce itself to salmo's notice in a genteel and natural manner. That is best accomplished by coolness; and if, coolness or not, his faculties are not at this moment all alive, and his pulses on the spring, true angler he is not.

So! The fly sped its distance, and alighted fairly well across and below, and if the angler allows the eddy from the jutting granite to take it in charge, it will be brought into position without any manœuvring on his part. Swish! It was a goodly rise, but the eager fisherman was too quick for the fish. To my thinking, that quiet intense boil in the dark current is *the* moment in salmon angling. There is a fervour in the mingling of hope, fear, and resolve that may be felt but not described, and that is not likely to recur during any of the subsequent stages of the contest. In this instance the moment of fervour would be followed by a temporary paroxysm of despair, to which the angler should not give way. He should put down his rod, seat himself on the rock, and smoke a cigarette. After all, it may have been that the salmon was too quick, and not the angler; and the fish may rise again.

The next attempt is successful, after two or three unheeded casts, but the fish rose more quietly, the fly not being so much under water, and though the rise was visible, the salmon sucked in rather than snapped at the Blue Doctor. Instead, therefore, of a boil, the fish went down with a swirling splash, and relieved the angler of half the duty of striking. Now for a brief space, to a great extent, leave the salmon to his own devices, the line never slack, the rod top well up and well curved, the winch free to respond to any demand. Nothing better could have happened than this. The fish has run at steady pace down stream. Next it may sulk or leap, requiring the angler, in the latter event, to lower his rod-point, and in the former to attach to the line the little ring which opens for the purpose, and which will run down and smite the salmon on the snout. It will be astonished and angry, but will make tracks, and so the great end is gained. Dangerous as the movement is, I rather prefer the pleasure of seeing a good fish break water, and flash his silver sides in the air, though the risk be a broken line. I would rather have a dozen somersaults than a prolonged sulk below, with that ominous trembling which so often ends in the gut being sawn off against a sharp stone. But our fish now hooked does neither. It runs up and down the pool, and continually returns to the spot where it met disaster. Finally it goes swiftly down stream, whither the angler has the opportunity of following it, and in twenty minutes the young man in attendance goes in knee deep and nets it, as it is on the point of steering once more into the stream—a fifteen-pounder, in immaculate condition.

Lucky for the angler that the finish was on that wise. Fifty yards down, the water was broken and rock-studded, and the nature of the bank fatal to any further pursuit on land. Salmon-fishing is full of such narrow escapes, and fish are not always taken with such ease. The exertion and tension of nerve undergone by the angler will nevertheless explain the possibility of a gentleman meaning what he says when he declares that, after the strike, and the first run or two, he has lost interest in the business. We have all heard of the angler who invariably hands his rod to the gillie, should the salmon play longer than ten minutes; and of the worthy who, the fish escaping after a vigorous play of forty minutes, exclaimed, "Thank God, that's over."

Salmon, however, are taken by other means than the artificial fly. Quite legitimately in Tay and other Scotch lochs, and in the Irish lakes, the fish in the spring, beginning with February, are taken with the phantom, spoon, and other artificial baits, and by spinning with the natural bait from the boat. This is, in truth, the only remunerative fashion of fishing at this period in these waters, and there is not a whisper to be breathed against the custom. But there is something unpleasant in the notion of the King of Game-fishes being done to death by a nasty blackheaded worm. Sinking and drawing with shrimp, perhaps, seems less objectionable, and when the fly is useless, as it often is in the hands of the best of anglers, conscience will tolerate minnow and par-tail rather than an empty creel. I should not like to go so far as to affirm that worm fishers for salmon and trout were poachers, but if I ever brought myself to such a pass, I would not talk about it, and should consider myself entitled to rank with the person who shoots a pheasant sitting. The end may justify the means, but it is not to be gloried in.

In February the trout angler, also welcomes his opening day. In numbers he is in the proportion of a hundred to one as compared with him of whom we have been speaking. As yet it is not the custom to impose a licence upon trout fishing, and the tickets issued by the local associations are a wholesome check upon malpractices, and no hard tax upon the fisherman. He is probably not a gentleman of leisure, or independent means, and must snatch his sport between turns at the mill-wheel of daily occupation. Very keenly, therefore, he looks forward to the opening of the rivers, and has furbished up his casts, and overhauled his rod, taken apart and oiled his winch, and arranged his flies long before the joyous day. He may have taken a preliminary Sunday ramble up the stream of his affections to make a mental map of the campaign, and be assured that the familiar scours and stickles have not been altered by the winter floods. For it will only be a dweller in the vicinity who takes earliest advantage of the February fishing—the local enthusiast who is aware that the first comer will find the trout ramping hungry in the strong currents, and so stand a good chance of sport however adverse the weather may be.

In such a climate as ours it is of course altogether too soon to talk about spring in the short, bleak, wintry February days, but for the purposes of this book we must assume that the spring begins with the 1st of February, because on many streams the close season for trout finishes on that date. At that time there are no visible signs that the winter is past, and the angler who makes up his mind to go forth must be quite independent of those sentimental thoughts which are supposed to have so large a share in the fascinations of angling. The chances are very much, however, that at the beginning of February the rivers will be unfishable. Even if frost and snow are not abroad, the streams are likely at this time of the year to be charged with flood-water, and therefore out of the question for angling.

But it is a long-established custom in Devonshire, where Nature begins to throb and move earlier than in most other parts of the country, to take advantage of the earliest fishable day after the termination of the fence months. True, the trout are seldom in condition, and ought not to be taken until March, but this is not always the case, for I myself on a frosty day on the Ottery, during a little midday sunshine, have taken at Shrovetide, which then fell in the middle of February, a brace of half-pound trout which were in as good order as any fish I have ever seen. Of course I need not remind the reader that there is no rule without an exception, and this perhaps might have been the exception. At least I made it the ground of a practical decision, acted upon in response to a dubious expression on the face of the keeper, who evidently viewed my capture of two trout from the same milky-coloured stickle with displeasure. He spoke not, but his eye most assuredly was fastened upon the second fish as he took it out of the landing-net in the hope of finding signs and tokens whereby he might invite me to return it to the water. I saw his desire, and at once pronounced the fish to be in splendid condition, a verdict with which he was bound to coincide, though he did so not very graciously, as he slipped the fish through the hole in the cover of the creel.

On the whole, therefore, though it would be impossible to pass by the month of February, we may fairly assume that it is not a valuable month for the angler, except in so far that it gives him the opportunity of getting together his tackle, and wandering out by the river side to try a few preliminary casts; and I have often been surprised to find how many anglers on the opening day of the season, let the weather be what it may, have equipped themselves, and hied them to the river, although there was not the slightest chance of getting a fish. All this, if amusing, is typical of the enthusiasm of the angler in Great Britain, and probably everywhere else. He has been waiting for this day; he has been preparing his apparatus; he has been making up his mind that now he shall have amends for the inaction of the dreary winter days. His waterproof boots are in prime order; his creel is sweet and natty; his rod has an extra polish; there is no flaw in landing-net or handle; and altogether our early angler has a very spruce appearance, when, with his heart full of hope, he goes out for the first time in the year to look for a trout. His real season, nevertheless, is more likely to begin with March.

Of Devonshire I have previously said that it still holds a first place amongst the trout-fishing counties to which the ordinary angler has access. The trout, if small, are plentiful, and there is a beauty in the county itself, and a charm in the forwardness of vegetation that make Devon very popular among anglers. The streams of Dartmoor may be taken as typical of the kind of trout stream which may be more properly termed a brook. Dartmoor, in fact, like its fishing, is a thing of itself; a wonderfully interesting solitude both for the rambler and angler. When the March brown is in its prime—although that fly may not be the best for Devonshire, where the anglers pin their faith to Meavy red, and blue upright, and hackles of various kinds—is the time to make for Dartmoor. Starting from the quiet town of Tavistock, which lies in a hollow, with the bare Cornish hills on one side and the billowy moorland on the other, you travel up-hill to Princetown, passing on the way little streams across which a strong man might easily leap, and out of which many a dish of small trout will be taken. These silvery streamlets tumble down from ledge to ledge, coming from various directions, purling through rocky little glens crowned with mystic tors, and all bound eventually to the Channel. The trout on the heights of Dartmoor are so small that the angler for awhile is ashamed to take them—ashamed until he learns how delicious the fingerlings are as served up by the Devonshire cooks, more after the fashion of whitebait, than any member of the *Salmo* family. For a man sound of wind and limb, well shod, with a small basket at his back and a light fly rod in his hand, with no necessity for carrying a landing-net, or being burdened with wading stockings or boots, a day on Dartmoor, when the wind blows well from the west on a March or April day, is a real treat, provided he be content to make it, so far as the trout are concerned, a day of small things.

March is, upon general trout streams, the first month in which fly-fishing may be hankered after in real earnest. A tempestuous, rude month it may be, but the weather is generally for the greater portion hopeful; for though the cold strengthens with the lengthening of the days, and gales prevail, there are glimpses of sunshine, and intervals of warmth which betoken the reviving year. The flies dance into life under the grateful influence, and the trout are on the look out. Later in the year you will have to ring the changes upon your stock of flies, which is generally three times as large as it need be. In March you may ordinarily rely upon the ever useful March-brown, the Blue-dun, the Olive-dun, Red Spinner, and the Marlow buzz *alias* Coch-y-bondu. Even at Lady-day the aspect of the river-side and its surroundings is bare and wintry; but when you take a short cut through the plantation to avoid the dead water, and reach the long rippling piece that murmurs down from the bridge, you will trample upon primroses and violets, and the little celandine. And the birds seem to join in a special carol of welcome to the March angler, and wish him the good fortune which often falls to his lot.

In April do not discard the above-named flies, but add to them the Grannom, Yellow-dun, Hawthorn, and Sedge, and cleave to them so long as trout-fishing lasts. April has proved to me invariably the month of months for trout in England and Wales, and would, I can fain believe, have proved so in Scotland and Ireland had I been able to subject them to the same test. If trout have feelings, they must, like the observer of nature abroad in the fields at this season, feel that it is good to be alive. They come with such a will at your flies, fight so gamely to the very end, and look so handsome in their brilliant vesture, that you linger in admiration over them in the landing-net. One or two streams in private hands are reserved for Mayday, but as a rule the British trout streams from John o' Groat's to Land's End, and from Lough Foyle to Bantry Bay, are in the prime of trout fishing in April.

Whether up-stream or down-stream fishing be the correct thing; whether gossamer casts are profitable in the long run; whether one, two or three flies should be used; whether the Alexandra fly is orthodox—these are amongst the topics the assembled fishermen discuss as they sit around on the spot to which the frugal luncheon has been brought, under shelter of the golden-blossomed gorse, their rods spiked hard by, and the flies streaming out before the breeze. If there are more than two present there is not likely to be unanimity upon any of these points.

It is well for the tackle makers that new notions—heresies in the eyes of anglers of the last generation—are so freely promulgated. I know some successful fishermen who habitually fish down-stream, and who use medium gut for their casts. In very rapid water, free from weeds (the Derbyshire rivers, and Welsh streams, for example,) a third fly may be added to the stretcher and dropper, but, on the whole, little good comes of more than two flies on the cast. In trout water where the fish do not rise well at the usual flies the Alexandra is as much in place as a spun minnow, but it spoils the fish for the artificial fly pure and simple. Upon all these matters the angler must form his own judgments from experience, and then I fancy he will take a delight, when wading, in casting straight up-stream with a short line; will always, otherwise, aim at casting across and allowing the flies to drift down without worrying them as they swim ; and when a quick current, or impediments ashore leave no alternative, will do the best within his power, down-stream, underhand, or by that curious pitch which the angler learns to make with effect when he has an obstacle at his back. When he has achieved the art of throwing a fly without frightening away the fish he has conquered the primary difficulty.

April brings an opening day for the Thames trout-fisher. The Thames trout, by careful preservation and the introduction of new stock, have not for many years given so good an account of themselves as during the season of 1883, and even after its close on the 15th September, a provokingly large quantity took a fancy to the baits of barbel-fishers, who returned them, as in duty bound, to the river. Trouting on the Thames is, however, indulged in by the few rather than the many. Only the most patient men follow it through evil and good report. It makes an abnormal draft upon human faith ; it is a somewhat sedentary occupation, as followed by modern masters. Now and then this notable fish is taken with an artificial fly, but fly-fishing is seldom practised by the regular Thames trout angler. You will find this worthy mostly perched above the head of one of the weirs, of which Boveney is a more than average sample, spinning a bleak in the streams and rough water under his feet, not, however, if he understand his business, leaving the bait to work its own restless will, and fruitlessly revolve on the top of the foam, but cleverly humouring it right and left, in eddies, down the current, and so making it dart and move that its action is calculated to deceive the very elect amongst Thames trout, the most knowing perhaps of any of the *Fario* family.

Spinning for Thames trout, whether from weir or boat,

is work for none but accomplished artists, and there are upon the river a few renowned specialists who day by day, and week by week, pursue their sport with untiring devotion, though a fish or two per week throughout the season would be considered very excellent sport. The Thames trout, however, is a gallant battler when once he feels the little triangles in his palate. While the rush lasts he outdoes even the salmon in his fierce charges and desperate tactics, so that, if he be discovered but rarely, when he does make a grave error he is a foeman worthy of the best steel ever fashioned into a fish-hook.

The game goes on until the 15th September, but the bloom is taken off the sport in a couple of months from the opening day. Every weir is spun persistently, and every weir, perhaps, if it could reveal its secrets, would testify to fish that had broken away, been pricked, or otherwise put upon their guard. Thus the trout, already cunning, get exceedingly wary, and hard to catch. Once upon a time the Thames anglers never dreamt of looking for trout in other than weirpools and rough, swift water, but modern men have found out that in reaches of the river where their presence was never suspected, an occasional lusty patriarch, retired from the noise and perpetual motion of lasher and weir, has taken up a quiet haunt; and as, in his more lively foraging expeditions, he is certain, sooner or later, to let his whereabouts be known—since the Thames is not hid in a corner—the process of live-baiting is applied to him, and not infrequently with fatal results.

CHAPTER III.

SUMMER.

SUMMER angling brings out new and more miscellaneous forces than heretofore to promote designs upon our freshwater fishes, and the English ladies are taking very kindly both to fly-fishing and general fishing. May they never be persuaded into pleading their sex as an excuse for establising unsportsmanlike practices against salmon and trout? Fly rods are made so daintily now, and casting a fly is really so easy, when once the knack is acquired of permitting the rod to do the major part of the work, that want of strength is no plea. And there is a still better argument. Not even the harp or the violin, nor the lawn-tennis racket, shows off the female figure to such positive advantage as the graceful manipulation of the fly-rod. In the summer evenings, therefore, when there is a saunter through the hay-field to the river and its forget-me-nots, listen not to the assurances of the youth (who knows better) that when ladies fish for the speckled beauties of the stream any bait may be used. He may be deprived of that coveted chance of impaling the worms for the fair fisherwoman, but his conscience will be at peace if he recommend and teach her the use of the fly.

The Mundella Act sets loose the fishing-punts on the 15th of June, when we may reasonably assume that summer smiles upon the land. On Thames, and such inland waters as come under the operations of the measure, the anglers swarm to renew their acquaintance with roach, dace, barbel, chub, perch, and (sad to add) with pike. Throughout the summer angling is made the occasion of happy water picnics. Hot bright days will mostly find all but the surface-feeding fish ensconced within the cool shady arbours of their subaqueous abodes, and morning and evening are the anglers' likeliest times for sport. The carp, however,—rarest of objects in the fisherman's basket—loves the blazing summer weather, and on intervening cloudy days may be hooked unawares. The long days are welcome to the angler on account of the spells of calm evening fishing afforded ; and a traveller rushing through the kingdom by any of the main lines of railway will be able to observe how universally popular is the amusement. By river, lake, canal, pond, clay-pit, and ditch, coming within ken of his carriage window, he will behold its persevering followers.

In the pond out of which the horses come to slake their thirst after the day's team-work is over, the schoolboy, having got through, at scampering pace, to-morrow's lessons, is allowed to make his first essays in angling ; and perhaps to the majority of us those juvenile snatches of fishing, with tackle of the most primitive kind, live longest in the memory, not only because of the singular passion for the sport which takes root in the boyish mind never to be eradicated, but because of the wonderful luck which proverbially falls to the neophyte's share. How often does it happen that the expert fisherman, with his delicate silk line and drawn gut links, with his carefully chosen baits, and working with all the wisdom of mature experience, has the mortification of seeing some untutored rustic walking away with a string of fish, while his basket remains untenanted ! And in some of those out-of-the-way ponds in rural England—ponds that have held fish from time immemorial—there is rare sport to be obtained on summer evenings with the mud-loving tench and the undaunted perch, descendants, may be, of the same fish which the Puritan lads caught in the days before their father's farm was drenched with the blood of Cavalier and Roundhead. On warm muggy days when all creation seems to sweat, and there is thunder in the air, that singular fish, the tench, bites well, and the largest and most plentiful of them are to be found in the most ancient of park lakes and monastic ponds. The sport is not particularly exciting, but it requires to be conducted with great care on account of the shyness of the fish. Different is it with the pond perch, which is a great encouragement to the youthful angler by the reckless readiness with which it will, in its hungry moments, assist him in imbibing a lifelong taste for the pastime.

In the vicinity of large towns the angler sits by the water side breathing at least fresh air, and surrounded by sights calculated to make him forget the petty cares of life, or the sordid belongings of a lot of poverty. He is content with even the smallest result in the way of sport. That sport is not of an extensive kind, nor of a high class, but he enjoys it, and appreciates his little show of roach or dace, or barbel, as much as the man of means appreciates his trout or salmon.

Summer time is also the period when that very remarkable collection of fresh-water lakes known as the broads of East Anglia are laid under contribution by anglers and cruisers. These broads have a character of their own in the angling of Great Britain, teeming as they do with bream and other coarse fish. It is no uncommon thing in a cruise up the waters from Lowestoft and Yarmouth, or from Wroxham Bridge, which is the starting-point for the upper broads, to pass hundreds of boats, each filled with its earnest angling party.

There are in these waters roach and perch and pike, bream and rudd, in untold quantities, but the reed thickets surrounding them are so dense that the pike are not generally enticed out of them until the winter, when the other kinds have retired to the deeps. The bream are so numerous that they are reckoned by the stone rather than by the brace or dozen, and although they are not highly-esteemed for table purposes after they are caught, they furnish a good deal of fun in the catching. This operation is somewhat disagreeable to a fastidious person. The angler provides himself with a huge bucket containing a sloppy mixture of grains and meal, and he protects himself from stray *débris* by wearing a white apron. This compound is thrown broadcast into a particular pitch—it should be done overnight—and the bream collect in herds around it. The hook is baited with a worm or with gentles, and the fish, when they are fairly on the feed, bite without cessation until the store net, which the East Anglian angler keeps suspended over the side of the punt, is full of large broad-sided, bronze-coloured bream, averaging 3 or 4 lbs.

These broads are also a favourite hunting-ground of the rudd, a fish often confounded with the roach. It is confined to a comparatively few localities, and there is no mistaking its lovely golden jacket and carmine fins and irides. Though commonly angled for on the same principle as roach, it will rise very freely at a fly in hot weather. In the quiet evenings, after the sun is down, I have moored my rude boat to the reeds that border one of these meres, and whipped out two half-pound rudd at a time, as fast as I could introduce to the shoal my small black gnat or red palmer, with a gentle on the tip of the hook. You could see the whole shoal rising at the small insects that were humming in the summer air.

Here a man is out of the noise and turmoil of the world. For leagues the eye roams over the tranquil waters, or upon the flat peculiar country converted by the slow running rivers, abundant windmills, and far-reaching broads, into a very Dutch-like kind of scenery. Nothing breaks the silence but the plunge of big fish amongst the reeds, or the constant passage of water-fowl, for which the region is as celebrated as for its coarse fish. When the gentlemen of Norfolk kindly invited the foreign commissioners at the International Fisheries Exhibition to go and inspect this region, Mr. Wilmot of the Canadian Court, and Professor Brown Goode of the United States Commission, expressed an opinion that the waters were very suitable for the introduction of the black bass. This fish has already been acclimatised by the Marquis of Exeter, and from its game qualities, its freedom in rising at a fly, or taking a spinning bait, it would be a very welcome addition to our fresh-water fishes, and would take an intermediate position between the pike and the perch, and the members of the Salmonidæ family. And it would be easy to confine the black bass to waters where it would not destroy more valuable species. Whether the gentlemen who have formed themselves into a society to protect the fisheries of these broads will entertain such an idea, or whether they will act upon a more recent suggestion and attempt the introduction of salmon, remains to be seen. The broads, at any rate, cannot be omitted from a description of our angling waters; they are visited every summer by thousands of anglers from various parts of the country, and are well worth visiting.

According to the terms of the Mundella Act, as I have stated, the Thames fisherman has his opening day on the 15th June, although it is much too soon to angle for pike. The other fish, if not in fair condition, are rapidly arriving at that stage, and from this date the professional fisherman hopes to have his regular customers, and each favourite station of the Thames will have its periodical visits from anglers. The efforts of the Thames Angling Preservation Society have undoubtedly been crowned with success, for the stock of fish has been improving year by year, and, as a passing reference in the previous chapter shows, the angling of the present season has been in all parts satisfactory. The Thames anglers are somewhat of a school to themselves, and, moreover, a very numerous class. They have a variety of fishing at their disposal. Roach and dace are plentiful everywhere from Kew to the source. Barbel are taken at certain stations in bulk. Pike too and perch are equally distributed along the whole length of the beautiful river, and the fly-fisher has plenty of room for the exercise of his abilities with chub and dace.

Fly-fishing for chub answers best in the hot summer months—say July and August; and along the willow and alder lined reaches, at odd times payable sport is obtained. It is a great boon after all for the man in the big city pent to be able to get away from business, and by an afternoon train arrive at any portion of the Thames below Oxford in time to have three or four of the best hours' fly-fishing which the day affords. The chub is not fastidious in its choice of flies. So long as the lure is large and hairy; so long as it bears some passing resemblance to a caterpillar or beetle, or large-winged moth, the angler's chances of big fish are good. The chub, however, is an easily scared fish, and it is a primary essential that the whipper shall keep out of sight.

The breadth of such rivers as the Thames at Moulsford,

or Ouse below St. Ives, and the out-of-the-way places in which the chub loves to lie, render the use of a boat imperative. In this the angler stations himself in the stern, his boatmen allowing the craft to drift slowly with the stream ten or twelve yards abreast of the overhanging branches, under which he knows the fish are lying. Let the fly touch the leaves, and then make believe to tumble accidentally into the water. There will be a straight rush made by the chub (which is not at all insulted in the old-fashioned appellation of logger-headed); he will take your fly at a gulp under water without the ceremony of a rise; and the leathery formation of the mouth makes the chances of escape very poor for the fish. The chub has no character for pluck, since after one pretty strong run by way of protest, it ceases to fight, and may be hauled into the landing-net without much trouble or the employment of any art on the part of the angler. I have known gentlemen in the course of a few hours' fishing in this manner take their 20 and 30 lbs. of chub, ranging from 2 to 4 lbs. In the Upper Verniew in the month of April three years ago, at one stand, fishing for trout with a small March brown, I took 18 chub of about a pound each. If they had weighed not more than a pennyweight I would have killed them in any trout water.

Trout-fishing I have dealt with in one or two phases in the chapter on spring. It need scarcely, however, be explained that this fish is the fly-fisher's idol during the entire summer. But the carnival of trout anglers may be said to occur when the May-fly is up. This anxiously looked for event generally happens early in June, and while it lasts the sport is indeed fast and furious. On preserved club waters, like the Hungerford water of the Kennet, and on the choice preserves of Hampshire, and other parts of the West of England, the sportsmen turn out with one consent to take advantage of the seven devils of gluttony which seem to enter into the strong-minded trout.

It is a glorious time of the year in which to be abroad on such a quest. The honey-suckle is opening its buds in the leafy lanes, the satin blossoms of the bramble are put forth, the rich meadows are ready for the haymakers, the foliage of the woods is developed upon nearly all our English trees, the wild flowers are spangling field and hedgerow in their glory, and the cuckoo, making the most of the little time that is left for song, "Tells his name to all the hills."

But I should say that at no season of the year has the sentimental angler less time than now to indulge in rhapsodies, for when the green and grey drake are what is technically termed "up," sport will demand all his attention. Lucky he if it make him not a butcher. There was a deal of human nature in that eminent divine who, upon being asked by his friend the bishop when an important work upon which he was engaged would be finished, replied—"My lord, I shall work steadily at it when the fly-fishing season is over." Such a reference, we may be permitted to believe, could only have been prompted by an unusually exuberant "great rise" in the May-fly season.

And no one has in pithier words described the peculiarities of this festival than Charles Kingsley, who, in his 'Chalk Stream Studies,' says :—" For is not the green drake on? And while he reigns, all hours, meals, decencies, and respectabilities must yield to his caprice. See here he sits, or rather tens of thousands of him, one on each stalk of grass, green drake, yellow drake, brown drake, white drake, each with his gauzy wings folded over his back, waiting for some unknown change of temperature or something else, in the afternoon, to wake him from his sleep, and send him fluttering over the stream ; while overhead the black drake, who has changed his skin and reproduced his species, dances in the sunshine, empty, hard, and happy, like Festus Bailey's great black crow, who

> 'All his life sings ho ! ho ! ho !
> For no one will eat him he well doth know.'"

The peculiarities of May-fly fishing are so well known, that there would be no excuse for pausing longer upon the subject. Bungling indeed must be the angler who cannot during this space of ten or twelve days catch fish, and the barefacedness with which, under favourable circumstances, the trick is done, rather leads one to regret that on any English stream the custom still prevails of fishing for trout with a living instead of artificial May-fly. The angler who cannot score with one of the perfect imitations now turned out, ought not to have a second chance.

It is different in the celebrated lakes of West Meath, where the big fish are not readily taken by the artificial fly, and where it has been an immemorial custom to use the impaled live insect with the blow line. Upon these lakes, for which Mullingar, some forty miles from Dublin, might be made convenient headquarters, the green drake comes up in myriads. The brown trout which the waters contain are in takeable condition as early as March, and are to be enticed with some of the common artificial flies used in the spring months. The most knowing fishermen in the drake season use two hooks tied back to back, and two flies so arranged that the head of one shall lie next to the tail of the other. The surface of the lakes, amongst which I may mention Ennel, or Belvidere, Owel, and Lough Ree (through which the Shannon runs), is agitated all over with the rising of fish that are seldom less than two pounds, and that run even to the maximum size of six and seven pounds. The boat is rowed up against the wind, and allowed to drift back broadside on.

The angler uplifts his moderately stiff rod, to which is attached the line of floss silk, very flimsy in appearance, but in reality strong enough for all necessary purposes. This the wind takes out, and the art is to allow the flies to dance upon the surface of the water as if a fancy-free insect were sailing along, tacking here and there with outspread wings, as is its pretty custom. It, however, requires a little experience to get into the way of striking the fish with a line which is naturally considerably bellied out at the time the bait is taken; but practice here, as in other things, soon makes perfect, and astonishing bags of trout are made.

This blow line fishing might in the summer be used with advantage to a greater extent than it is at present in English waters. In the Lea I have seen masterful baskets of roach, chub, and dace, acquired by this device; the hook attached to the blow-line in such cases, however, being very small, and the insect a house fly, or some other creature of no more formidable size and character. Roach will occasionally, I may mention in passing, take the artificial fly, especially when to it is appended the luscious gentle; but this only happens in the very hottest weather, when the fish are lazy on the shallows. But the blow-line invariably agitates, and often catches them.

On the disappearance of the May-fly the trout become demoralized. They have gorged to their heart's content, and probably a little more, for their voracity during the term (it is commemoration term with the angler) in which the fly is up is such that you often take the fish crammed with them, and with a little bunch of flies waiting at the threshold of the gullet for a favourable opportunity of being absorbed into the stomach. I have seen a May-fly crawl out of the half-opened mouth of a trout in my basket.

It is not to be wondered at that after this debauchery a certain supineness intervenes, and that the trout lie about in a depressed state of mind, such as should always follow immoderation of appetite. Upon some rivers, indeed, the pick of the trout fishing is over after the May-fly time, while in others, as in the Gloucestershire Coln, the really best fishing does not begin until the trout have recovered from their periodical feast. As the summer advances the trout fisher enters into another phase of his artistic sport, perhaps the most delicate of all. The rivers run low, the weeds form thickets and forests in the streams. The trout, much whipped over during the preceding three or four months, have become disagreeably artful, and if they are to be caught at all they must be caught by guile.

Guile in this particular instance takes the shape of what is termed fishing with a dry fly. Of late years the tacklemakers have arrived at the perfection of art in manufacturing what should be to the fish the most ravishing of artificial flies, whose upstanding wings materially assist the angler in this very artful angling operation. At the same time, I ask permission to believe that trout fishermen are apt to ride the dry fly notion to death. When once some of us get into the habit of using the dry fly, and wax proud of our ability, we become wedded to the method, and in season and out of season adhere to it. At times it is unquestionably absolutely necessary to use the dry fly, for the best of all reasons—the fish will look at no other. But I have frequently seen experienced anglers persevere with their floating fancies, yet do nothing, when other persons who were allowing their flies to sink and swim in the usual way down the stream were rewarded with trout.

It is always useful, nevertheless, to have your supply of dry flies at hand, and in case of non-success in the other method, to put them up. But, I repeat, too much is oftentimes made of the dry-fly theory. Perhaps this is because of a consciousness on the part of the angler that it requires the acme of skill to be successful with it. Perhaps, also, it may be partly accounted for by the said angler being used to waters where dry-fly fishing in the later months of the summer is a *sine quâ non*.

There are no more skilful trout anglers than those accustomed to the streams which flow tranquilly through the fat Hampshire meadows. The rivers contain beautiful fish, but they are extremely difficult to take, and the Hampshireman is quite justified in his boast that the angler who can kill in Itchen or Test need not be ashamed to exhibit his prowess anywhere. It requires a good deal of experience to learn how, after whipping the fly four or five times through the air, to secure the requisite dryness, to dispatch it across underneath the further bank, and make it alight so that it shall float some distance down the stream without being checked by the line.

The situation necessarily involves a certain slackness of line, and with the fine tackle that must be used, the extra skill, of which I have just spoken, must be extended to the striking, else a long farewell to fly and fish. There is no doubt that a large percentage of trout hooked in dry-fly fishing by defect at this crisis get away. I know of no more pleasant form of angling for trout on a fine summer's evening, when a mere zephyr skims over the water, when the swallows are hawking low upon it, and the voice of the corncrake is heard in the uplands, than to kneel warily amongst the flowering comfrey, meadow sweet, willow herb, and loosestrife, and mark a rising trout close under the rank sedges fringing yonder bank. The artificial sedge fly, with its artistic ribbing, though not made expressly to float, is capital for dry-fly fishing, and all things being favourable there is no more telling way of adding to the contents of your basket than by finishing up a day's fishing in laying siege to that fish till he capitulates.

Then in August the red and black ant come in, and all through the summer three specific flies should never be out of the angler's book, to wit the Wickham, Hoflands, and the Francis Francis Fancies. During the past season I was introduced by my friend Mr. Marston to a new fly, new at least to me, the wings of which are made of pike scales. It is manufactured by McNee of Pitlochrie, and I have found it answer, and seen it answer, when the trout allowed every other kind of fly to pass by unheeded. The theory is that the pike scale, when it becomes wet, has the unctuous appearance of a gelatinous wing, and it may be so. At any rate, on streams as opposite in their character as the Chatsworth Derwent, the Little Stour in Kent, and the Lambourne in Berkshire, I have reason to be thankful that this addition to our list of flies was made known to me. It is certainly worth a trial.

Loch fishing is a fashionable and essential item of the general summer programme, and on Loch Leven the club competitions for which the lake is celebrated are decided. It is truly astonishing that the trout in this lake show no signs of diminution, for although careful restocking is attended to, there is no more thoroughly thrashed water in Scotland; and amongst the gentlemen who make such pleasant parties in the boats you generally find one who has never handled rod before, and whose flies do *not* fall like the traditional thistledown upon the water. Yet the sport, if not what it was when an angler was disgusted if he came ashore at Kinross without his twenty or thirty pounds of fish, is maintained above an ordinary level. In the year before last, I can recall one day in May, when seventeen boats were on the lake—a full complement. The wind and water were favourable, and the boats finished in the evening with 212 trout, weighing 213 lbs. The Loch Leven trout always seem to average one pound; and as I have watched anglers from Edinburgh, Dundee, Glasgow, Stirling, Perth, Kirkcaldy, and Dunfermline, I have often thought that their tackle is unnecessarily coarse. No doubt they know their own business best. They get fine sport certainly.

Different from Leven are the lochs away in the unbeaten districts of the Highlands. There is the small lake swarming with yellow trout of three to the pound (game little fellows to angle for on a summer day), and there is the larger loch in which the pike keep down the small fish, so that the angler will get none under two pounds. The brown trout attain a heavy size—five, six, and seven pounds—in these waters, and, unlike the *ferox*, they will take a large fly with gusto. Spinning with a phantom minnow of medium size, when the natural bait cannot be procured, is useful for all these large trout, and for salmon. In the streams the summer warrants the use of Stewart's tackle, a most telling method, which one may almost describe as fly-fishing with worm. I have seen it applied by southerners in southern waters with surprising results in perch and chub fishing.

CHAPTER IV.

AUTUMN.

THERE is a charm in the English autumn to which the angler ought to be peculiarly sensible. The late coming salmon and sea-trout fishing, wind and weather permitting, is the best of the year, since it is not, in the natural order of things, interfered with by the turbulent floods which follow the melting of the snow, nor reduced by the netters, nor ruined by the low, bright waters of the summer weeks Autumn is more often reliable, I have noticed, as to weather than other seasons, though there was a miserable exception to the rule in 1882. When the elements are favourable, the water is in excellent condition for the Scotch, Irish, English and Welsh streams visited by the migratory salmon.

The days, which rapidly close in long before the swallows depart or the leaves fall, are all too short, however, for such out-of-door sports as angling, because the fish have now no inclination to move freely until the forenoon is well advanced. Against this drawback must be written the exquisite tints of the trees, and the bracing air, in which the more active exercises of angling may be conducted in comfort. For spinning or trolling, for wielding the big greenheart, the double-handed hickory, or the split cane single-hander, there are no better months than September and October; and as to landscape, I am one of those who love spring, revel in summer, but adore autumn, with its corn and wine and oil, its golden plenty emphasised by a framework of gentle decay.

The salmon fisher has seen the brown hills brighten with green, and blaze into the regal purple of the heather, and now the rowan tree hangs out its scarlet lamps, and the firs assume a deeper hue. The trout fisher in the bright May days was gladdened by the fragrant hawthorn, and noticed how strong the briony clasped the hedgerow. He saw the blossoms of the wild guelder rose shaken to earth by the lightest summer shower, and the true wild rose in full bearing. Their berries now gleam black and red, those of the guelder rose clustered like drops of blood, while its leaves are veined with every colour of the rainbow. The village children, who months back stood shyly by to watch the landing of the two-pounder that had taken the Red Spinner in the smooth stream above the ford, had sprigs of immature travellers' joy round their hats, and their hands were full of cowslip, ragged robbin, and lady smocks. Their faces are smeared with blackberry stain, and their pinafores turned into receptacles for hazel nuts, as they wonder why, on that late September evening, you cast your fly so many times through the air before allowing it to touch the water. The punt fisher moored in the Thames above Maidenhead, has, in Bisham, and incomparable Cliveden, a mixture of colours upon the densely wooded hillsides such as mortal hand could never compound.

The sea-trout fisher is in his glory in the autumn. That last run up of the fish is generally the briskest, and the sea-trout angler has therefore the privilege of leaving off for the season without the consciousness that it was convenient to make a virtue of necessity. So long as the *Salmo trutta* is in the river, you do not wear out your welcome. This fish gives super-excellent sport. Your equipment is heavier than that used for brown trout, and lighter than salmon gear. A well-balanced double-handed rod that will answer also for grilse is the weapon, and there is no need whatever for the coarse gut footline which in both Scotland and Ireland the native anglers deem essential. The gut must be of the purest quality, but medium size is ample. The difficulty here is to obtain flies that are tied upon gut to correspond, and this is a difficulty which causes annoyance to all classes of anglers. It is a forcible argument in favour of the new fashion of eyed flies for every description of fly fishing. The sea-trout is found in most salmon rivers, of course, and in the lakes, but his chief recommendation to me is that he runs up small streams, which but for him would never be visited by any of the silvery visitors.

There is in my mind's eye at the present a narrow river, if I may so term it, which has no name upon the map. Within a hundred yards of the sea I could leap across it in two places. You can reach its infant stage by tramping a couple of miles up the moor through a heathery bog, and follow it down through, at first, a series of rough, rocky leaps, next through a sequestered glen, and finally through a descending mile of turning and twisting. This streamlet, up to the heaped-up rocklets, is a succession of pools and streams, alternating with perfectly dull water. In the autumn the sea-trout swarm in every one of them, though they do not reach the maximum size. In the next river on the same coast, and not twenty miles distant, five-pound fish are not rare, but in my nameless stream you create a sensation at the village post-office—which is the Rialto of that Highland community—if you kill one of three pounds. Two pounds seems to be an average, and may I never

An English grayling of about 1½ lbs. weight is as handsome in his own peculiar style of beauty as the trout, for if he lack the crimson spots and golden burnishment, he has a fine admixture of blue and silver, while his shape is faultless.

There is another kind of fly-fishing to be followed during September and October, of which I for one am extremely fond, albeit it has a somewhat unpretentious object, being directed to nothing more important than the common dace. The dace is really one of our surface feeders. He may be found during the winter time in deep water, keeping company with the roach, and he congregates in force in deep mill-tails and weir-pools, where he will take the small red worm or the gentle with very much the boldness of the perch. In Autumn, however, the dace still lingers upon the shallows, and rises well at almost any small fly. Take two examples of dace-fishing in the autumn. The first was in the Thames, above Richmond Bridge. All the shallows, from Twickenham downwards, have a well deserved repute for fly-fishing for dace, and the Thames-side urchins, with willow-wands, lengths of whipcord, and anything in the shape of a fly which they can beg or borrow, make nice little strings of fish, running to about seven or eight inches in length. A sunshiny day, with a soft ripple, is the best for this sport, and one might pass away four or five hours in worse amusement than wading into the Thames opposite Ham Lane, and whipping down upon the shallows with the fancy black and red flies manufactured for the purpose, their speciality being tiny strips of washleather, in place of tail. There is a continual procession of pleasure-boats up this gay reach of the Thames, and the familiar features of Richmond Hill are an elevated background to the picture which the downward moving angler looks upon. It is useless fishing for dace in the Thames, except at particular times of the tide, and the regular plan is to begin when the tide is at half-ebb, and leave off when the flood makes. A working-man angler, who was standing a few yards above me, on the last occasion I indulged in this amusement, whipped out, with very indifferent tackle, his four dozen of fish, and I myself, had something over three dozen of the silvery little fellows in my basket.

A seven-inch, however, or even a nine-inch dace (and you will seldom get larger specimens while fly-fishing on the Thames shallows) is very indifferent game as compared with the really good-looking and gamesome fish of the same species which are to be had in the Colne and in the Lea. On the second occasion to which I have referred, I was taken by a gentleman to a choice club water on the Lea, between Hertford and Ware. A mill pool was pointed out to me as full of dace. The mill was silent, and there was no stream from the pool; but a light breeze tickled its surface, and the sun was shining in a cloudless sky. The sides of the mill pool were solid masonry, and the pool terminated in a somewhat sudden shelf. The stream thenceforward, for some hundred yards, was of the shallowest description. One does not often get the opportunity of fly-fishing from a seat, but I was in an indolent humour on this particular morning, and sat me down on the edge of the wall, with my feet dangling over the stream, some 10 yards below the tail of the pool. The fish, for an hour or so, were perfectly ravenous, and gave me much entertainment. There were very few dace under $\frac{1}{2}$ lb., and fat lively white fellows of that kind upon a drawn-gut cast, and with the smallest trout-rod that is made, will treat you to no indifferent sport. Within a short space of time I contrived to get from the pool, or from the two-inch shallows down stream, nine and a half brace of specimen dace, which, with the addition of a few others contributed by my friend, made the total weight nearly 10 lbs.

We have glanced at the grand salmon rivers and the swift trout streams, and at the more sluggish rivers by which the general angler watches his travelling float, or keeps the tightened leger line well in hand. Lakes and ponds, amidst the "tall ancestral trees" of country domains, have not been forgotten. But autumn reminds me of yet another haunt of the English angler. It is the millpool, within the upper wall of which the waterwheel drippingly revolves, grinding the corn of the miller and his men. Not less dear to the angler than the poet and artist is the English mill. Above the mill head there is often a quiet reach, permanently tenanted by pike and perch.

From the pool miscellaneous bags are extracted. The live bait works on its own accord on the other side under the graceful willows, while the angler, with his ordinary rod, line, and float, angles promiscuously. Out of such a millpool I have seen, lying in one heap upon the grass behind some old woodwork upon which the angler sat, a representative sample of many British fresh-water fishes, and as they were caught on an October day, they were all, with one exception, in their healthiest hues and forms. The heap comprised a 7 lb. pike, four or five burly perch, a brown and a white bream, several roach and dace, one gudgeon, four minnows, and a small barbel. The exception indicated was an indiscreet trout, which had taken a gudgeon on the live-bait apparatus, and since the hook used was the gorge affair that is threddled under the skin of the side, the case was hopeless, and the kindly miller, on being appealed to, decided that the fish should not be returned to die a painful death.

The autumnal general-fishing of the rivers produces, as a rule, larger fish than are taken in the summer. The weeds soon begin to rot after Michaelmas, and most of the coarse fish betake themselves, without more ado, to their winter quarters in the deeps. The prettiest hour's roach fishing I ever saw was on a September evening, on returning from whipping a ford where the large dace were in the habit of congregating. Above one of those small noisy weirs which are laid across our lesser rivers, there meandered through the meadow some 200 yards of even current, still but deep. There were three rustic seats stationed upon the bank, for the convenience of the members of the club who rented the fishery. Upon one of these sat a veteran angler, who had had his share of the more energetic descriptions of sport for half a century, and who was now content with the tranquil amusement of roach fishing. He thoroughly understood the art, and would have deemed that the roach were insulted if angled for with other than a tight hair line and a long bamboo rod. His process was troublesome, but remunerative. At every swim he enveloped his paste bait with a thin wrapping of the bran composition with which he had been ground-baiting, and it was a liberal education to watch his fortunes. The float, shotted down to a quarter of an inch of the surface, to my eye indicated no bite, but invariably, when the end of the swim had been reached, within a foot or so, my good friend was somehow playing a fish, following it hither and thither under the point of his rod. The 20-foot bamboo was unshipped after the orthodox Lea style, reducing its length, and the angler netted his fish without a splash or alarming movement.

The essence of roach fishing, under these circumstances, is to be quiet, and so well did this successful angler comply with the requirement, that a pretty brown water-rat opposite went on diving for, and returning to land with, some kind of ribbon weed, and audibly munching it on the balcony of his sandy abode in the bank. In less than three-quarters of an hour I witnessed, by this clever tight-line fishing, the taking of ten roach, of which the largest was nearly a pound and a half, and the smallest three-quarters of a pound. I enjoyed the watching, I am sure, as much as the veteran enjoyed the catching. As an illustration of the precarious nature of roach fishing, it is incumbent upon me to add that the whole of the morning and afternoon, to that evening hour when the mellow sun was setting over the church spire and its adjacent rookery, had yielded only half-a-dozen small fish.

CHAPTER V.

WINTER.

WHEN the salmon, by legislative enactment, are hunted no more by net or by rod, but are allowed to perform their spawning operations in peace and security; when the trout are also left undisturbed, to increase and multiply, and get into condition by the time that spring returns again, there is still a good deal worth having left for the English angler. Fair-weather fishermen will put away their rods and console themselves during the short winter days, and long winter nights, by their firesides; but there will be in town and country a decided majority of enthusiastic English anglers, who will brave the frost, snow, rain, and fog, and never abandon, until compelled to do so, their raids upon the fish that are in season.

As in treating of the Salmonidæ I have placed the *Salmo salar* at the head of the list, so in a concluding chapter upon winter angling, I cannot do less than give prominence to the pike.

The humanitarian question of angling, I may confess, without apology, never troubles me, and there will be time enough to meet it and deal with it, or shirk it, when, should the Pigeon Shooting Bill become law, consequential attempts are made to interfere in other directions. During the debate in Parliament upon that remarkable measure, it may be remembered that references were made to the pastime of angling. Until actually forced to defend themselves, I should recommend anglers to hold their tongues upon the subject. It is very plausible to argue, as many do, that it is vouchsafed to fishes to enjoy a minimum of pain; and there are some who are so convinced of this great gift to the finny race, that they have at last apparently persuaded themselves that fish rather like the sensation of being hooked and played than otherwise. It may be so. With regard to the pike I do not, however, hesitate to declare that I have no bowels of mercy for him. Last year I read a singularly interesting book by a lady, who described her travels by fell and fiord in Iceland. The authoress was a confessed fly-fisherwoman, and she, as might be expected from one of the tender-hearted sex, seemed to be a little troubled in mind upon the question of cruelty. One argument of hers struck me as being so apposite, that I entered it in my note-book, and, in beginning this chapter, which is virtually one upon pike fishing, I will take the liberty to quote it :—

"Fish are outside our circle altogether, and we may have the further satisfaction of thinking that though they seem to live particularly careless, jolly lives, they all end in being eaten, either by us or by each other, unless they meet with great ill-luck, such as chemical waste in rivers, and are poisoned. Now, for every big fish we kill, and it is these we aim at, a number of merry little fishes have longer lives; so we anglers are really benevolent institutions from a purely fishy point of view. Real fish, too, as distinguished from whales and seals, have no attachment to each other—they are only rivals. Witness the fighting for bait in a shoal; witness the withered old carp wrestling with each other in ancient palace waters. Therefore, in catching a fish you make no home desolate, you bereave no fond creature of a friend. Cool, calm, and selfish, the fish goes on his glittering way like a regular man of the world; he misses nobody out of his water home, and, when he ends an easy life by an easy death, nobody misses him."

The character of the fresh-water shark is especially exemplified in the closing sentence of the extract, and the authoress might have gone further and described *Esox lucius* as a systematic and professional marauder. He respects not his own kith and kin; he prowls up and down, seeking what he may devour; and he has no claim upon our consideration except as a furnisher of sport. There are few waters that are exclusively devoted to the breeding and preservation of pike, and, in the majority of rivers and lakes with which I am acquainted, where they are to be found, keeping down these creatures is a general good.

Spinning is in pike-fishing what the use of the artificial fly is with salmon, trout, and grayling; it is the most artistic branch of the sport. Pike fishers in one respect resemble their brethren of the salmon rod, for they are continually inventing new fancies, laying down new theories, trying new experiments, and dogmatising upon them all with a profundity of faith that in these sceptical days is most refreshing to witness. Artificial baits have been invented without end, and for each and all there is something to be said. I shall not venture to discuss them, but I may remark in passing, that artificial baits, from the oldest to the newest, are very useful to the pike angler.

There are times when it is impossible to procure the natural food of the fish, and there are times, as every angler knows, when a spoon-bait or artificial dace or gudgeon, or one of those beautifully finished imitations of fish in brass, silver, and other less solid compositions, answer better than anything else. But, when the natural baits are to be obtained, let the angler give them a fair trial before he takes out his artificial bait-case. I will illustrate, to the best of my ability, the principal methods of pike-angling by casual recollections which it is pleasant for me to recall.

The first scene is a lake in one of those old English estates which have been in the possession of one family for generations. As I wait for the keeper to open the doors of the boat-house and bring out the little fishing-boat from which I am to operate, I can descry over the tree-tops the turrets of a castle of modern build, and behind me, peeping through the leafless branches of another plantation, I can see, beyond a group of noble cedars, the ivy-covered ruins of a building in which Sir Walter Raleigh spent a portion of his time, and which was made short work of by Cromwell, who placed his cannon upon the hill yonder, at the bottom of which is the deer fence. In the home park a choice herd of Jersey cattle are grazing, and as I put my pike fishing-tackle together, I notice the Squire, an octogenarian within a month or two, drive down the chestnut avenue with his workmanlike four-in-hand.

An angler here, who had the necessary permission, might fish all the year round. Beginning with January, there is not only this lake, with its coarse fish, but a grayling stream within three miles. When, in spring, the trout are in condition, there is a river within an hour's drive behind a fast-stepping dog-cart horse. Roach last until the "ides of March" are over, and they may be caught even in winter in shoals around the promontory on the lawn where the swans are fed. Tench of enormous size infest the waters, biting well in spring, and timing their domestic duties, as an old writer intended them to do, with the blossoming of wheat. The head of the extensive house of Cyprinidæ Brothers may be left out of consideration, for the fat, lazy rascal seldom comes from his hiding-place until the winter is over and gone; yet in the under-keeper's garden there is a rudely-stuffed specimen of a carp of 24 lbs., set up as a scare-crow. Perch may be taken up to the middle of March. By the time trout-fishing is over, which in the stream in question is virtually at the end of July, the coarse fish are ready again, and the grayling almost fit, in the stream into which they were introduced some years ago. There is finally an estuary not very far away where salmon peel are occasionally taken.

The centre, however, of all this fishing is the serpentine lake, out of which, last Christmas, the nephew of the old squire, in a short December afternoon, killed 80 lbs. weight of pike. It is with no ordinary hope, therefore, that I enter the boat and am pushed out upon the surface. Some men are born to be unlucky, and, in angling, I have often thought that I am one of them. There is not to-day a breath of wind to ruffle the surface, or scatter the light mist which still broods over the water. Although the thin blue smoke which floats over the trees from the castle chimneys shows that what little upper current of air there is comes from the bleak north-easterly quarter, which anglers never pray for, there may yet be a chance, for, if the wind be verily honest and constant, you need not, in pike-fishing, seriously trouble as to the point of the compass from which it blows. Wind of some sort, however, is a prime necessity in pike-fishing.

I had rigged up without loss of time my spinning apparatus. As the reader is probably aware, there are many spinning flights of different sizes, of different patterns, but they are all based upon the one supposition that by their means the bait is made to spin without an ugly motion, and as nearly as possible to resemble the swimming of a natural fish. I have tried all the flights that have been invented, and having listened carefully to all the arguments advanced in their favour, have at last decided in favour, first, of one which has no other name, to my knowledge, than "Storr's flight"; and the other, I believe, is called Wood's Chapman spinner. The latter has a lead weight moulded around a length of brass wire, which is sharpened at the end, and armed with a small hook. At the head of the weight are a couple of flanges to give the requisite spinning motion. The sharply-pointed leaded wire, with its little hook, is thrust into the interior of the fish until the flanges protrude on either side of the mouth. Two sets of flights then lie along the sides of the bait. The whole arrangement is of course kept from slipping out by the aforementioned small hook attached to the wire.

This bait spins beautifully, and it has the very desirable advantage of making but one splash when thrown into the water, because, the weight being within the bait, the usual lead attached to the trace, a foot or so from the bait, is dispensed with. The disadvantage of the Chapman spinner is that after being in action a short time the tender interior of the fish with which you are spinning yields to the constant pressure of the tiny hook, and there is a gradual withdrawal of the flanges from the mouth. Still it is an excellent bait, because you can at least make sure that it will always revolve steady and straight, while the disposition of the flights gives the pike very little chance when once he has closed his jaws upon it.

Storr's flight is a simple and convenient, yet at the same time effective, arrangement. It consists of one large triangle, two of the hooks standing out laterally. This is attached to a piece of gimp half an inch longer than the bait to be used. By means of a baiting-needle the gimp is passed through and out of the mouth, the large triangle jamming against the vent, and there remaining. It will be found convenient to have a small triangle attached to an inch and a quarter of gimp, slipping over, and flying loose above the shoulders of the bait. Sometimes a difficulty is found when the bait is other than dace or gudgeon, in getting the proper spinning motion; but you soon learn how to act.

It is always best in pike-fishing to use a trace of twisted gut. Our forefathers considered that anything would do for pike, but this is an exploded idea. The use of coarse gimp is now generally acknowledged to be a mistake, and the deterioration of the quality of gimp some little time ago led to a more general adoption of the twisted or double gut trace. Gimp, however, for the hooks, is essential in angling for a fish with such a formidable furnishing of teeth as the pike.

On a day like the one in which we are supposed to be fishing the Squire's lake, fine tackle is more than ever a necessity, for not only is there an absence of wind, but the water is unfortunately abnormally clear. The direful *anacharis* has, as usual, installed itself in the lake, and, but for the free use of an ingenious steam ploughing machine, would render pike fishing an impossibility, so densely has it taken possession. The first few casts produce nothing. In fact, to be truthful, I must confess that two hours pass before any sign of sport is forthcoming. This in a choice preserve known to be, as the saying goes, full of pike, is ominous, for the voracious nature of the fish is such that if he means taking he does not waste time in pondering over the how and wherefore. But fate relents towards the afternoon, and a pretty ripple dances over the more exposed portions of the lake. A long cast into one of the open spaces brings me the first fish. It moves, nevertheless, in a most mysterious way. Upon feeling the attack you of course strike sharply. Anglers are earnestly impressed with the duty in fishing for pike of striking hard, so as to plunge the barbs into the bony palate; and they are recommended, if in doubt, to strike a second time. There is little necessity for the advice. The rousing shake which a hungry pike gives to a spinning bait acts upon the angler as if he had received a violent blow in the face, and he will assuredly strike back again; in other words, he involuntarily gives his line a quick twitch. The pike then shakes his head angrily, as if he would worry the bait into pieces, and the arm of the angler again involuntarily responds to this by another sharp strike.

Our fish at present, however, seems to be indulging in a relay of rotatory movements that are incomprehensible, but they are partly explained when the captive is brought to the side of the boat; the line is wound six times round the body of the fish so tightly that in one of the circles it has cut into the belly. The boat is next slowly pulled about in the deeper water, where in winter time the fish lie; but the wind has dropped again, and the day seems to yield nothing heavier than seven or eight pounds, and there are only some eight or ten fish lying at the bottom of the half boat half punt. Allusion has been made to a little promontory jutting out from the lawn, at the end of which the food is thrown in for the swans; and although the water there is shallow, it is a reasonable supposition that the clustering of small fry, picking up grains of barley and what not, may have induced a cunning pike to sneak around in the rear. Just half-an-hour before dark, putting this theory to the proof, we get towards that quarter, and a fresh dace, bright as silver, falls into the water about a yard from the land. Apparently from the outer fringe of a mass of decayed weeds, and in not more than a foot depth of water, something arrow-like speeds straight away, churning up the water as it goes. There is no half-heartedness about the smack bang of the transaction.

The fish, as you may wager without seeing the result, has taken every one of the hooks into his safe keeping, and has only to be allowed to take his own course to be added to the spoil already accumulated. Given strong tackle, well tried before the day's angling begins, there is little excuse for the loss, by breaking away, of a well-hooked pike, however large it may be; barring such accidents as fouling with trees, or hanging the line up in some irretrievable position. And a sixteen-pound pike on a spinning flight does not give in all of a moment. Your pike never fights out the battle like some of the fish that have been spoken of in the course of these pages, but he puts out all his strength and speed when hooked only with snap tackle, and is by no means a contemptible antagonist. This fellow leaps out of the water after a thirty yards gallop, and plunges into a weed bank. But I winch up to him in the boat, dislodge him, and gaff him, to put the crowning weight to the sum total, which the keeper's man bears, staggering, away with me in a rush basket to the station.

The venerable practice of trolling with the dead gorge has latterly gone a good deal out of fashion, and it cannot be denied that its deadly nature is a fair argument against it when the preservation of the pike is in question. Let the fish be ever so small, after it has taken the murderous gorge into its gullet, its career is ended, and even pike must have sportsman's law, and the youngsters be returned to the water when possible. But I must plead guilty to a sneaking kindness for this form of pike-fishing, upon which, in the seventeenth century, old Robert Nobbes wrote a very quaint treatise. Trolling is the kind of artifice that suits a half-indolent man, or one who, through age or inclination, does not care to enter into the fatiguing labour which is involved in a day's spinning.

Trolling is an appropriately effective method of angling for pike in a river. The angler, with bag and gaff slung at his back, sallies forth on a winter day, crackling the frozen snow, perhaps, beneath his feet as he trudges to the river-side. His trolling bait may be dropped here and there into holes and eddies, the proceeding being just sufficient to keep his blood in active circulation, the exercise enough to bring all his muscles into play, and yet all being conducted with a dignified action that adds not a little to the enjoyment of the sport. There is also something particularly entertaining in the manner in which the movements of the pike are to be studied when trolling.

You have thrown your bait out ten, twelve, or fifteen yards, as the case may be; it sinks to the bottom, and by a series of gentle draws up and down and ever onwards, it is gradually worked towards you, the line meanwhile being neatly coiled on the ground at your left side, unless you have acquired the art of casting, Nottingham style, from the winch, which is the poetry of the process.

Something on the way seems to touch the bait. Is it a loose weed? It may be a submerged branch. Here, then, is the first sensation—to determine whether the slight check proceeds from a fish. At any rate, you have paused in action. Sometimes the angler is held in doubt for several seconds. The pike on grabbing the bait (across the middle) has a habit of keeping still, as if to gloat over the certainty of a meal which Providence has at last placed in his way. Before long, however, he will begin to move away, the line running meanwhile free through the rings. The art of trolling lies not a little in calculating the amount of freedom which it is necessary to allow the fish. The general rule is that the pike, having struck the bait, proceeds forthwith with the pleasing movement technically known as "a run." The theory is that, not to be disturbed or pounced upon by a big brother, he retires to his lodgings, which may be near or which may be a long distance off, to pouch at leisure.

On no account should the line be checked; and it is the safest plan to allow the fish to pouch at even inordinate leisure, if such be his inclination, and then move off on a second excursion. By this time it will be safe to tighten the line, striking being unnecessary with this particular process, and to bring the fish in. The two hooks are not in trolling affixed to the bony walls of the jaws, but in the soft linings of the gullet, and there is no shaking them off or breaking them. This is the general rule, but the experienced troller is aware that when the pike is a large one it often takes the bait, slews it round, and swallows it at a gulp, and then darts swiftly, and may be repentant, away. Some five or ten minutes are generally consumed in waiting for the moment when it is safe to bring to his senses a fish that has taken your trolling bait in the regular way, and this prolonged sensation of hope and doubt may be fairly set off against the more acute excitement of playing a fish struck with the spinning flights.

The live bait gorge is open to the same objections as are urged against the trolling hook, but it is a very convenient method of commanding broad water upon which there is no boat, and where your float should be despatched on a mission of not less than thirty yards, the line being kept up, while the bait is working, by three or four smaller floats unattached. This is the only justification for using it, there being no ground for the excuse pleaded by the troller, that he can work between weeds and cover water, impracticable for spinning. Jardine's snap-tackle has been now generally adopted, in preference to the saddle and other rigs familiar to pike fishermen for many years.

A final word as to useful winter occupation for the angler. When the low-lying lands are a yellow sea, and the heads of the trees in which you were wont to entangle your fly-cast in the summer, seem to be floating on a watery expanse; when the river has forgotten its bounds, and the landmarks are swept away, there is no angling, save in a few exceptional lakes which never become discoloured. At home, you will be tired, sooner or later, of gazing at those stuffed fish that day by day remind your admiring household of your genius. The fondling of your rods and books, and general impedimenta, palls after a while. But, from the thoroughly practical books which have been published, exhausting every phase of the subject of angling, there is always something to be learned: and in the lighter literature of the sport, which is part study of human nature, part communion with nature, animate and inanimate, other than human, and part rehearsal of angling experiences, we may, through the darkest night and most inclement day, be led to continue our recreation in the spirit, if not in the flesh.

International Fisheries Exhibition,
LONDON, 1883.

THE

CULTIVATION

OF

FRESHWATER FISH

OTHER THAN

SALMONIDÆ.

BY

R. B. MARSTON.

[*PRIZE ESSAY.*]

LONDON:
WILLIAM CLOWES AND SONS, LIMITED,
13 CHARING CROSS, S.W.
1884.

LONDON:
PRINTED BY WILLIAM CLOWES AND SONS, Limited,
STAMFORD STREET AND CHARING CROSS.

THE CULTIVATION OF FRESHWATER FISH.

ONE of the most remarkable things in connection with the ancient art of angling is the amazing increase of its disciples which has taken place within the last few years. And although this increase has been large among salmon, trout, and grayling anglers, it has been far greater among those who, not having the means or opportunity to angle for the salmonidæ, give their attention to our other freshwater fish, such as pike, perch, roach, bream, carp, chub, &c. A few years ago the angling clubs of London and Sheffield could be counted by the dozen, now they number many hundreds with many thousands of members. A few years ago angling clubs of the kind referred to here hardly existed in the provinces—to-day we find them springing up on all sides and in all parts of the country. But, while anglers have been increasing in this wonderful manner, the fish have been most certainly decreasing. The cry from the clubs is: How can we get fish?

Something must be done for these thousands upon thousands of anglers, for without fish their recreation is gone, and that they should be encouraged will be admitted by every one who gives the matter a moment's reflection. The larger portion of these coarse-fish anglers are working men and youths, mechanics, artizans, miners, toilers in our mills and factories in the great centres of industry,—men to whom every inducement should be held out to attract them into fresh air and scenes in their spare time. How, then, is the decrease in those fish, in the capture of which they take such delight, to be stopped? and how can the thousands of miles of water which might yield them sport be replenished? To answer these questions will be the object of this essay.

That these questions need answering at all proves that, in this country at least, very little has been done in the direction of cultivation of coarse fish, though, as a matter of fact, in the case of most of them it presents far less difficulty and expense than is attendant on the breeding of the salmonidæ.

The first thing to be recognised is that, consequent on the great difference in the modes of spawning of the salmonidæ and coarse fish, a widely different method must be adopted. Salmon, trout, and grayling eggs are non-adhesive, and each egg can thus be manipulated separately —they take many months to hatch out. The eggs of the coarse fish are adhesive, making their manipulation extremely difficult—so much so, that while ninety-five per cent. of salmon and trout eggs can be hatched out, those who have attempted to treat coarse fish eggs in the same way have rarely succeeded in rearing even five per cent. The eggs of the coarse fish hatch out in a very short time, a week or ten days being the average time required. If, then, we had to look to what is called artificial breeding to enable us to increase our coarse fish, the prospect would not be an encouraging one.

But, fortunately perhaps, artificial breeding is not necessary in the case of coarse fish; all we need do is to give nature a certain amount of aid, and she will do the rest for us.

In the Berlin Fisheries Exhibition, 1880, there was

XI.–18.
Plate I

exhibited in the Swedish department the model of a box, known as Lund's hatching box, for some kinds of coarse fish. This box was described for the first time in England by Mr. R. B. Marston, Editor of the *Fishing Gazette*, in a Paper he read before a meeting of London anglers at the Society of Arts Room last year.*

It is simply an ordinary box—its size depending on the number of fish it is to hold—with holes drilled in the sides to permit of a free current of water through it. The interior is lined with fir branches, and in Sweden, where it has been in use for over a century, it is used thus : Shortly before their spawning time a few pairs of male and female fish (perch are principally cultivated in this way) are placed in the box, which has previously been anchored in a pond, or lake, or stream. The water is not allowed to flow over the top of the box, which is kept some inches above the water level. The box either rests on the ground, or, by means of wooden floats, is kept at a proper level. The parent fish deposit their ova on the fir branches, and they are then taken out; in a few days the young fish hatch out and are found in millions amongst the branches. They can then be either liberated in the lake or other water they are in, or transported to some other water it may be desired to stock, or the fecundated ova can be transported in the same way. Here, then, we have a most simple and inexpensive way of obtaining any quantity of that most valuable fish, the perch. The box ensures that the incredibly vast number of ova deposited by a few fish are protected from the numberless enemies which would attack them in the open, even supposing that the parent

* It is also described in a paper read by Mr. Marston on the same subject at one of the Conferences of the International Fisheries Exhibition (ED.).

fish had been able to find a suitable and undisturbed place in which to deposit them. It is simply aiding nature, for the whole operation goes on exactly as in the ordinary way. Sun, air, wind and waves can exert their beneficial influences, while the ravages of storm and flood are provided against. M. Lundeberg, the Swedish Inspector of Fisheries, says that although used chiefly for perch, they can (with slight modifications of the material on which the spawn is to be deposited) be equally well used for roach, bream, and some other fish. The successful use of this box in Sweden shows clearly that if properly tried in this country many of our coarse fish can be cultivated to any extent. But there are some kinds of coarse fish which require different treatment. To confine pike in a box of this kind would not be difficult, but it would necessitate the use of such a large one, and the growth of such a comparatively large quantity of water weeds, as might not often be practicable. To obtain a stock of pike, probably the best plan would be to place in a small pond, or in an enclosed part of a larger one, a dozen or so of male and two or three dozen female fish, as nearly alike in size as possible. The place selected should be chiefly shallow, well overgrown with water-plants, and with a deep place for the fish to retire to when disturbed. As soon as the spawning is over, the parent fish should be removed, and in a few days the young pike will hatch out. If they are in a small pond, they will require feeding with freshwater shrimps, worms, &c.; they grow very rapidly if well fed, and in two or three months' time can be netted out and sent to any part of the country. In the case of their being wanted to stock a large water, by removing the fine wire netting forming the enclosure above referred to, they will be able to spread out and find their own living along its shores.

To cultivate carp the best plan is to place twenty or thirty pairs of parent fish in a pond from which *all other* fish have been removed. As an instance of what wonderful results can be obtained in carp culture, may be mentioned the fact that last summer, Herr Max v. d. Borne, the well-known German pisciculturist, placed some dozens of pairs of parent fish in a pond on his estate, and in the autumn, when the water was drawn off, *over ninety thousand young carp were found.* Another instance of the possibilities of coarse-fish culture is afforded by the fact, that whereas a few years ago there was not a single carp proper in America, now they exist there in millions—the progeny of a very few parent fish imported from Germany by the United States Fish Commission. In the face of results like these, what need is there to fear that the coarse fish will disappear? Their abundant increase is *only* a question of judicious farming.

The chub is a fish which it would probably be difficult to breed in a Lund-box; in the first place, it is an extremely shy fish; and, secondly, it, like the dace, barbel, and gudgeon, prefers a sandy and stony bed in a stream on which to deposit its ova. But given a small stream of good water, and a bed suitable for these fish can be most easily formed. It is then only a question of protecting them efficiently from water-fowl and other destroying and disturbing influences, and confining the fish placed in the streamlet as much as possible to one kind. A few dozen parent fish protected in this way will produce hundreds of thousands of fry, and directly they have done so they should be removed, or they will commence to destroy it. The fry will require feeding on finely-minced offal, as is done in the case of trout. Supposing, for instance, such a society as the National Fish Culture Association possessed a fish farm which included one or two streams, what difficulty would there be in their adapting the streams to the not very varied requirements of such coarse fish as could not well be bred in the Lund-box ? Any one who has seen what Mr. Silk has accomplished for Lord Exeter at Burleigh Park will know that a very small stream of water, with a flow of hardly more than a gallon per minute, can be utilised in forming a series of most excellent breeding and feeding ponds.

But in addition to the Lund-box and the breeding-ponds, there are yet other methods by which coarse fish may be increased, and they are specially useful in those waters where there are no good natural spawning-grounds, or where, when they exist, they cannot, for some reason or other, be made use of. The water traffic on many rivers prevents the fish getting that undisturbed rest they so much require at this time. In such a river breeding-hurdles can often be used with great advantage. Ordinary hurdles, with branches interlaced, are sunk in such places as offer the best chance of quiet and protection for the fish while spawning. These hurdles are in use in many parts of France and Sweden; they are more suited to increasing the native stock of a river than for general breeding purposes like Lund's box.

Our English freshwater fish are of such various and valuable kinds, that the question of introducing foreign fish is one which should be most carefully considered. But there is one candidate for naturalization—if indeed it is not already naturalized—which, provided it is placed in suitable waters, appears to be eminently likely to provide sport for coarse-fish anglers, and sport of a kind which they could only get otherwise from the salmonidæ. This fish is the black bass of the North American Continent, a fish esteemed by American anglers even above the trout. It is a fish of prey, like the perch, and should, of course, not be placed in trout or grayling streams; indeed, it thrives best in ponds and lakes. In sport and food qualities it is undoubtedly superior to any of our coarse fish. The successful importations of it made by the Marquis of Exeter and some other gentlemen prove conclusively that it will do well in this country; indeed it is doubtful if there exists a more hardy fish, or one which can be more easily cultivated. This will be made evident by a short description of the wonderful manner in which the black bass provides for the safety of its young—in striking contrast to the habits of nearly all other fish in this respect. The black bass spawns in May or June, according as the season is early or late. The parent fish go in pairs, and select some place where the bed of the water they inhabit rises nearly to the surface, where the sun's warmth may reach the eggs. If they can find no convenient shallow, they will heap up stones on the bottom and make one. Before the eggs are deposited, the parent fish most carefully clean the space they have selected by brushing it with their fins, and by carrying away from it with their mouths all *débris*, such as twigs, stones, &c. These cleaned spaces are readily distinguished by their contrast to the dark weed-covered ground around them, and many of them may be seen in the lake (White Water) in Burleigh Park, in which the Marquis of Exeter placed some hundreds of black bass a few years ago.

American observers of the black bass have placed things on these cleaned spaces, and have seen them carried away and deposited outside by the black bass. The nest prepared, the female deposits her eggs in it, and the male impregnates them. Then both fish keep jealous guard over them for some ten days, when the young hatch out. Every intruder is fiercely driven away; nor does their care cease here, for, keeping their young together, as a hen does her chickens, they convoy them to some shallow place amongst reeds and weeds, where they will be safest from the attacks of other fish. This care is continued for some days, until the fry are strong enough to scatter and look after themselves. It will thus be seen that a few parent fish will speedily stock a water without aid of any kind. But inasmuch as the cost of bringing over these fish from America has hitherto been at the rate of about ten shillings each, it will be evident that the cost is too great to permit of many fish being used for stocking purposes. To place a very limited number of fish in a large sheet of water might result in their becoming too much scattered to get together again in the breeding season, therefore it is advisable to place them in very small ponds, or else to enclose with wire netting a portion of a large sheet of water, and keep them there until they have spawned. A great recommendation in the eyes of anglers should be the fact that the black bass rises freely to the fly, and will also take baits of every description, and, when hooked, affords superlative sport. It is as free from bones as the trout, the flesh is firm, white, crisp, and delicious, with curd between the flakes. At the same time it would be most unwise to advocate its general and indiscriminate introduction into our waters. Let it be confined to some of those numberless ponds and lakes which now afford no sport to the angler.

A question intimately connected with the cultivation of fish is that of the best and cheapest way of feeding them. On the Continent fish culturists are beginning to realise the fact that the cultivation of their natural food—freshwater crustacea, insects, frogs, flies, worms, larvæ, &c.—offers the simplest and best solution of the question ; in fact, the cultivation of the food of fish should keep pace with the cultivation of the fish themselves.

LONDON:
PRINTED BY WILLIAM CLOWES AND SONS, Limited,
STAMFORD STREET AND CHARING CROSS.

International Fisheries Exhibition
LONDON, 1883

COARSE FISH CULTURE

BY

R. B. MARSTON

EDITOR OF THE FISHING GAZETTE, MEMBER OF THE EXECUTIVE COMMITTEE OF
THE NATIONAL FISH CULTURE ASSOCIATION.

LONDON
WILLIAM CLOWES AND SONS, LIMITED
INTERNATIONAL FISHERIES EXHIBITION
AND 13 CHARING CROSS, S.W.
1883

International Fisheries Exhibition,
LONDON, 1883.

CONFERENCE ON 29TH JUNE, 1883.

MR. THOMAS SPRECKLEY (Chairman of the Thames Angling Preservation Society) presided. In introducing Mr. Marston, he said he was a gentleman who had descended from the higher realms of piscatorialism on this occasion ; for, though he was a trout and salmon fisherman, he had now come to tell them what he knew of the coarser kinds of fish, which give great pleasure to tens of thousands of their poorer brethren as anglers who could not afford to fish for trout or salmon. He himself knew very little of what was called the science of fish breeding, but he believed that no one could feel more than he did the necessity of protection for the fish. He had seen rivers where you could scarcely get a fish worth taking, and yet when he had four or five miles under his care, at the end of four years, without the aid of anything foreign, simply by protection, by having a book of rules and laws, it had been so improved that the last time he fished there he took a jack of eleven pounds, and three over seven pounds, besides smaller ones which he put back. At the same time he never refused permission to fish but once.

COARSE FISH CULTURE.

Before proceeding to give you some description of the various methods in which what are generally, but I think incorrectly, termed coarse fish may be propagated, it may be well to point out as briefly as possible the reasons why they should be propagated.

This is the more necessary because the majority of those who are interested only in the Salmonidæ, as a rule consider all other fresh water fish as useless, or worse than useless. As a trout angler myself, and much preferring that branch of sport to any other, I am perfectly ready to admit that coarse fish of almost any kind, in a trout or grayling stream, are indeed worse than useless. That there are circumstances, however, in which coarse fish are not only useful, but extremely valuable, I hope to· be able in the course of my remarks to demonstrate to you.

There is a maxim, attributed I think to Jeremy Bentham, for which I have always had great respect, "The greatest good of the greatest number." I take this to mean that though a thing may not be good for all, yet if it be for the benefit of the majority its *raison d'être* is established. There are many thousands of anglers in this country, how many thousands it is difficult to say, but the fact that the vast majority of them are coarse fish anglers is beyond question. In London and Sheffield alone there are some twenty thousand coarse fish anglers enrolled as members of angling clubs, and in addition to these there are many thousands who fish only for coarse fish who do not belong to any club. I will not enlarge on this matter of the vast number of coarse fish anglers, because my friend Mr. Wheeldon is preparing an exhibition handbook on the angling clubs of London and the provinces, and I am sure that the statistics he will give you respecting their number, nature, and organisation will astonish and interest you, and fully bear out the statement that of the two classes of anglers, those who fish for salmon and trout and those who fish for other fresh-water fish, the latter are by far the most numerous.

The first reason, then, why we should cultivate coarse fish is because they afford sport and healthful recreation to many thousands of our fellow men—the majority of them being working men who have neither means nor opportnnity for trout or salmon fishing.

The second reason is one which I think will be new to many of you, and it has the advantage of recommending itself strongly, I think, to all who are interested in the culture of Salmonidæ. This highest branch of pisciculture has been brought to such perfection that, as we were informed in the admirable paper on the subject read by Sir James Maitland last week, fully ninety-five per cent. of eggs can be successfully hatched and reared by artificial means. But to rear Salmonidæ successfully in captivity * you must feed them, and the question of food is an all important one, inasmuch as on it depends in great measure the quality of the fish and the price at which they can be profitably sold. The trout, I need scarcely tell you, is a fish of prey, provided by nature with a capacious mouth armed with rows of sharp teeth, and it is a fact well known to trout anglers that large trout feed almost exclusively on smaller trout and other fish.

I am indebted to Dr. Zenk, president of the Unterfränkischen Kreisfischerei-vereins, for the suggestion that

* By "in captivity" I mean those cases where a large number of trout are kept in a small body of water, in which they would starve unless food is provided for them.

coarse fish can be most advantageously cultivated with a view to obtaining food for Salmonidæ. Dr. Zenk, who had hoped to have been present with us to-day, is the proprietor of one of the largest fish-breeding establishments on the continent, viz., that of Zeewiese, near Gemünden in Bavaria. The fishery comprises about thirty miles of water, including a portion of the river Saale well stocked with coarse fish, almost the whole of the Schondra, with many smaller brooks stocked with trout and grayling. I may mention that Dr. Zenk entertains no doubt whatever as to the possibility of breeding almost infinite numbers of any kind of coarse fish, and some of his ponds are devoted entirely to the cultivation of coarse fish for the purpose of obtaining food for his vast stock of Salmonidæ.

I will now pass on to the practical part of my subject, and endeavour to describe to you the various ways in which coarse fish, or, as they are called in Germany, summer spawning fish, may be propagated.

It must be borne in mind that it has not been found possible to cultivate these fish in the way that the Salmonidæ are cultivated. It is not only difficult to manipulate the eggs in troughs and trays, but the difficulty of rearing the young fry is even much greater. They are hatched out as perfect fish, at once requiring extraneous food, and they are so extremely small that all attempts to feed them artificially have failed. They appear to require that as soon as they leave the egg they should be able to seek their own sustenance on the almost invisible animalculæ present in their native waters. But to cultivate these fish artificially is not only difficult, but unnecessary. All that is necessary is to aid nature to a certain extent by placing parent fish in suitable places for spawning, and then protecting the eggs until the fry hatch out.

We have here some diagrams, which were kindly prepared for me by my friend Mr. Hobden, to illustrate a Paper on this subject which I read last year to a meeting of London anglers at the Society of Arts Room, on which occasion Mr. Birkbeck very kindly took the chair. The outcome of that meeting was the establishment of the United London Anglers' Fisheries Association, to which I shall refer presently, and whose objects are to obtain suitable fishing waters for the London anglers, and to stock them with fish.

This diagram represents what is known in Sweden as

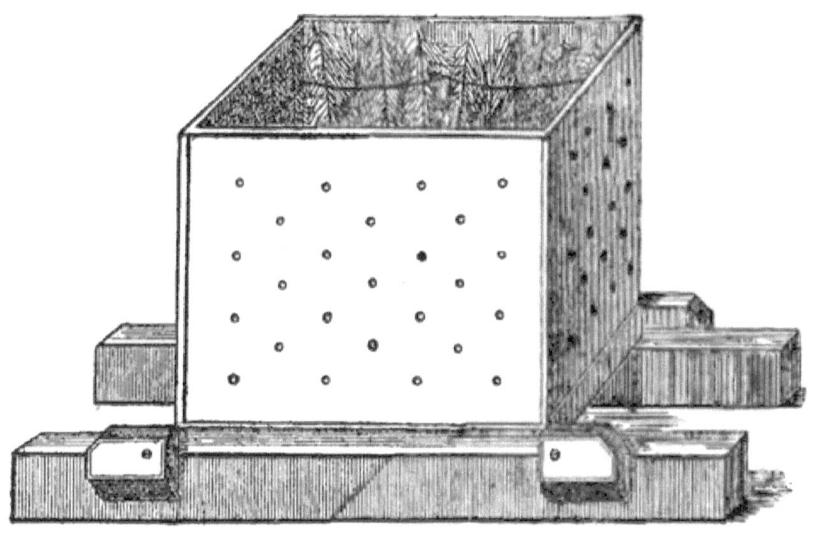

LUND'S HATCHING BOX.

Lund's hatching-box. It was invented more than a hundred years ago by a Mr. Lund, of Linköping. The Swedish inspector kindly furnished me, in February last year, with information about this box, which is in general use in Sweden. He says:—"Replying to your letter of the 25th of February, in which you request me to give you some particulars respecting Lund's hatching-box for the propagation of summer-spawning fish, I herewith hasten to give you all the information I can. Lund's apparatus is remarkable on account of its being, for aught I know, the first attempt in Europe to promote the propagation of the above-mentioned fish with human assistance. As you rightly suppose, the box is to be placed in shallow water near the bank, so that the water does not flow over it. Lund has not given any dimensions for his box, which may be of any size. The sides are hinged, so that they can be let down, and they are perforated with numerous small holes, so that the water can circulate through. The inside should be charred by fire to preserve it. The bottom of the box and the sides are lined with fir branches. As you will see from the sketch I send you, the box should rest on blocks, so as to be raised a little from the bed of the water. With some modifications—for instance it is not necessary to have the sides hinged— Lund's box has been adopted here in Sweden with success, and, in my opinion, for the hatching of perch, it is the most practical that has yet been invented. In a box of this kind, 6 feet square, and with sides 2 feet high, we place fifty female and from twenty to thirty male fish. These fish must be placed in the hatching-box as near their spawning time as possible, and are taken out again as soon as the spawning is finished. The fish deposit the spawn on the branches. It is of great importance that the sides are well perforated, to ensure free circulation of the water. We use these boxes chiefly for perch, but they can also be used, with some modifications, for other fish."

You will see, gentlemen, that it is an easy matter to transport spawn which has been obtained in this way to almost any distance, as it adheres to the boughs; so that you can either let the fry develop in the box, and then go free in the water you desire to stock, or you can carry the fertilised spawn to some place, perhaps a hundred miles away, and then place it in a similar box in the water you desire to stock. In a week or ten days' time the fry will hatch out in countless numbers, and must then be liberated and allowed to begin their fight for life alone. In the Swedish exhibit in the present Exhibition, you will see some models of Lund's box. Here is one which the Swedish Commissioner has very kindly lent me to show you to-day. These models were exhibited in the Berlin International Fisheries Exhibition, and are thus referred to, in the German Official Report on that Exhibition, by Dr. Haack, .director of the great fish breeding establishment at Huningen. In dealing with the Swedish exhibit he says :—" In the Swedish exhibit there were two insignificant-looking models, which were quite overlooked by the majority of visitors, but which were of the very greatest interest to every thinking pisciculturist. These models, in spite of their simplicity and insignificance, show us the way we, in future, most simply, easily, and inexpensively may carry on the propagation of our summer-spawning fish to any extent." He then describes the manner in which the box is used, and refers to its advantages as follows :—" As will be evident to every one, the eggs which have been deposited and impregnated in the box develop in a perfectly natural manner . . . air, light, and sun are able to exert their influences on the eggs in exactly the same way as if they had been deposited on water-plants in the open water in the ordinary way. Wind and waves can in like manner exert their beneficial influence on the eggs, which at the same time are protected from the violence of the storm, from which cause alone millions of eggs are frequently destroyed in the open water. The sides of the box and the branches effectually prevent this destruction." Further, the numberless enemies of the egg are shut out, for by placing a piece of wire netting over the top, the ravages of swans, ducks, and wild fowl—those great destroyers of spawn—are provided against. When I described Lund's box to the meeting at the Society of Arts Room last year, to which I just now referred, its manifest advantages for coarse fish culture were fully appreciated, and a society was formed, of which I am glad to see we have here present to-day the President, Mr. Philip Geen, and the Hon. Secretary, Mr. T. Hoole. This society was formed with the object of renting waters and stocking them with fish, and it decided this spring to experiment with Lund's box. Six boxes were made and used, and I think I may say that in spite of some errors inseparable from a first experiment of this kind, they proved fairly successful. Spawn in large quantities was deposited in some of the boxes, and large quantities of fry were afterwards observed in and around them. The only difficulty experienced was in obtaining the parent fish, but as I trust the gentlemen who had charge of these boxes will give us some account of their experiences, I will not refer to them further than to mention that in a box the Society kindly lent me, and which I hope to make better use of next year, I placed one female perch, of about three quarters of a pound, and two very small perch. After about ten days I found a band of perch spawn containing many thousand eggs in the box, but as they remained unfertilised for want of male fish, of course they perished. I tried everywhere to obtain perch just before they spawned, but was unsuccessful. But from what I have seen of its practical working, I am perfectly assured that, provided you can get an adequate stock of parent fish, the Lund box is a most admirable contrivance for obtaining any quantity of fry.

Another, and in some respects even more simple contrivance for breeding these fish, is the breeding-hurdle. It consists of an ordinary hurdle, on which branches have been intertwined; it is sunk in a pond, lake, or stream, in any shallow undisturbed spot, and the fish find it a convenient place on which to cast their spawn, which can then be taken out and transferred to other waters, or left to hatch out. It is chiefly advantageous where natural spawning places are deficient, and is used to a considerable extent in France and Sweden.

Where some primary expense is not a matter of consideration, the next method I shall describe to you is perhaps the best and most satisfactory of all. I refer to the pond system of cultivation, which is carried on to such an enormous extent in Germany. The diagram (p. 12), most kindly made for me by Mr. G. A. Audsley, represents a small coarse fish farm, such as I venture to suggest might be most advantageously instituted by the National Fish Culture Association, for the purpose of hatching and rearing fry of all kinds of coarse fish, for distribution to angling clubs and private individuals requiring these fish. I am so often asked by secretaries of angling clubs and others where they can obtain coarse fish for stocking their waters, that I feel certain if the association was in a position to supply the fry of coarse fish in large quantities, the demand would be very large indeed. What holds good in the case of Salmonidæ will equally hold good in the case of coarse fish, for to one angler for the former fish there are a hundred anglers for the latter. It will be seen from the diagram that in the arrangement I propose each pond, although supplied from the same stream, is entirely separate from the others. The water flows from the river into the pond, and from the pond into the waste water stream. It would be almost impossible if the water flowed from one

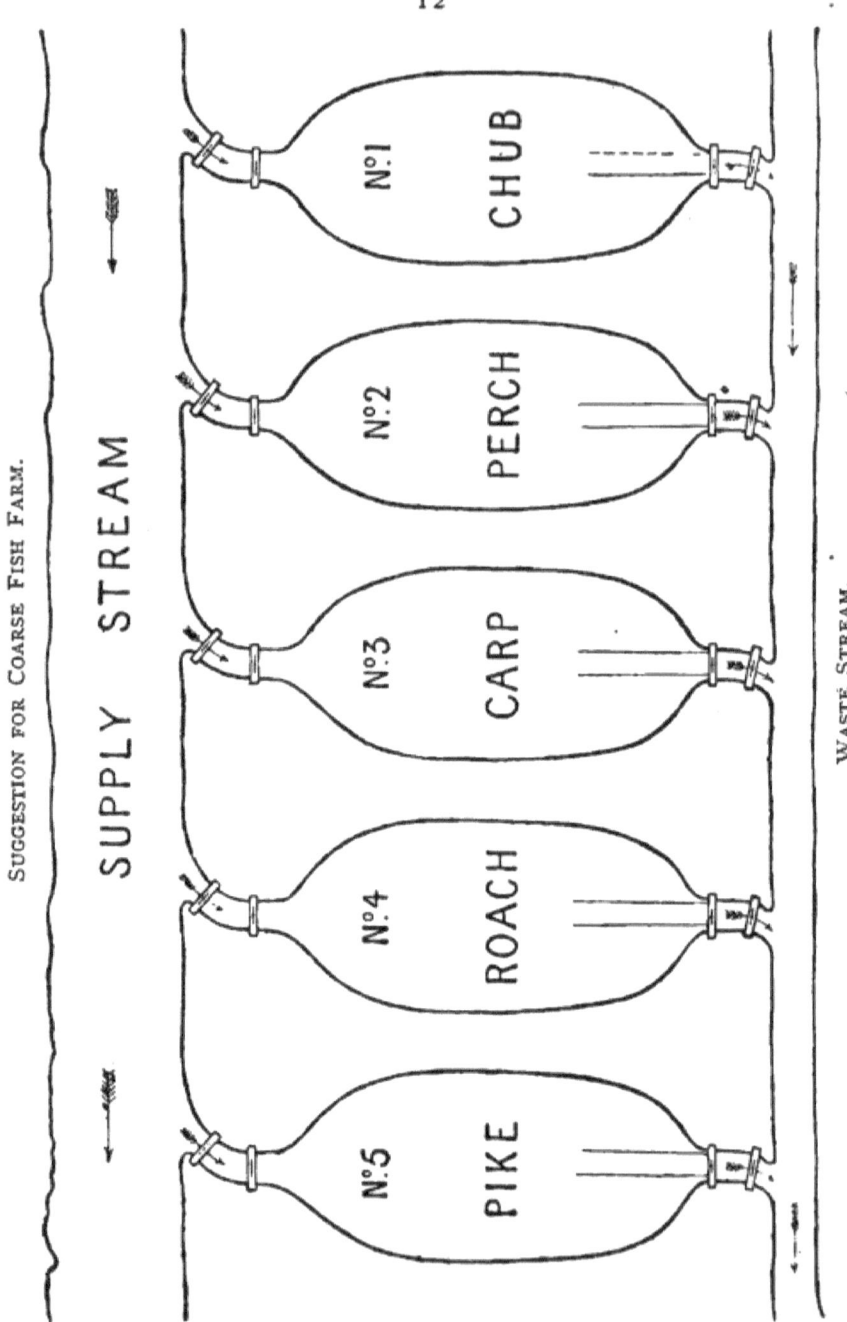

NOTE.—The ponds can of course be of any dimensions, according to requirements—50 yards long by 25 broad would be a convenient size. The faint lines at the lower end of the ponds represent a drain as deep as the deepest part of the pond, so that all the water can be drawn off when necessary.

pond into the next, as is the case in trout-breeding ponds, to keep the various kinds of fish distinct. The fry are so small that they will find their way through the finest grating, and it would manifestly never do to send a customer who had ordered roach, bream, or carp fry, a number of young pike or perch as well! The ponds, and the amount of water passing through them, should of course be adapted to the nature of the fish to be reared in them, and only one kind of fish, or fish similar in their habits, should be bred in a pond. As an instance of what may be accomplished with coarse fish in this way, I may mention that last spring Herr Max von dem Borne, the well-known German pisciculturist, placed about five hundred carp (spawners and milters) in one of his ponds, and in the autumn, when he drew the water off before a large company he had invited to witness the result, more than eighty thousand fine young carp were found.

I have referred to the difficulty experienced in obtaining parent fish for breeding purposes; there are hundreds of streams and other waters in this country which contain coarse fish, which are considered by the proprietors of these waters as, I was going to say, vermin; at any rate, they do all they can to get rid of them, to make room for their trout and grayling. Now I venture to suggest that the United London Anglers' Fisheries Society, and the National Fish Culture Association, would find this a most profitable field to work. I am perfectly certain that the proprietors of trout and grayling fisheries would be only too glad to give these societies all the coarse fish they could catch in their waters, and the very finest pike, perch, chub, roach, &c., are those which are bred in a trout stream. The expense of netting and fish-carriers would not be great. I am led to make this suggestion because, when on a trout-fishing excursion, I have often thought how welcome these shoals of despised coarse fish would be if transported to some of the depleted waters fished by London and other coarse fish anglers. Our worthy and much-respected chairman, Mr. Spreckley, President of the Thames Angling Preservation Society, and the other officers of that society, have done a grand work of this kind by netting the reservoirs of the water companies along the Thames and other waters, and turning their stores of fish into the Thames.

Having described the methods in which coarse fish culture may be carried on, I will now, with your permission, give a brief general account of the natural conditions under which some of these fish breed—to give a complete list would occupy too much time. In coarse fish culture the more closely we follow the conditions laid down by nature, the more likely are we to meet with success. Being fully aware of the scantiness of our knowledge respecting the breeding of many of our coarse fish, I wish to disclaim any pretension to complete accuracy in what I state respecting this matter. I have got my information, such as it is, partly from personal observation, and partly from foreign works which refer to the subject.

SPAWNING TIMES OF COARSE FISH.

Nature of places they choose, and time it requires the young to hatch out.

The Pike spawns in February and March; the eggs, which are small, hatch in from fourteen to twenty-one days, and are deposited on mud, rushes, sedges, and other water plants in shallow quiet bays and ditches. The parent fish usually go in pairs.

The Perch spawns from March to May ; the eggs, which hang together in bands like rows of beads on a coral necklace, are very small at first, but gradually swell, and the young fish escapes in from ten to twenty days according to the temperature of the water. The eggs are deposited on water plants and submerged boughs, and are then fertilised by the milt of the male fish.

The Loach spawns in December and January ; the eggs, which are deposited on gravel in running water, hatch out in from thirty to forty days.

The Carp spawns in May and June ; the eggs are deposited on water plants, and hatch out in from fourteen to twenty days. There are three kinds of carp; the common carp, which is covered with large scales ; the mirror carp, which has one row of very large scales along the back, and another along the side, the rest of its body being covered with a leather-like skin free from scales ; and the leather carp in which scales are entirely absent. Specimens of the two last-named fish, which are not common in England, can be seen in the aquarium of the Exhibition.

The Tench is another powerful and handsome pond fish which would well repay cultivation. It prefers stagnant and weedy waters. Like the carp and eel it buries itself in the mud in the cold months. Its food consists of larvæ, water plants, and worms. Like carp and all other muddy-flavoured fish, it eats well, and loses the muddy flavour if kept for a time in clear running water. It spawns from May to July on water plants, and the young fish hatch out in a week or ten days.

The Gudgeon, Minnow, Loach, and Bullhead spawn from May to July, selecting very shallow streams, and depositing their eggs on the gravel and stones. These fish all form admirable food for Salmonidæ, and can be easily cultivated in any small clear stream.

The food of the carp consists chiefly of the larvæ of water insects, worms, sprouts of water plants, and decaying vegetable matter. Kitchen refuse forms very fattening food for carp. To rear carp with the greatest success the parent fish should be placed in a suitable pond in which there are no other fish; they spawn in May and June; the parent fish should then be netted out, and in the autumn, under suitable conditions, there will be an immense crop of young carp from two to three inches in length. The carp is a powerful fish affording great sport to the angler, and its cultivation might be most profitably carried on in England. In fact before the advent of Protestantism in England fish stews for the natural propagation of carp and other fish were very common.

The *Roach, Rudd*, and *Bream* spawn in May or early in June on water weeds; the eggs hatch out in a week or ten days.

The *Chub* spawns at the end of April or beginning of May, on shallow sandy or gravelly places, and the eggs hatch out in a very short time.

The *Barbel* spawns on stones and gravel, in a sharp stream from one to three or more feet deep; how long the eggs take to hatch out I have not been able to ascertain, but probably in a week or ten days.

The *Dace* spawns in March or the beginning of April, also in sharp shallow streams. There are some valuable foreign coarse fish which I think might be advantageously introduced into this country; but as my friend Mr. Oldham Chambers is to give us a Paper on the acclimatisation of foreign fishes, I will only refer to one of these, viz. the American black bass, because this fish—thanks chiefly to

the great interest taken in it by the Marquis of Exeter—
may be said to be acclimatised here already. There are
probably many thousands of them now in the fine sheet of
water called White-water, near Burleigh House, Stamford,
the country residence of his lordship. In 1878 and 1879, Mr.
Silk, the able pisciculturist to the Marquis, brought over
from the United States nearly one thousand young bass;
and he informs me that the fish have spawned the last two
or three seasons. Last year Mr. Silk was sent to the States
to obtain a further supply of these fish, and they were distributed among some half-dozen gentlemen who had subscribed towards the expenses of getting them over. I received thirty of this lot, ranging in size from one and a
half pounds to a few ounces, and they appear to be doing
very well in a small sheet of water in which I have placed
them. Having for some years past strongly advocated the
introduction of this fine game and food fish into suitable
English waters, I was, in common with others interested
in this fish, extremely sorry to see, from the reports in the
papers, that Mr. Goode, the United States Commissioner,
had "warned English anglers against the black bass." I
felt convinced that Mr. Goode did not intend to warn us
against the introduction of this fish into *any* of our waters,
but only such as were suitable for Salmonidæ. Knowing
that an expression of opinion on this matter from so high
an authority would have very great weight in this country,
I wrote to Mr. Goode to ask him if he intended his remarks
to apply to the introduction of the fish generally. His
reply was exactly what I expected it would be; and I have
very great pleasure in reading it to you, because it will do
far more to remove any prejudice against the introduction
of the black bass into *suitable* English waters than anything I can say :—

Mr. Goode says :—

"DEAR MR. MARSTON,—I am much annoyed—with myself chiefly, for I ought to have expressed myself more explicitly—that my remarks upon the black bass were so misinterpreted. I was speaking solely in reference to planting black bass in salmon streams, and in comment upon Sir James Gibson Maitland's paper upon the culture of *Salmonidæ*. The entire drift of my remarks was to the effect that the black bass is a fish with which public fish-culture had nothing to do, being purely an angler's fish, and not one which professional fishermen can take in large quantities for the supply of the public markets. As an angler's fish I believe the black bass to be superior in every respect to any fish you have in Great Britain outside of the salmon family, and I believe that its introduction into streams where pike, perch, roach, and bream are now the principal occupants, can do no possible harm, and would probably be a benefit to all anglers. It is also well suited for large ponds and small lakes, where there is an abundant supply of 'coarse fish,' which a school of them will soon convert into fish by no means 'coarse.' If you will kindly refer to my 'Game Fishes of the United States,' p. 12, you will find that my views as to the value of the black bass in my own country are already on record, and I can see no reason why this fish should not be equally valuable in Great Britain. I quote from my own essay as follows :—

"'Fish culturists have made many efforts to hatch the eggs of the black bass, but have never succeeded. . . . This failure is the less to be regretted since young bass may easily be transported from place to place in barrels of cool water, and when once introduced they soon multiply, if protected, to any desired number. The first experiment in their transportation seems to have been that of Mr. S. T. Tisdale, of East Wareham, Massachusetts, who, in 1850, carried 27 Large-mouths from Saratoga Lake, N.Y., to Agawam, Mass. The custom of stocking streams soon became popular, and, through private enterprise and the labour of State commissioners, nearly every available body of water in New England and the United States has been filled with these fish, and in 1877 they were successfully carried to the Pacific coast.

This movement has not met with universal approval, for by the ill-advised enthusiasm of some of its advocates a number of trout and bream have been destroyed, and complaints are heard that the fisheries of certain rivers have been injured. The general results, however, have been very beneficial. The black bass will never become the food of the millions, as may be judged from the fact that New York market receives probably less than 60,000 lbs. annually; yet hundreds of bodies are now stocked with them in sufficient numbers to afford pleasant sport and considerable quantities of excellent food. 'Valued as the brook-trout is for its game qualities,' writes Mr. Halloch; 'widely distributed as it is, and much extolled in song as it has been, the black bass has a wider range, and being common to both cold and warm waters, and to northern and southern climes, seems destined to become the leading game fish of America, and to take the place of the wild brook-trout, which vanishes like the aborigines before civilization and settlements.'"

"I shall try to be present at the reading of your paper on Friday, but fear that I may be detained by another engagement. I shall be very glad, then, if you will quote this letter as fully as your space will allow, in justice to the black bass and its advocates, as well as to myself.—I am, sir, yours truly,

"G. BROWN GOODE,
"*Commissioner.*"

I am sure, gentlemen, nothing could be more satisfactory than this letter. As an enthusiastic angler for all kinds of fish, I should be the last to advocate the introduction of a fish which would spoil our sport. Nor would I have anything to say for it if it were a fish like the trout, affording sport chiefly to the rich; but the black bass is essentially a poor man's fish; it will take any kind of bait freely, affords superb sport, and thrives best in just those waters which are not suited to trout and salmon, viz., ponds, lakes, and slow, deep streams.

In conclusion, gentlemen, I thank you sincerely for the

patient and kind manner in which you have listened to my Paper, and I trust that some of the facts I have given you in connection with a subject which is really of vast importance to many thousands of anglers, viz., the increase of our sport-affording coarse fish, will counterbalance to some extent the deficiency of my Paper in other respects.

DISCUSSION.

Mr. J. C. BLOOMFIELD said, coming from Ireland, he should like to say a word or two upon this matter. Like the Chairman he had been for many years endeavouring all he possibly could to protect fish ; and possibly there might be some present who had come across, at Lough Erne, in the north of Ireland, the results of his labours. He had been a salmon and trout fisher himself, and no one would wish to associate them with such fish as they were dealing with to-day. But he agreed with Mr. Marston that you could not touch anything that was of more importance to the country than this coarse fish question. In this country there were a vast number of poor people who visited the different ponds and small rivers for the purpose of angling, and no one would grudge them the pleasure and the exhilaration they would feel on those occasions, and which they appreciated all the more from the confined nature of their occupation during so many months of the year. The salmon fisherman who knew what it was to have a twenty-pound fish at the end of his line must be a churl if he would not like to see a ten-pound pike at the end of the line of his poorer brother. He had in his mind's eye a spot in the north of Ireland where, from one hill, you had a view of twenty-seven mountain lakes all containing pike, perch, roach, or trout. He was not sure that it was worth preserving the trout, because, although there was sufficient running water for them to live in, they were not in good condition for the table. But of those twenty-seven lakes not five pounds'-worth of food was taken out of them from year's end to year's end. If some of their German and French friends had those lakes, what would they make out of them? The fact was there were millions of acres of water in Ireland lying neglected. A man in Manchester who took all his rabbits for two years, came over, and saw him one day drawing for bream. In one day he brought out about twelve tons. He was very much astonished, and said there were a great many Irishmen in Manchester and Liverpool and there was not one of them who, at certain times of the week and many times of the year, did not want fish, and if these fish could be sent to Manchester, he should be very glad to pay well for them. That showed the desirability of the cultivation of these coarse fish. It would be an immense benefit to numbers of poor people whose conscience did not allow them to eat meat at certain times and who could get nothing else. London was the great centre, as he hoped it always would remain, of Imperial interest, and they had all been delighted to see the interest which had been taken in this matter by their Royal Highnesses the Prince of Wales and the Duke of Connaught; but he hoped that the interests of Ireland would not be left out in the cold.

Mr. MANN, as a fish culturist from the age of fifteen, could not allow Mr. Marston's Paper to pass without offering him a tribute of thanks for the information he had conveyed. Ten years ago he should have objected that the cultivation of coarse fish was not necessary, but when he came to think of the enormous increase of rod-fishers, the steam-launches on the Thames, and the enormous interest some people seemed to take in the introduction of swans, Brent geese, ducks, and other individuals which shovelled up ova when deposited in the spawning-beds, he was free to confess that two years ago he withdrew unreservedly his opposition, and as far as it lay in his power he should be happy to give any association with which Mr. Marston was connected his utmost support. Mr. Chambers' fish box was like Lund's, only that the sides were covered with galvanised wire, the insides being lined with the points of the pine. He remembered one day in his sixteenth year, having got tired of fishing he turned up his sleeves and went along the bank trying to catch a few cray-fish. He came to the roots of an old willow-tree, and there discovered large rods of spawn attached to and intermingled amongst the roots of the willow. He got the man who was with him to cut off the roots, put them in his bait tin, and took them home and put them into a pond through which flowed a slight stream of water. Every morning he examined these under the microscope, and was delighted to see the gradual development of the perch. The recollection of the fact suggested to him, when he saw Mr. Chambers' box, that it might be improved by interlacing the roots of the willow into the uprights of these boxes in place of the points of the pine-tree, which he thought were hardly to be found at the bottom of a river. They were very slippery, and where the point was broken off there was always a resinous flow into the water, which would at once be fatal to the germ. He had put this forward as a suggestion which he hoped would be tried. As an illustration of what swans, geese, and ducks would do he might say that there was a certain nobleman in the south of England who was kind enough to grant him permission to fish his streams. Some years ago he came to a fine shallow and there found four swans with their heads down going along on the scour. The man who was with him said, "I am afraid you will not get any fish off there to-day;" and his reply was "No; and who is going to get any three years hence?" He drove the swans away, went in and sifted the gravel, and there was not one-tenth part of the ova left; they had gobbled it up by pints, and what was the result? Later on the same nobleman granted him a day's fishing, and, instead of catching fifteen or sixteen pounds of trout, he killed only five takeable fish, and in two years the stream would not be worth throwing a fly upon. They had heard from Professor Huxley that the destruction of man did not matter, and that nature would balance itself. He was willing to grant that with regard to the herring and the cod it might be so, but with regard to the crustacea inshore and trawl fish, which they were not now discussing, he entirely denied it from his own practical observation. He knew of one ledge of rocks on which a family could once gain a livelihood of £6 a week, and it was now not worth fishing.

Mr. WHEELDON, while thoroughly indorsing what had been said with regard to the Paper, confessed to some disappointment that Mr. Marston had not suggested some practical scheme which might be placed in due time before the National Association of Fish Culture, of which he had the honour to be on the Council. He should like to have heard of some thoroughly well-developed scheme for which they might have asked the co-operation and assistance of the Legislature. He had very little belief personally in the idea that the angling clubs of London would be the greater supporters to this scheme, because, unfortunately, however hearty their sportsman-like spirit might be, they did not develop the great spirit of co-operation. If they did, they might be the most powerful body of men in the kingdom. There was very little doubt that the anglers would be found in overwhelming numbers compared to fox-hunters, pigeon-shooters, coursers, or any other description of sportsmen, and it was inevitable that it should be so, because in a great manufacturing country like England, it was certain that the men who had to spend their lives in hard work, would devote their leisure more frequently to the sport of angling, which had a peaceful tendency. With regard to the introduction of the black bass, he did not gather from what Mr. Goode said, that he desired it to be introduced into any body of water containing salmonidæ, because such a course would be simply suicidal. They might as well let out all the pike and perch of the Avon into some of the Hampshire trout streams, or other waters tenanted by trout, and hope to have the race of trout prosper. He recognised most fully the fact that the black bass was a grand sporting fish, and a good food fish, and a fish which might be of essential use if introduced into such waters as the Serpentine, or some of the ornamental park waters, such as the Welsh Harp and other places of like character. Why the powers that be should debar London anglers from fishing in the Serpentine and other waters of a like character, he did not know, and if they had the black bass thoroughly established, in due time they might have as many black bass clubs as there were in America. With regard to the question of swans on the Thames, he would say a word or two. The previous day he went out fishing on the Thames, and saw to his great regret, that in spite of the immense amount of damage done by swans, not only were the swans on the Thames increasing, but there were absolutely bills posted prohibiting any one taking the eggs or destroying the young birds. Perhaps that might be necessary, but he did really think the Legislature should be asked to cause the number of swans on the Thames to be reduced to some extent, because they did an immense amount of evil. With regard to the traffic on the Thames, he hoped a bill would soon be passed in Parliament for its better regulation; but he did not think it applied exclusively to launches. No doubt they did a large amount of harm, but it was certain that every boating season, although the anglers of London have very few rights, they were certainly despoiled of them by boating crews continually practising on the Thames. On the previous day he was fishing, when an eight-oared boat of some kind came down, manned by a crew of College boys; Eton boys were grand young fellows, but they were a very great nuisance on the Thames, and to anglers generally all oarsmen were of the same character. These young fellows came down the stream, and though they were not in the way, deliberately rowed smack into the punt, nearly cut their own boat in two, broke two outriggers, and then assailed them with a volley of Eton abuse. It was quite certain the question of anglers' rights and privileges and coarse fish culture was one which ought to receive more attention.

The CHAIRMAN informed the Conference that a bill for regulating steam-launches passed both Houses of Parliament, as he had just been informed by a letter from the Solicitor to the bill. He must say he should like to see the discussion get more practical. If they could persuade the owners of waters to do all they could to produce fish for the pleasure and food of man, it would be a great thing, and his opinion was, that you could fish as much as you liked, provided you fished fairly. With respect to Mr. Wheeldon's remarks about the swans, there were only three and a-half swans per mile between Richmond and Staines bridge, and he did not think that was a very great excess. They might do some harm of course, as they always would. He looked forward to the time when there would be a society formed, when their own keepers would have authority from the Conservancy to watch and see the boats and launches maintained a fair speed only. He remembered a good many years ago fishing in some splendid waters about five miles from Nuneaton, some hundreds of acres altogether, and saw there lots of small fish which had been taken out with the net lying on the bank dead. It was simply murder, because if that water had been preserved, it would have been a source of pleasure to thousands. He only wished he had that water under his control. If this Paper could be made more public, and the lessons it contained impressed on the minds of those who owned the waters, what a grand thing it would be. He had no hesitation in saying that he could make it pay splendidly, simply by charging a small sum for the privilege of fishing, dealing fairly with people, and laying down proper regulations.

Mr. GEEN had also listened with great pleasure to the Paper; but could not help expressing regret that it did not lead up to some practical issue. No doubt it was Mr. Marston's intention and desire that the discussion should lead to some resolution which would bear fruit, otherwise it would be like many other meetings of anglers, which left the question precisely where they found it. The first thing was, whether it was desirable to cultivate coarse fish. If it was, the next question arose, was it possible; and thirdly, if it was desirable and possible, what were the most practicable means of carrying it out. He did not think there could be any question in any one's mind who had heard the eloquent speech of the gentleman from Ireland, who referred not only to the importance of these fish as a means of sport, but as food. As to the first point, they were told that the man who made two blades of grass grow where only one grew before, was a benefactor, and the same principle applied to those who not only provided food, but also provided another great need of the labouring classes, and that was some health-giving sport or recreation giving them absolute relaxation from the turmoil of their every day life. He did not think there was any sport within the reach of the working-classes so innocent and health-giving as that of angling, and if it were possible to stock the numerous depleted waters in and around all our large manufacturing centres, it was certainly desirable to do so. As to the question if it were possible —he could not help fancying that people who wrote and talked so much about the Salmonidæ, thought it was equally practicable to reproduce artificial coarse or summer spawning fish; but it was not so. Some four years ago, it was brought forward at a meeting of the Thames Angling Preservation Society by Mr. Benningfield, who asked him (Mr. Geen), to consider it, and it was to be brought forward at the next meeting, but to his surprise the subject dropped; but from a conversation he had had with him, the result was, that it was perfectly practicable to artificially spawn perch; but no other summer spawning fish. The reason was this, the Salmonidæ gave a solid egg, which you could handle, and send to the uttermost parts of the world if necessary; but the spawn of the coarse fish was something you could not handle without destruction. The roach, for instance, deposited their spawn with the greatest care in suitable spots; they would go up day after day with the intention of shooting the spawn; but if the weather turned dark and cold they would go back again into deep water. Mr. Marston had said that the eggs took seven or eight days to come out; but that was not so. They came out in twenty-four hours in favourable weather,* and that was an instance which showed how impossible it was to deal artificially with these fish except perch. Still, Nature might be assisted, and if they could possibly get a series of ponds partaking somewhat of the nature of a fish farm (because small meddling never came to any good), something might be done. It was all very well to talk of fishery associations, and Mr. Marston had given the tremendous success which attended his box, but it was only a success so far, that the female was there without the male. They must have them both there, or it would not be any good, and that was very much the result with all other boxes. They must put them in the boxes, and a certain proportion would vivify; but they would come out of the holes where the water went in. The only effectual means would be a system of ponds, and it must be taken up by somebody besides the anglers of London. They might give it their support, and no doubt they would; but he should like to see the National Fish Culture Association take up the question. If they would not, what on earth were they constituted for? He hoped that Mr. Marston and others, himself included, would be able to induce the Council to take the matter up, and then the

---

* I doubt this assertion. I have made inquiries in various directions since I read this Paper, and the result has been to confirm my own statement. The fish do not all spawn at once, and the eggs first deposited of course hatch out soonest. I fancy this fact has misled Mr. Geen, who may have seen the eggs of a first deposit hatching soon after a second or third deposit had taken place.—R. B. M.

anglers of London must put their hands in their pockets and give them proper support.

Mr. SENIOR remarked that some gentlemen seemed to forget that the National Fish Culture Association was at the present moment only in its infancy, and although it was really established to do what they had heard should be done and must be done, up to the present it had had no possible time for formulating a scheme. He must differ from his friend who had preceded him as to Mr. Marston's paper. There was nothing easier than to criticise a paper written and read by another man, but he considered they were all much indebted to Mr. Marston for what he had done, and it was not for him to put his head into a hornet's nest by formulating a scheme for other people to pick to pieces. If there was anything which he hated more than another it was a long speech or a long sermon, and it was a very admirable rule that papers read there should not exceed half an hour. Now in his half hour paper Mr. Marston had given the result of a good deal of study; he had told them what had been done on the continent, and what had been done in this country. There were other papers which would deal with the scientific possibilities of the question of fish culture, and he thought it very wise in Mr. Marston not to attempt a scheme, but to allow scientific men of greater age and experience to put their heads together and furnish the scheme. He had been asked by Mr. Oldham Chambers, secretary to the Fish Culture Association, to apologise for his inability to be present, he having had to go down to Norfolk in order to arrange for a little excursion for the Foreign Commissioners and others to the broads of East Anglia, which teemed with coarse fish, and which he hoped some day would be stocked with black bass. The Angling Preservation Societies, the parent of which the Chairman represented, had done a great deal towards the culture of coarse fish. Preservation meant culture to a great extent, and the splendid takes of trout registered in the Thames during the present season, of a grand total quite unprecedented, might be considered to be due entirely to preservation. There were some grounds therefore to go upon. The Marquis of Exeter had done something towards the acclimatisation of the bass, and others had acclimatised other kinds of fish. Notwithstanding what Mr. Geen had said he still believed it was as possible to cultivate the carp and tench in ponds, lakes, or rivers, as the perch. The first thing wanted was that the public mind should be educated on this question, and such papers as that now read and as had been read at angling clubs during the past winter, would prepare the ground for the seed which would be sown. The next thing wanted would be the sinews of war, and with regard to that he would only say that Mr. Oldham Chambers would be very happy to receive cheques or contributions, and it would then be for those who had subscribed to the society and supported it to complain if it did not make some progress towards realising what had been promised.

Mr. CRUMPLEN wished to add a word or two with regard to the breeding boxes which had been described by Mr. Marston, and had been used by several anglers. The Fisheries Society resolved to take up the question, and a certain number of the Lund breeding boxes were distributed. One which was tried at Ponders End had proved a perfect success, but he differed from Mr. Geen when he said it was artificial, there was nothing artificial about it beyond this, that it rendered assistance to nature ; and if you gave other fish the same assistance—it might not be in a box—but if you provided proper receptacles, and placed food for the spawn, and took care to give them what nature would give them, he had not the slightest doubt but that similar results would be obtained. To the limited extent to which the culture of coarse fish had been attempted it had been successful, and they should be encouraged to persevere. It was not altogether a question of cost; London anglers had not much to spend, and they might be careful what they spent, but if their money was well spent in an experiment which might not be successful this year, but was likely to be successful in another, he was sure they were sufficiently intelligent to be satisfied with the result. With regard to the black bass, he was not at all opposed to its introduction under certain circumstances, but until their knowledge of it was more complete he thought it desirable· to proceed with extreme caution before introducing it to any large extent. His impression was that in this matter they should be very conservative, and not run a risk which at present they were not prepared for. He would warmly advocate the introduction of any fish likely to be useful, but never until it was perfectly certain that it was not going to injure the existing stock.

Dr. SEYMOUR HADEN said a very good illustration of the extreme facility with which coarse fish were bred was shown by the way in which the town of Lyons was furnished with coarse fish before the time of railways. As a boy he was well acquainted with the neighbourhood of Lyons, and in the immediate vicinity there were six lakes one above another. They were never known to have been stocked with fish by anyone, but they were treated in this way. After a certain number of years the lower lake was dragged, and the fish sent to market. The next year the lake above it was drawn, the next year the one above that, and so on until the whole six had been drawn in turn. In every case the lakes stocked themselves with fresh *ova*, and kept the whole of these six lakes perpetually stocked with vast quantities of coarse fish, carp, bream, tench, and jack, which were taken to Lyons market, and in fact the people of Lyons had no other fish supply whatever. There must be some mistake on the part of those who said that there was great difficulty in propagating coarse fish.

Mr. BRADY, Inspector of Irish Fisheries, then proposed a vote of thanks to Mr. Marston for his very able paper, the importance of which was shown by the lengthy discussion which had arisen. His countryman, Mr. Bloomfield, had shown how important fish culture might be made in certain parts of Ireland as food for the million, and also for the recreation of the large classes of people which could not afford the sport of salmon fishing. Whatever difference of opinion there might be with regard to the difficulties of culture, there could not be any as to the importance of it as a question of food. Mr. Bloomfield had spoken of the spot from whence he could see 27 lakes ; he could go to hills from which you could look on 1027 lakes, the whole of which did not provide £5 worth of food, which might be made very valuable if only there were greater facilities for transit, for after all this was the great difficulty.

Mr. WILMOT, Superintendent of Canadian Fisheries, said it afforded him great pleasure to indorse the sentiments contained in the Paper. If anything, it was more desirable to cultivate coarse fish than the higher orders, for, speaking from an experience of 16 or 18 years, the higher orders of fish could not exist without the lower orders. The Almighty, in His providence, had thought proper to put into the same waters fish of high order and of a low order, and it was invariably found that the high order lived on the low order. If the latter were exterminated, the former would disappear. All the finest salmon rivers had in them certain species of fish of a very low order; they entered the river at a different period to the salmon, to reproduce their species, and the young went down the rivers to the sea, and there in turn were fed upon by the salmon which frequented the same river. It was said by some gentlemen that you could not produce the lower orders of fish, but he maintained that you could produce a thousand to one of the lower orders, because they deposited their ova in the spring months, when the weather was warm, whilst the higher orders deposited theirs in the autumn months, when the weather was cold, and took from three to six or seven months to reproduce, whilst the lower orders were hatched in from three days to three weeks. Consequently nature had given the lower orders the greater preponderance. Throughout nature, as a rule, the lower orders supported the higher, and therefore it became the duty of man to carry out that which Providence had ordained. Carp was a poor man's fish altogether; it could be produced in ponds and small preserves, and ought to be protected and cultivated almost above every other, whilst the salmon and trout were the rich man's fish, because those who sought them had to spend a large amount of money on the sport. With regard to bass, it was a very bad voracious fish to introduce amongst others of a better quality, and he said this coming from a country where it was more famous than in any other part of the world. Where they found the black bass they never found the salmon or trout. There were lakes innumerable in Canada, where the bass, the pike, and other fish of the same character abounded, but they never found in those lakes any of the higher orders of fish. There were also magnificent rivers, teeming originally with salmon and trout, and they never found black bass in them until lately, when, in consequence of man having killed all the salmon and trout, black bass had been introduced, and in consequence there was nothing but black bass there now. Black bass was a good game fish and a food fish, but they should be put into waters by themselves, or where there was plenty of inferior fish for them to feed upon, but not where they could interfere with better kinds. There was a lake in Canada which teemed with black bass, pike, perch, sunfish, and other of the lower orders, and being a small lake, the temperature in summer was 80° to 90°, and there the black bass abounded; but the inhabitants fished it to such an extent that they exterminated the bass. A petition was sent in to the Legislature about it, and an order was passed that there should be no netting for three years. When that period expired there was an abundance. No one was permitted to spear in it or to net; none but anglers fished it, and there was abundance for all. You never could destroy fish by angling, but in one year they could be destroyed by netting. Still it was no use for an intelligent man to read such an instructive Paper as they had heard to-day, or for other people to discuss it, if men of science, holding the highest positions in the country, told them that it was useless to protect the fish, and that they could take care of themselves. He could only say, if such views were to prevail, the time would come when there would be no fish in Great Britain or any other part of the world.

The resolution having been carried unanimously,

Mr. MARSTON, in reply, said there was no intention whatever to introduce the black bass into trout or salmon streams, any more than they thought of putting the pike into a trout stream; but there were thousands of acres of water where there were no fish at present, where bass could be put, and would afford magnificent sport. The Sheffield anglers had to go about 30 miles to get their fishing, and every year paid about £15,000 for it, when they might have abundant fishing in their own neighbourhood, if only the streams were populated. With regard to the point mentioned by Mr. Mann, he believed that pine branches were used because they were found to answer admirably, and did not rot; but his suggestion was a very good one, and he hoped next year to try it. Mr. Wheeldon and Mr. Geen had been somewhat disappointed that he had not set forth a more complete scheme, but the scope of this Paper only allowed him to give an outline of the subject. He took it that they considered the matter even more urgent than he did, and no doubt they would help to formulate a scheme and support it. Mr. Geen was right, to a certain extent, in saying that coarse fish could not be cultivated artificially; but in his Paper he had insisted on this fact, and had referred particularly to pond culture, by which means any of these fish could be cultivated. Carp was cultivated to a great extent in Germany, and fetched more money even than sea fish, but he believed other kinds had not been cultivated there, because they were not wanted. There were not many anglers in Germany, and it was for anglers principally that he suggested these fish should be cultivated.

Mr. CROSSMAN moved a vote of thanks to the Chairman, who had been the principal agent in persuading the Conservators of the Thames to prevent the capture of small immature fish. Mr. Wilmot had referred to the opinion expressed on the platform by a gentleman high in the scientific world, but he would say that the great object of these conferences was to bring together men who were not only scientific but practical, to hear their opinions expressed in the boldest manner possible, so that they might be able to arrive at the truth with regard to any subject connected with fisheries. The salient points in connection with all the fisheries would be thoroughly considered by the most competent men, and he trusted the results would be of the most practical kind. Whoever stood on that platform, whether he were a scientific man, a practical, or a theoretical man, would not, he hoped, be afraid of expressing his opinion on any subject, however antagonistic it might be to the one which seemed to prevail at the moment, because in the end the truth must prevail. The subject brought forward by Mr. Marston was one in which he had taken a great interest, and he might say that the only prize offered at the Exhibition for the cultivation of fish in fresh-water ponds was offered by himself. He saw in Germany and Austria the importance of that cultivation, and in all these matters history seemed to repeat itself. They knew that the ancient Romans were famous for fish culture in ponds. Their tables were provided with carp and every kind of fresh-water fish, and so valuable were they that it was said that one of the fish-ponds of the poet Lucullus actually realised £20,000 after his death. Dr. Seymour Haden had shown what was actually carried on in Lyons, and the same system could be adopted in this country. Wherever there were low-lying meadows, with streams or rivulets running through them, these ponds could be easily constructed. The monks in the older days, who knew how to place their abbeys in the most lovely spots in creation, also knew which were the most valuable fish, and they always had carp ponds, because they knew it was about the best fresh-water fish, the one most tenacious of life, not carnivorous, but living on weeds and insects. There were in this country canals of several miles in length, and numerous lakes, utterly devoid of fish, and there were ponds in nearly every field which could, under a wise system, be stocked with fresh-water fish. He was sure this Paper would draw the attention of those who took an interest in these matters to the necessity of cultivating these kinds of fish, and there was no country in the world where it could be cultivated to a more profitable extent than in England, Scotland, and Ireland.

Mr. C. E. FRYER seconded the motion. He did not wish to import a note of discord at the last moment, but he could not miss the opportunity of saying that Mr. Wilmot seemed to have slightly misunderstood the position which Professor Huxley had taken with regard to the question of fisheries. He did not come there as the apologist or defender of Professor Huxley, who was perfectly capable of taking care of himself, but it was most undesirable that any misconception should exist. Professor Huxley held the opinion that, as regards the power of man to interfere with fisheries, they were divisible into three distinct classes ; those which might be destroyed, those which could be partially destroyed, and those which we have no proof that it was possible for man to destroy. With regard to the special subject under discussion to-day, Professor Huxley joined the National Fish Culture Association on the ground that it would afford the opportunity of taking up fish culture, more especially with regard to fresh-water fish, that branch being more susceptible of assistance than deep sea fisheries ; the fresh-water fish would come under the general category of fisheries that were capable of being destroyed; the littoral fisheries would come under the second category, which it was possible for man to interfere with and seriously injure, if not altogether to destroy, such, for instance, as Lobster, Crab, and Oyster fisheries, and with regard to Lobster fisheries, Professor Huxley had himself within the last year recommended that very stringent regulations should be enforced on the coast of Norfolk, in the hope that, all the circumstances being very favourable, some general idea might be arrived at as to the effect of restrictive legislation, whether it was really beneficial or not. Coming back to the subject of the Paper, and he regretted he had not been able to attend early enough to listen to it, it appeared to him they should run before they walked, and before taking up difficult and intricate systems of ponds and boxes, and apparatus of various kinds, a great deal might be done by inducing the owners of fish-ponds to treat those fish-ponds exactly as they found them ;* not

---

* I regret that Mr. Fryer was not present in time to hear my paper, because he would then have seen that my object in advocating coarse-fish culture is, that we can only by this means re-stock the rivers, canals, lakes, ponds, &c., which have been depleted by unfair fishing, over-fishing, and poaching. It will not much assist the thousands of working-men anglers if those gentlemen who have ponds cultivate them again in the way their ancestors did, as referred to in my Paper; how will that help the many thousands of club anglers? They find it usually most difficult to get permission to fish in a private pond, which is often not worth fishing; it would be more hopeless still if the owner of the water had spent money on it in cultivating it. Nor will I admit that the Lund-box, the hurdle, and the system of ponds I described can in any way be fairly designated "intricate." Their simplicity is obvious, for they merely aid nature. Finally, it will be seen Mr. Fryer recommends the German pond system, which in my Paper I had referred to as being by far the best way in which to cultivate coarse fish of all kinds, where some primary expense was not an object (see p. 11 *et seq.*). Of course I do not suppose Mr. Fryer intended to knock my skittles down merely to set them up again himself in this way; but I think it was a pity he deprecated my suggestions without having heard what I had said about them, and then proposed as a substitute the very thing I had advocated most strongly—except that my pond farm would be less "intricate." than those he proposed. I proposed one pond for one kind of fish; his suggestion would require three ponds for each kind of fish.—R. B. M.

to leave them fallow, and utterly ignore them, but to cultivate them as they would a field. A man who owned a field did not leave his sheep and cattle to run wild and starve, but fed them, and killed them when necessary; so with fish, a man who owned a fish-pond had a source of food supply which was inexhaustible if properly managed. Fresh-water fish were not like salmon; salmon lived in the sea, and in the head waters of rivers, but coarse fish were always on the spot. You had a pond with fish in it, and they did not want to run away; they were not eels who climbed out and ran over the grass. They would remain there and breed and fatten if properly treated. Without going minutely into the question, he might throw out the suggestion that gentlemen having ponds should, without going to any great expense—for the idea of expense and scientific apparatus frightened many people—endeavour to cultivate the fish as they found them, dividing the pond into one or two portions, keeping the breeding fish in one portion, the yearling fish in another, and fattening and feeding them in another. They might be netted if thought desirable, only taking care that a proper proportion were left for breeding. In saying this he did not wish to throw cold water on any scientific attempt to increase fresh-water fish in any way whatever, because the further they went in making scientific and practical investigations in this matter, the better it would be in the end; but without going to the trouble of making special ponds and apparatus, many gentlemen had the opportunity of doing a great deal towards increasing the food supply, simply by utilising the stock of fish they had in their own private grounds.

The resolution having been carried unanimously,

The CHAIRMAN in responding said it was a fair answer

to a great deal that had been said, that a few years ago between London and Staines scarcely a fish was to be caught in the Thames. This year there had been the finest takes of trout ever known. Within the last fortnight more fish than ever had been taken in the Thames. This was accomplished simply by preservation, care, and attention. He hoped the time would soon come when children would be taught not to kill young fish, just as they were taught not to kill a calf or a lamb directly it was born.

International Fisheries Exhibition,
LONDON, 1883.

THE

PROPAGATION

OF

FRESHWATER FISH

EXCLUDING SALMONIDÆ.

BY

W. OLDHAM CHAMBERS, F.L.S., F.R.I.B.A.

[*PRIZE ESSAY.*]

LONDON:
WILLIAM CLOWES AND SONS, Limited,
13 CHARING CROSS, S.W.
1884.

LONDON:
PRINTED BY WILLIAM CLOWES AND SONS, Limited,
STAMFORD STREET AND CHARING CROSS.

THE
PROPAGATION OF FRESHWATER FISH.

THE measures by which our food fishes can best be multiplied have more or less from the earliest periods of time received the consideration of mankind. *Introduction.*

The first attempts at breeding, rearing and cultivating fish were made by the Chinese, and can be traced back to periods of the greatest antiquity; it was a national source of wealth, and proved of great value in the supply of daily food and in relieving distress in time of famine. *Early history.*

Several instances are mentioned in the Bible as far back as 2000 years B.C.

The Romans spent large sums of money in the culture of fish and construction of ponds and lakes, notably that *bon vivant* Lucullus, history informing us that he bored through the sides of a mountain to introduce sea-water into his fish-ponds. *Roman works.*

During the middle ages pisciculture had many patrons, and the monks contributed in no small degree to its success, as it presented them with the means of food during their religious feasts and ordinances. *Ponds of middle ages.*

In many parts of the country very fine examples of ponds or stews are visible, showing great engineering skill in their construction.

4   THE PROPAGATION OF FRESHWATER FISH.

No trace of fish culture in modern periods.

Although means have been adopted for the artificial propagation of salmonidæ during comparatively modern periods, we are devoid of any reliable data as to practical endeavours in this country to cultivate any of our national coarse fish for the purpose of restocking our depleted rivers and food-producing acres.

The science of fish culture is now no longer a question of experiment based on scientific results, but one of national economy in the production of a cheap and wholesome aliment for our densely populated cities and manufacturing towns, and in this respect we are bound to consider the science.

Harmony of nature.

The laws effecting the harmony of nature are governed not only in view of the countless dangers fish in their embryo and alevin condition have to encounter before being able to contribute to the reproduction of species, but also to the innumerable difficulties attending the fecundation of the eggs in their natural condition.

Impregnation.

The direct contact of the milt with the ova is of course necessary to create the development of the germ. Eggs, therefore, failing to receive this impregnation soon decompose in ordinary or natural spawning, and a very high percentage of loss may from the above cause be anticipated.

Enemies.

After the eggs are hatched, the enemies that prey upon the young are very numerous. The natural desire to feed on each other, the attacks of fish-eating birds, water insects, crustaceans, &c., all tend to retard reproduction.

Fish have, therefore, to contend against all these calamities before being able to take their place in the repopulation of our waters.

The purport of this essay is to show how we can assist

nature in the restocking of our waters by the adoption of certain simple measures tending to that end. *Assist nature in stocking.*

The species of our national coarse fishes best adapted for cultivation must be well considered, and the writer would venture to suggest, *inter alia*, the following, not only in giving sport to the angler, but in furnishing food to the people, namely, pike, perch, carp, roach, tench, bream, dace, &c. *Species to cultivate.*

These may be divided into carnivorous and herbivorous feeders, and an undue increase of the former will, in the ordinary law of nature, represent a corresponding decrease in the latter.

To meet this, we find a greater fecundity is given to herbivorous fish than to their carnivorous *confrères;* while the latter in their turn prevent a too great increase over the former; so is the balance of nature preserved.

In considering the question of the restocking of rivers, this feature must not be lost sight of, that as food fishes the carnivorous species are infinitely superior to the herbivorous: great care must be exercised in selecting a fair proportion of each species, in order to retain an equitable balance. *Food fishes.*

The spawning of British coarse fishes varies from the salmonidæ in this respect, that whereas the latter shed their ova in the winter free, or non-adhesive, on gravelly bottoms of streams, the latter yield their ova in the spring or summer months, and select stones, trunks of trees, weeds, rushes, &c., upon which to attach the eggs, which are adhesive in character. *Spawning.*

They delight in moderately still waters, and select shallows for the better incubation of their eggs; also on account of the minute insectile life found therein, for the young fish to feed upon when hatched.

E. 19. B 2

Propagation. In considering the question of propagation, it has been shown in the former part of this essay that the natural enemies of our fishes are multitudinous, not only in their ovum and embryo stages, but also in their alevin condition, and measures should therefore be adopted, as far as possible, to guard against the difficulties that are known to exist in carrying out a scheme for the cultivation of our coarse fishes.

Artificial fecundation. Experiments have been made in the artificial fecundation of the eggs of coarse fishes, and apparatus have been constructed for the hatching of adhesive ova upon wooden frames over which linen has been stretched; also upon sheets of glass placed in boxes with water allowed to pass through, until the eggs are hatched, when the young fish are removed, as may be desired; but these experiments are not to be relied upon in leading to results of a satisfactory nature, for unless a uniform and natural temperature of soft water is obtained, considerable disappointment will follow.

The hurdle hatcher. Reference must be made to a German invention, known as the wooden "hurdle," through which branches of the fir tree are intertwined, and the framework is then sunk in suitable places for the fish to spawn upon.

Hatching box. Special reference must be made to an apparatus which forms a leading feature in this essay; it is so designed that fish may be placed in it to spawn, after which the ova can be either left to hatch in the natural course, or removed to distant waters.

Form of the apparatus. Such an apparatus the writer of this essay has had the honour to invent, a drawing of which is given on the other side. By reference thereto it will be seen that the structure is oblong in form, the length being about five feet, the width two feet six inches, and the depth two feet.

PLAN OF
COARSE FISH HATCHER
(Looking down.)

XI.–19. Plate II.

ELEVATION OF
COARSE FISH HATCHER

The outer framework has strips of perforated zinc inserted, three inches in width, for the free passage of the water.

In the centre of the box is a division for the purpose of separating the species if desired.

Round the interior of the box, including the bottom, are provided light frames, upon which is stretched galvanized netting of $1\frac{1}{2}$ inches mesh; into this netting are intertwined young fir branches, and a lid formed with galvanized-wire netting closes the whole of the apparatus, which is then ready for use.

Previous to spawning, the box is secured on the margin of a lake, small tributary, or other approved position; a few pairs of carefully selected ripe fish are then placed in the box, and in due course the spawn is deposited on the fir branches; if it is intended to stock the water in which the box is situated, it is simply retained *in situ* until the young fish are hatched; a small door in the side is then removed, and in due course the fish find their way into the waters; but supposing the intention is to transfer the eggs to a distant part of the country, the frames are then drawn out, with the fir branches and deposited spawn, and placed in a carrier filled with water, and forwarded to their ultimate destination. The frames are taken out, and sunk in the new waters until the eggs are hatched. *How to use the apparatus.*

The whole of the woodwork used in the construction is charred, to prevent fungoid growth.

In Sweden for more than a century there has been an apparatus in partial use, known as the "Lund" hatching-box. *The Lund hatcher.*

The writer claims for himself the originality of design in the above-described box, both in the construction of the invention, and also for the purposes to which the same can be applied with so much simplicity.

This essay upon the cultivation of fish can hardly be considered complete without a few words on the formation of artificial ponds.

<small>Artificial ponds.</small>
In designing and superintending the construction of fish ponds, the writer has always upheld the principle that the most convenient and profitable form is to have a series—namely, nursery, yearling, and stock ponds.

The whole should be designed so as to enable the water to be easily drawn off by means of sluices, thus placing under entire control the whole of the ponds, as may be required from time to time.

It is highly desirable, where space will admit, to have more than one nursery pond, in order to separate the herbivorous from the carnivorous fishes, and thus regulate the number in each species in stocking waters.

<small>Nursery ponds.</small>
The nursery pond should be shallow; three feet wide at the bottom, six feet at the top, and about fifty feet in length.

Gravel should be spread along the bottom to six inches in depth, weeds and drain-pipes may be dispersed about for shelter; the depth of water should vary from four inches at one end to ten inches at the other. A very slight current of water will be sufficient to retain life; a few bushes planted round the edges will be of service for shade.

When the sluice is lowered and the water drawn off, provision must be made to catch the fish in a "receiver," five feet long and one foot deep, incapable of being drained; protection must be given by perforated zinc placed at an angle of 45° to prevent the fish passing through in the pond at a lower level.

<small>Yearling ponds.</small>
The yearling pond must be much larger, and constructed in a similar way, with a depth of water from six inches to two feet: gravel the bottom in places, and provide suitable water-plants and "hides" for the fish.

A ditch three feet wide and one foot deep should be formed in the centre leading to the "receiver," as before described; the ditch will assist in conducting the fish to the receiver when the water is drained off at the sluice.

It is necessary, in addition to the "hides" named, that stumps of trees should be fixed in the banks at places, thus affording suitable shady spots for the young fish in the summer months.

Bushes must also be planted round the banks with overhanging branches.

The stock ponds should be considerably larger than the last described, and constructed similar to the yearling pond; they must be provided with shallows one foot in depth, as they afford means for the growth of insects. *Stock ponds.*

The average depth of water in the ponds should be about three feet; there is no benefit in deep ponds; holes can be sunk six feet deep for the larger fish.

Little bye-streams round the sides are of great advantage, and they should be supplied with water-plants, upon which the fish may spawn.

It will much facilitate the growth of the fish, more especially in the cultivation of the carp, if the ponds can be laid dry periodically during the spring and summer months, and planted with oats and rye-grass. *Management of ponds.*

No pond should be used longer than three years for aqua-culture; the bottom becomes foul and rank from the alluvial deposits; these should be raked off and removed, and the surface ploughed up. The oftener a pond is laid dry and exposed, the faster the fish will grow.

A great advantage will be gained by having a set of three ponds for stock or fattening purposes, and alternate them, as before described, with agri-culture. *Advantage of the series system.*

It is difficult to lay down a hard-and-fast rule as to the number of fish to be placed in a given area of water.

As it is with pastures so it is with waters, some are rich and productive in the extreme in supplying nourishing food, whereas in other instances the opposite we find to be the case.

Dangers of overcrowding. Broadly speaking, every care must be exercised by a frequent examination of the condition of the fishes, to avoid overcrowding; it will be far better to err on the side of over-caution in this respect, than heedlessly to stock the waters with a superabundance of fish, that would only result in a supply of lean, starved, and ill-formed fish, fit neither for the rod, nor for the table.

Food. Suitable food should be given at regular intervals avoiding large quantities at a time, which would only sink to the bottom and soon decompose, causing fungoid growth to the inhabitants of the waters.

The best food for our coarse fishes generally is large and small lobworms, brewers' grains, meal, oilcake, &c., cut to sizes according to the age of the fish.

The warmer the weather, the fleeter the water to distribute the food, and the colder the weather, the deeper must be the feeding. Very young fish only feed on minute insects, which may be encouraged by placing in the water newly made hay or old grass.

LONDON:
PRINTED BY WILLIAM CLOWES AND SONS, Limited,
STAMFORD STREET AND CHARING CROSS.

www.ingramcontent.com/pod-product-compliance
Lightning Source LLC
Chambersburg PA
CBHW030017240426
43672CB00007B/988